NEW ESSAYS ON CANADIAN THEATRE
VOLUME TWELVE

POWER MOVES

ALSO IN THIS SERIES

ASIAN CANADIAN THEATRE
EDITED BY NINA LEE AQUINO AND RIC KNOWLES

NEW CANADIAN REALISMS
EDITED BY ROBERTA BARKER AND KIM SOLGA

LATINA/O CANADIAN THEATRE AND PERFORMANCE
EDITED BY NATALIE ÁLVAREZ

THEATRES OF AFFECT
EDITED BY ERIN HURLEY

DANIEL MacIVOR
EDITED BY RICHIE WILCOX

PERFORMING INDIGENEITY
EDITED BY YVETTE NOLAN AND RIC KNOWLES

CANADIAN PERFORMANCE HISTORIES AND HISTORIOGRAPHIES
EDITED BY HEATHER DAVIS-FISCH

Q2Q: QUEER CANADIAN THEATRE AND PERFORMANCE
EDITED BY PETER DICKINSON, C.E. GATCHALIAN, KATHLEEN OLIVER, AND DALBIR SINGH

LINDA GRIFFITHS
EDITED BY JACQUELINE PETROPOULOS

THEATRE AND (IM)MIGRATION
EDITED BY YANA MEERZON

DIGITAL PERFORMANCE IN CANADA
EDITED BY DAVID OWEN

NEW ESSAYS ON CANADIAN THEATRE
VOLUME TWELVE

POWER MOVES: DANCE, CULTURE, POLITICS

EDITED BY SEIKA BOYE AND MJ THOMPSON

PLAYWRIGHTS CANADA PRESS
TORONTO

First edition: February 2025
Printed and bound in Canada by Imprimerie Gauvin Ltée, Gatineau

Jacket design by Leon Aureus
Jacket photo of Ellen Furey and Malik Nashad Sharpe © Ian Douglas, provided courtesy of American Realness

Playwrights Canada Press
202-269 Richmond St. W., Toronto, ON M5V 1X1
416.703.0013 | info@playwrightscanada.com | www.playwrightscanada.com

LIBRARY AND ARCHIVES CANADA CATALOGUING IN PUBLICATION
Title: Power moves : dance, culture, politics / edited by Seika Boye and MJ Thompson.
Other titles: Power moves (2024)
Names: Boye, Seika, editor. | Thompson, M. J. (Mary Jo), editor.
Series: New essays on Canadian theatre ; v. 12.
Description: Series statement: New essays on Canadian theatre ; volume 12 | Includes bibliographical references and index.
Identifiers: Canadiana 20240451937 | ISBN 9780369103697 (softcover)
Subjects: LCSH: Dance—Political aspects—Canada. | LCSH: Dance—Canada—Sociological aspects.
Classification: LCC GV1588.45 .P69 2024 | DDC 792.80971—dc23

Playwrights Canada Press staff work across Turtle Island, on Treaty 7, Treaty 13, and Treaty 20 territories, which are the current and ancestral homes of the Anishinaabe Nations (Ojibwe / Chippewa, Odawa, Potawatomi, Algonquin, Saulteaux, Nipissing, and Mississauga / Michi Saagiig), the Blackfoot Confederacy (Kainai, Piikani, and Siksika), néhiyaw, Sioux, Stoney Nakoda, Tsuut'ina, Wendat, and members of the Haudenosaunee Confederacy (Mohawk, Oneida, Onondaga, Cayuga, Seneca, and Tuscarora), as well as Metis and Inuit peoples. It always was and always will be Indigenous land.

We acknowledge the financial support of the Canada Council for the Arts, the Ontario Arts Council (OAC), Ontario Creates, the Government of Ontario, and the Government of Canada for our publishing activities.

To the dancers
however you dance
whyever you dance
don't stop
power moves.

CONTENTS

GENERAL EDITOR'S PREFACE

ROBERTA BARKER

When Ric Knowles founded New Essays on Canadian Theatre in 2011, he set out to complement his previous book series for Playwrights Canada Press, Critical Perspectives on Canadian Theatre in English (CPCTE). Each volume of the CPCTE series offered a critical history of a key topic in Canadian theatre studies; most of the essays featured in these volumes were reprints of important articles in the field, though they were supplemented by newly commissioned works that brought novel perspectives to the questions at hand. With NECT, Knowles chose to foreground new work, underexplored subjects, and fresh viewpoints. As he wrote in his general editor's preface for *Performing Indigeneity* (2016), these volumes

> are designed to fill what I perceive to be gaps in the critical record, often . . . taking new approaches, often . . . from minoritized and under-represented perspectives, and in almost every case introducing topics that have not received book-length coverage . . . They are designed at once to follow, lead, and instantiate new and emerging developments in the field. (v)

Responding to major questions of the present as well as to silences in the past, these books strive to shape the future of the field by opening exciting new avenues of exploration for artists, students, and scholars of Canadian theatre.

The six volumes published under Knowles's editorship richly fulfill this mandate, covering in the process a wide range of topics and approaches. Some, like *Asian Canadian Theatre* (edited by Nina Lee Aquino and Knowles) and *Latina/o Canadian Theatre and Performance* (edited by Natalie Álvarez), illuminate the vibrant and important work of key communities within the Canadian theatrical ecosystem. Others, like *New Canadian Realisms* (edited by Kim Solga and myself) and *Theatres of Affect* (edited by Erin Hurley), strive to reconsider established genres and forms of theatre through new theoretical lenses. The 2015 volume, *Daniel MacIvor* (edited by Richie Wilcox), brings long overdue scholarly attention to the work of one of Canada's most beloved and innovative theatre artists. Finally, 2016's volume makes a particularly mighty contribution: *Performing Indigeneity*, edited by Yvette Nolan (Algonquin) and Knowles, is the first collection of essays on performance in Turtle Island to offer an all-Indigenous list of contributors. Many of these volumes, or the articles they feature, have been garlanded with scholarly prizes and awards: a fitting tribute to their impact on the field.

Since taking over the general editorship of NECT in 2017, I have been continually inspired by the work of Knowles, his collaborators, and the many other brilliant scholars and artists who continue to transform our understanding of the field of Canadian theatre and performance. The editors with whom I have been fortunate enough to work have responded thoughtfully to the goals that shape the series. In the 2017 volume of NECT, *Canadian Performance Histories and Historiographies*, editor Heather Davis-Fisch and her collaborators set out to rethink the subject we have been used to calling "Canadian theatre history." The following year represented an epoch in the history of NECT, marking the first time Playwrights Canada Press published two volumes in the NECT series within the span of one calendar year. The first 2018 volume, *Q2Q: Queer Canadian Theatre and Performance* (edited by Peter Dickinson, C.E. Gatchalian, Kathleen Oliver, and Dalbir Singh), brings together the voices of many of this country's leading makers and scholars of queer theatre and performance to explore, celebrate, debate, and redefine the ways in which 2SLGBT2Q+ identities and perspectives have shaped theatre and performance on this land mass. The second, *Linda Griffiths* (edited by Jacqueline Petropoulos), is the first edited collection ever to focus solely on the work of one of Canada's most multi-talented, influential, and complex theatre artists. The 2019 volume, *Theatre and (Im)migration* (edited by Yana Meerzon), offers a groundbreaking exploration of the complex and transformative roles played by immigrant artists and perspectives in the ongoing development of theatre and performance across Canada: an exploration in which the voices of immigrant Canadians take centre stage. The next volume, *Digital Performance in Canada* (edited by David Owen), was published in 2021. When David first proposed this collection, we could never have predicted just how timely its multi-faceted exploration of performance's interactions with digital technologies would prove amid the COVID-19 pandemic.

After a hiatus occasioned by that same pandemic and the many other challenges of the past few years, it is thrilling to see NECT return with a new volume that speaks eloquently to the series' core mandate. *Power Moves: Dance, Culture, Politics* explores the crucial but long underexplored field of dance and movement studies on and beyond the lands currently known as Canada through a range of vital perspectives. Seika Boye and MJ Thompson, the editors of the volume, bring to their work a wealth not only of scholarly knowledge but also of lived experience of dance, movement, and their socially liberatory potential. Their diverse and insightful contributors speak to topics as wide-ranging as the histories and futures of Indigenous movement(s) on these lands, dramaturgies of Black corporeality, choreographies of power in police training, dance as a method for unsettling white settler discourses, and the arrival of breaking within the athletic bastion of the Olympic Games, among many others.

The explorations and conversations within this volume show that, in the words of the editors, "dance offers an alternative entry into discourse, emphasizing a materiality of body, technique, social, religious and cultural histories, community, and more." Too long under-represented (as the title of a 2015 conference that Seika Boye co-organized with Evadne Kelly, Heather Fitzsimmons Frey, and T. Nikki Cesare Schotzko put it) as "the other D" of drama, theatre, and performance studies on these lands, dance and movement studies emerges in this work as a complex and transformative force for social dialogue and change. I am so grateful to Seika, MJ, and all the volume's authors, both for their perseverance in keeping this important project alive through trying times and for the many ways in which their work invites us to move more thoughtfully and bravely into the future.

WORKS CITED

Knowles, Ric. General Editor's Preface. *Performing Indigeneity*, edited by Yvette Nolan and Knowles, Playwrights Canada, 2016, pp. v-vii. New Essays on Canadian Theatre 6.

INTRODUCTION: DANCING KNOWLEDGE IN THE CANADIAN CONTEXT

SEIKA BOYE AND MJ THOMPSON

As editors of this collection, our lifelong engagements with dance as practice and profession include Seika's early training at her neighbourhood studio in jazz, tap, ballet, and musical theatre, which led to years of competitive dancing and community stages. Her dancing life outside of the studio was in the living room with her parents' record collection; in front of the TV watching MuchMusic and programs like *Toronto Rocks* and *Electric Circus*; in the all-ages clubs of late-1980s in Hamilton, Ontario; and in the early-1990s mosh pits of Lollapalooza and Hamilton's grunge and indie music scene. These worlds often felt at odds with each other and, after quitting dance to pursue a career in journalism, a recreational modern dance class at the University of Toronto's Hart House offered Seika a middle ground—a place where the politics of life could enter the expression of dancing. Of course, this notion is fraught with many of the binaries and discussions that continue to shape dance studies and dance-focused research today. Both discoveries and disappointments followed, but it was a first for her that placed the politics of life in overt conversation with the act of dancing. It was formative in a manner that finds echoes in several essays in this volume. Today as a dance scholar these questions are central to Seika's research, curatorial practice, and pedagogy.

MJ's focus on the body begins with a broad work history—among other jobs, a hospital worker, a hotel cleaner, a waitress, a journalist, an academic—in a family that emphasized manual labour as at once critical and, not unproblematically, redemptive; her love of dance emerged primarily through writing assignments that lead to her work at the Canadian magazine *Dance Connection*, in print from 1983–1996, and her doctoral research at New York University, where she wrote about how choreographers work with ordinary forms of movement and why. Movement knowledge, found at work and alongside social dancing, recreational dance classes, and a sustained practice in yoga, became sharpened for MJ in dialogue with many artists over many years. What remains is an understanding of the moving body as a primary site through which to consider the full range of social, cultural, and political phenomena that make up a life.

Through these personal and political trajectories, dance methodologies offer critical ways of doing, seeing, and thinking about bodies: as phenomena, as constructs, and always in relation to others, the world, and history (Martin, *Critical Moves*). At the same time, dance as a methodology for research offers pathways toward knowing and unknowing, providing ways to find, present, and challenge knowledge. Some of these methodologies are on view in this collection: practice as research and mobilization; first-person observation and movement analysis; oral histories and lived experience; historical and archival research; narrative, documentary, and experimental accounts; image-making, including photography and filmmaking; and always, first and foremost, dancing.

We write this introduction in the wake of the COVID-19 pandemic (2020–), the murder of George Floyd at the hands of the Minneapolis police (2020), and so many attacks on critical thinking and post-secondary education in the humanities, from the François Legault government in Québec to the Ron DeSantis regime in Florida. During the COVID-19 pandemic, responses to scientific innovation in the prevention and treatment of the virus were distorted into accusations of conspiracy that were used to justify racist attacks and assaults on public health practitioners across the country. Amid the widespread circulation of disinformation, when the meaning of language is bent and distorted at every turn, dance offers an alternative entry into discourse, emphasizing a materiality of body; technique; social, religious, and cultural histories; community; and more. At its best, dance is an invitation to move and know differently, along new pathways, independently and together, with love.

Yet dance's unique powers of presence, action, and relationality make it a clear target for state control. Canada's history demonstrates repeated state attacks on dancing, including a ban on Indigenous dancing issued by the federal government in the early twentieth century through the anti-Potlatch proclamation in 1883 that was made law in 1885 ("Potlach Ban"). This violent veto was a critical tactic in the nation-state's agenda to construct the "ideal" citizen and to control what that citizen could and could not do in celebration, ritual, artistic expression, and community gathering. Dance appears as a target in part because of its relation to the body as a contested political site, and in part because of its extraordinary powers of asserting agency, mobility, and assembly. At any point in history, to ask who was allowed to dance and where is to learn the values of that society at that given moment.[1]

The title of this volume, *Power Moves*, refers to the shifting location of power that is so acutely visible in the close observation of dancing. A person who has limited social and political power on civic streets may dominate on the dance floor, in cypher or ballroom couple, and in their social dancing community. It also refers to the powerful moves made by individuals and communities through dance. Dancing in secret during the Potlatch ban so that older generations could pass on sacred and secular dances to younger generations is a power move that is reaping the benefits of Indigenous regeneration across Turtle Island today (see "Elder Magaret Harris"). Despite perpetual attempts to extinguish and contain dance, it persists, proving a need and capacity for the durable embodied knowledge that fuels resilience.

DANCING IN AND ACROSS THE DISCIPLINES

This collection builds on robust histories of scholarship in dance and ongoing inquiry into the contours of the field. Of course our own identities, education, and career pathways, as well as our artistic training and experiences, inform our perspectives. MJ's lived experience is as an Irish-Italian, formerly Roman

1 See also Boye, "Legislation," for relationships between legislation and dancing for racialized populations in the twentieth century.

Catholic, white anglo settler descendent currently living in Tiohtiá:ke/Montreal. She received a Ph.D. in Performance Studies from New York University in 2008. Seika is a middle-aged, mixed-heritage Black woman, mother, partner, educator, and artist. She is a first-generation Canadian, descendent on her maternal side of Scottish German colonial settlers in Aotearoa/New Zealand and on her paternal side of Ghanaian West Africans. She has degrees in Dance and English (BFA at York, 1999), Dance (M.A. at York, 2006), and Theatre and Performance Studies (Ph.D. at University of Toronto, 2016). These identities have shaped considerations in trying to map the unwieldy and proliferating contours of where dance scholarship is happening in Canada.

As a doctoral student in 2015, Seika co-organized with Evadne Kelly, Heather Fitzsimmons Frey, and Nikki Cesare Schotzko the symposium The Other D: Locating Dance in Drama, Theatre and Performance Studies in Canada,[2] hosted within the Centre for Drama, Theatre and Performance Studies at the University of Toronto. Part of the impetus of this symposium was an effort to understand, as the title suggests, the place of dance within post-secondary education in Canada, especially in light of emergent performance studies and performing arts umbrella programs. The two invited keynote speakers, dance and cultural historians Dr. Susan Manning and Dr. Allana Lindgren, were tasked with mapping the development of dance studies in the US and Canada, respectively. Eight years later their comments still provide a useful record. Manning presented "How We Got Here: The View from the US Academy" and Lindgren presented "Disciplinarity and the Future of Dance in Canadian Universities." We have opted to quote from these interventions at length, as this new collection may be seen as a continuation of the thinking that was invited and offered at the Other D. Manning writes,

> The US dance department was established in the years between the two world wars as an integral part of the patronage system for modern dance. Although the curriculum included historical, cultural, and

2 See the full website, program, schedule, and keynotes at "The Other D." The Other D was supported by a SSHRC Connection Grant.

> theoretical topics as supplements to training in modern dance technique and composition, the dance department could not absorb the boom in dance studies that started in the 1970s and has continued into the present. Beginning in the 1980s, a significant number of aspiring dance scholars pursued advanced degrees in theatre and performance studies, drawn by the field's new openness to research on nondramatic, unscripted genres of performance, including dance. This openness resulted from an internal critique within theatre studies that exploded the study of the Western dramatic canon in the name of performance studies. In other words, it was the dynamic tension between scripted drama and unscripted performance that enabled dance studies to cohabit departments of theatre and performance studies. (151)

Whereas the US story is relatively well-known, the Canadian story is less so.[3] The day after Manning's keynote, Lindgren reflected on her own interdisciplinary dance studies education in Canada, noting that at the time Canada had only nine degree-granting programs compared to 655 in the US. She writes,

> If interdisciplinarity has been central to my personal path, it is worth acknowledging this situation parallels the institutional history of post-secondary dance in Canada. Dance in Canadian universities has always been interdisciplinary in nature, though the experiences and engagement with interdisciplinarity are individual to each institution. (85–86)

Lindgren continues through a survey of the long-standing degree-granting dance programs in Canada at York University (est. 1970); Simon Fraser University (est. 1975); *Université de Montréal* (est. 1978); Concordia University (est. 1979); and the University of Calgary, where dance was housed in both the School of Physical Education and the Faculty of Fine Arts and only in

3 See too Anne Flynn's essay on the history of dance studies as an emergent field in Canada and the US.

1995 was a B.A. formed and offered through the newly established School of Creative and Performing Arts (88).[4] Through this overview, Lindgren highlights the common tensions that emerge within dance programs: their expense due to the need for space and musical accompaniment; philosophical differences about disciplinary location, often either in health sciences or fine arts; disciplinary domination when dance is analyzed with critical tools intended for other disciplines such as visual arts or literature; the tendency to hire dance faculty sessionally rather than as full-time faculty within the creative-arts umbrella; curricular and hiring decisions being made by non-dance specialists; and precarities of hiring for practice-based teachers. She continues:

> We need to be strategic and careful in how we position dance in order to avoid potential headaches and misfortune. It is worth noting that the place of dance within universities has been debated in the US, Britain, and Europe, with arguments coalescing around two main issues (Bales and Eliot). On the one hand, there have been critiques of dance as too specialized and a call for interdisciplinary approaches to help "bring dance closer to the intellectual mainstream" (Koritz 89). On the other hand, some dance scholars have lamented a perceived loss of fluency in the languages of dance due to an emphasis on interdisciplinarity (Bales and Eliot 4). (88)

These anxieties remain in Canadian institutions today and, at the time of writing, all dance-specific degree-granting programs are undergraduate. At the graduate level, dance is now exclusively incorporated into theatre and performance studies or interdisciplinary graduate programs. Returning to Lindgren, she cautioned about what she perceived as the risks of unexamined interdisciplinarity: superficial scholarship, dance scholarship without dance, the under/devaluing of historical archival sources in embodied dance

4 See Lindgren's full keynote for details on historical trajectories of undergraduate and graduate degrees. The M.A. and Ph.D. programs in Dance at York University were folded into the Theatre and Performance Studies program in 2022–23.

research, and the subsuming of dance by other disciplines. All of these concerns remain and yet, as this volume demonstrates, dance studies in Canada continues to emerge in new places. The presence of dance-focused research is alive and happening in dialogue with other disciplines; this continues to be a source of new ideas, collaborations, and performances.

POWER MOVES: DANCING POLITICS AND CULTURE

Interdisciplinary approaches, driven by the largesse of how dance presents, whether in social, theatrical, or everyday settings, circulate across the country and certainly within the pages of this book. These testify to the range of academic and performance contexts in which dance scholars in Canada work, as well as to the ingenuity of writers and artists making language and dancing politics across divides. This collection embraces movement-based research that may happen outside academic or dance studies contexts per se, yet nevertheless prioritizes the specificity of method, history, and performance central to the field. We are inspired and influenced by essay collections focused on Canada and/or by dance scholars working in Canada, including *Dancing Bodies, Living Histories: New Writings about Dance and Culture* (ed. Lisa Doolittle and Anne Flynn, 2000); *Canadian Dance: Visions and Stories* (ed. Selma Landen Odom and Mary Jane Warner, 2004); *Renegade Bodies: Canadian Dance in the 1970s* (ed. Allana Lindgren and Kaija Pepper, 2012); and, more recently, *The Oxford Handbook of Hip Hop Dance Studies* (ed. Mary Fogarty and Imani Kai Johnson, 2022).

Power Moves: Dance, Culture, Politics stitches together relays between research methodologies, practices, and theories, attending to the specificity and singularity of cultural practices and power as these are made in Canada. One important model in the field is Thomas F. DeFrantz and Philipa Rothfield's collection *Choreography and Corporeality: Relay in Motion* (2016), which, in its discussion of the relations between theory and practice, underscores how the conceptual is formed culturally and, what's more, with material effects; their collection pays close attention to the way "concepts are mobilized and put to work, amid very different concerns, embodied histories, and motivations" (8).

Foundational scholarship within the field of dance studies, building on the practices of dance artists, has also shaped and informed this collection. Dance studies scholar Randy Martin has neatly theorized the political potential of dance as a model of assembly and pointed out dance's capacity as a tool for making movement/s in the political sense of the word. He writes,

> Against the facile dismissal of political aspirations as forever insufficient to what they face, dance offers a surfeit of possibility, it makes legible the very means by which action is joined, measures taken, steps carried through. An ensemble that manufactures a social body that releases its own excess, that orients practical accomplishment toward itself, this expansive sense of the social that exists in and for itself, grounds a socialism that issues from the loins and beads of sweat made in movement together. ("Between Intervention" 29)

After Martin's pivotal embrace of the ensemble as social body, numerous scholars and artists have further sharpened considerations of dance as politics, including but not limited to recent work by Jens Richard Giersdorf and Yutian Wong ("Remobilizing Dance Studies" in *Dance Research Journal*, 2016) and Gabriele Klein and Sandra Noeth (*Emerging Bodies: The Performance of Worldmaking in Dance and Choreography*, 2011).

Since the 1990s, scholarship at the intersection of dance ethnography and cultural studies has affirmed the ways in which dance constitutes culture. Cynthia Novack's ethnography of contact improvisation is exemplary here; she writes,

> Culture is embodied . . . Movement constitutes an ever-present reality in which we constantly participate. We perform movement, invent it, interpret it, and reinterpret it, on conscious and unconscious levels. In these actions we participate in and reinforce culture, and we also create it. (8)

Countless scholars working in dance, history, anthropology, and performance studies have further developed this perspective in order to analyze and theorize theatrical dance, cultural forms, movement subcultures, and embodiment as method, practice, and theory. For example, in her 2007 book *Sensational Knowledge: Embodying Culture Through Japanese Dance*, ethnomusicologist and dance artist Tomie Hahn uses the tools of ethnography—both participation and observation—to understand the body as educated sensorium. Reflecting on her own experience of learning Japanese fan dancing through individual sensory experiences, she writes, "I strongly believe that an observation of how dance is taught reveals a great deal about that culture as well as the individual dancers practicing tradition" (1). Observation and ethnography function in Hahn's research to reveal the multi-faceted process of "dance transmission and how cultural knowledge is embodied" (1). Hahn's work emphasizes all that is contained in and manifested from the exchange between the teacher/dancer dynamic and constitutes a granular analysis of how culture shapes embodiment.

This pulsing between disciplines, methods, and all manner of binaries—studies and practices, the collective and the individual, the abstract and the material—marks the scope of this collection. In the essays that follow, we aim to gather diverse understandings of dance and movement, written by authors from a range of disciplines and with a range of expertise. As editors, we actively sought out voices that moved from reflection to history to theory, across and/or within essays. We sought work that might challenge the contours of dance studies and/or academic scholarship as these have looked historically. The abundance of new writing about dance across the country was truly exciting; this collection, by no means exhaustive of the robust scholarship happening, gathers authors whose work explicitly engages with dance's relation to politics—dance both as a lens on culture and as an agent of change.

In addition to the scholars listed above we are inspired by and indebted to many more dance writers, journalists, editors, publications,[5] presenters,[6]

---

5 See Bowrig.

6 See "About Us" to learn more about the CanDance Network, a service organization for Canadian dance presenters.

service organizations,[7] audiences, students, and funders who have shaped the field. More than ever, we note a dialogue between those working in dance professions and those working through dance in universities. The social and protest movements Idle No More, #MeToo, and Black Lives Matter have impacted cultural and artistic organizations and forced acknowledgement and reckoning in ways we had not seen before in our lifetimes. We believe the authors of the work to follow are integral to the future of dance-focused scholarship and environments of dance participation—curricular and non-curricular—facilitated through post-secondary resources.

Several of the authors here focus on dance as culture, movement as theory, and the body as a political site. Angélique Willkie, a professor of dance at Concordia University and long-time interpreter and dramaturge, offers first notes toward a Black dramaturgy in a diary-like set of reflections moving between her career in dance, Black performance theory, and the limits of identity as category. The robust presence of dance groups in British Columbia, discussed by the Tsimshian dancer/scholar Mique'l Dangeli, underscores the power of dance as cultural knowledge and cautions against readings that replay traditional/innovative colonial binaries. Emily Johnson, Karyn Recollet, Joseph M. Pierce, and Camille Georgeson-Usher share a conversation reflecting on Johnson's collaborative, site-specific dance work *The Ways We Love and the Ways We Love Better—Monumental Movement Toward Being Future Being(s)* which focuses on renewal, transformation, and Indigenous presence in Lenapehoking—homeland of the Lenapeyok people.

A number of authors consider dance's pedagogic potential as a way to gather, reflect, and move toward revised futures. Ahalya Satkunaratnam describes her experience of cultivating a pedagogy informed by feminist dance ethnography while teaching at Quest University, located on the ancestral, traditional, and unceded territories of the Sḵwx̱wú7mesh people. Theatremaker/teacher/writer/musician Gabe Levine follows the work of interdisciplinary Kanien'kehá:kan performing artist Ange Loft, from Kahnawake

7 Of note is Dance Collection Danse, Canada's only dedicated dance archive and publisher. See "Welcome to Dance Collection Danse."

Mohawk Territory, whose Talking Treaties project foregrounds the histories of Indigenous treaties on the lands in and around Tkaronto/Toronto as ongoing and collective embodied practice. An essay co-authored by Natalie Álvarez, Greg Hodge, and Jennifer Lavoie considers scenario-based training with an emphasis on gestural and movement codifications that aims to educate police officers toward more sensitive interactions with mentally ill people experiencing a crisis. Independent scholar Evadne Kelly infuses a cautionary note around ideas of improvement, building on her own research history and combining dance, ethnographic, and archival research strategies to craft an essay on settler-colonial notions of "betterment" as they have played out through eugenics, right-to-die movements, and, inevitably, dance. Grounded in personal narrative and critical theory, Kelly asks us to question dance's appetite for space, ground, and land through the lens of the Truth and Reconciliation Commission reports.

Still others examine the political structures that impose order on movement forms and speculate on how dance might counter such forces. Serouj Aprahamian examines the absorption of breakdancing into the Olympics via a 2016 decision that assigned the World DanceSport Federation (WDSF) administrative power over the "dancesport"; with an eye to potential benefits of increased resources and support for dancers, he speculates on what is lost when context, terminology, and values shift. MJ Thompson looks at legal documents that codified so-called "furtive movements" during the height of New York City's stop-and-frisk policy (2003–2013) and considers how dancing know-how works against biased assumptions about what and how movement means.

Finally, to work with dance whether as performer, writer, teacher, activist, or archivist—with hyphens between these as not-discrete categories—is to think and do movement as a way of pulling closer to the world. Where would we be without dancers on the land and on the dance floor, in the underground and in the cypher and in the streets, on the stage and on our screens, in the hallways of our universities (because studios are too few and in high demand), and in our imaginations, our living rooms, bedrooms, and basements, in the reflections of mirrors and windows, and in our hearts? In closing, and following

Seika's invitation back in 2016, the question remains: What is one thing you can do tomorrow to support dancers and dancing, and advocate for its value? If you are reading this and don't know where to start, or how to continue, we offer this call. We have found that there is almost always someone else who will join you in the dance.

WORKS CITED

"About Us." *CanDance Network*, candance.ca/about/.

Bales, Melanie, and Karen Eliot. Introduction. *Dance on Its Own Terms: Histories and Methodologies*, edited by Bales and Eliot, Oxford UP, 2013, pp. 3–7.

Bowrig, Amy. "Footprints: A Recent History of Dance Publishing in Canada." Foothills and Footsteps: New Writings in Dance Studies Conference. U of Calgary, January 5–9, 1999.

Boye, Seika. "IT'S ABOUT TIME: Dancing Black in Canada 1900–1970." *IT'S ABOUT TIME: Dancing Black in Canada 1900–1970*, 2017, dancingblackcanada.ca.

———. "Legislation and Protest." *IT'S ABOUT TIME: Dancing Black in Canada 1900–1970*, 2017, dancingblackcanada.ca/legislation-and-protest.

DeFrantz, Thomas F., and Philipa Rothfield, editors. *Choreography and Corporeality: Relay in Motion*. U of Wisconsin P, 2016.

Doolittle, Lisa, and Anne Flynn, editors. *Dancing Bodies, Living Histories: New Writing About Dance and Culture*. Banff Centre P, 2000.

"Elder Magaret Harris." *Dancers of Damelahamid*, damelahamid.ca/our-team/elder-margaret-harris/.

Flynn, Anne. "Shape, Sense, Shift: Organizational and Disciplinary Changes in Dance Scholarship." *Canadian Theatre Review*, vol. 184, fall 2020, pp. 86–89.

Fogarty, Mary, and Imani Kai Johnson, editors. *The Oxford Handbook of Hip Hop Dance Studies*. Oxford UP, 2022.

Giersdorf, Jens Richard, and Yutian Wong. "Remobilizing Dance Studies." *Dance Research Journal*, vol. 48, no. 3, 2016, pp. 70–84.

Hahn, Tomie. *Sensational Knowledge: Embodying Culture Through Japanese Dance*. Wesleyan UP, 2007.

Klein, Gabriele, and Sandra Noeth, editors. *Emerging Bodies: The Performance of Worldmaking in Dance and Choreography*. Transcript, 2011.

Koritz, Amy. "Re/Moving Boundaries: From Dance History to Cultural Studies." *Moving Words: Re-Writing Dance*, edited by Gay Morris, Routledge, 1996, pp. 88–103.

Lindgren, Allana. "'The Other "D"' Keynote Address: Disciplinarity and the Future of Dance in Canadian Universities." *Performance Matters*, vol. 2, no. 2, 2016, pp. 84–94.

Lindgren, Allana, and Kaija Pepper, editors. *Renegade Bodies: Canadian Dance in the 1970s*. Dance Collection Danse P, 2012.

Manning, Susan. "How We Got Here: A View from the US Academy." *Performance Matters*, vol. 2, no. 2, 2016, pp. 151–58.

Martin, Randy. "Between Intervention and Utopia: Dance Politics." Klein and Noeth, pp. 29–46.

———. *Critical Moves: Dance Studies in Theory and Politics*. Duke UP, 1998.

Novack, Cynthia. *Sharing the Dance: Contact Improvisation and American Culture*. U of Wisconsin P, 1990.

Odom, Selma Landen, and Mary Jane Warner, editors. *Canadian Dance: Visions and Stories*. Dance Collection Danse P, 2004.

"The Other D." *Institute for Dance Studies*, dancestudies.artsci.utoronto.ca/?page_id=534.

"Potlach Ban." *U'mista Potlach*, umistapotlatch.ca/potlatch_interdire-potlatch_ban-eng.php.

"Welcome to Dance Collection Danse." *Dance Collection Danse*, dcd.ca/.

CHOREOGRAPHIES OF POWER: DE-HABITUATING OFFICER PRESENCE IN SCENARIO-BASED, DE-ESCALATION TRAINING

NATALIE ÁLVAREZ, GREG HODGE, AND JENNIFER LAVOIE

Can scenario-based training improve police response to individuals in mental health crisis? What happens when officers are taken through a stop-rewind-replay rehearsal process that asks them to "inhabit the role" of an officer in front of their peers and subject-matter experts, where they see themselves being seen and how they are being seen?

In 2017 we embarked on a four-year study funded by the Social Sciences and Humanities Research Council in an effort to investigate these questions. The study coincided with a wave of independent reviews and reports—such as the 2016 Ontario Ombudsman Paul Dubé's report, the Honourable Frank Iacobucci's 2014 report, and the 2014 Mental Health Commission report authored by two of our collaborators, Terry Coleman and Dorothy Cotton—sparked by the 2013 shooting of Sammy Yatim by Constable James Forcillo on a streetcar in Toronto. The shooting was, at the time, the most recent in a long history of police use of force incidents involving fatal shootings that disproportionately impact racialized persons in mental health crisis.[1] These reports overwhelmingly and consistently insist that standardized training

1 See "Deadly Force" by Marcoux and Nicholson, an investigation by the Canadian Broadcasting Corporation (CBC) that found that more than 460 people died in encounters with police from 2000 to 2017. The majority of those were in a state of mental-health crisis and Indigenous and Black populations were "overwhelmingly over-represented in these encounters."

in de-escalation and mental health crisis response needs to be implemented across the province. Those calls have not yet been realized. In Ontario and, indeed, across Canada, we have not yet seen or experienced what it would be like to have a police force trained and *evaluated* in de-escalation competencies, antiracism, and mental health crisis response in a standardized, validated, and sustained way.

In response to these calls, Natalie Álvarez, alongside co-investigators Jennifer Lavoie and Yasmine Kandil, assembled a multidisciplinary, national team of people with lived experience of mental illness (co-author Greg Hodge among them), peer support workers, theatre practitioners, researchers, forensic psychologists, mental health clinicians, de-escalation trainers, and Indigenous cultural-safety experts to co-design and co-deliver a forty-hour scenario-based training program. The team collectively created an evaluation framework, the De-escalating Persons in Crisis Competencies Tool (DePICT), consisting of fourteen core competencies in de-escalation and mental health crisis response to be used for assessment purposes that hold police officers to a professional standard.[2] The study takes officers through a spectrum of scenarios featuring a diversity of individuals and mental health crisis encounters, beginning with a high-intensity ten-minute scenario to capture a baseline measure of skill set to a series of three ninety-minute "Forum Scenarios" (adapted from the Forum Theatre methods of Brazilian director Augusto Boal) and on to a circuit of four ten-minute, high-affect scenarios in which officers are assessed using the DePICT framework on their ability to demonstrate the core de-escalation competencies.

The signature feature of the study, the Forum Scenario, is a form of stop-rewind-replay observer-participant scene work in which officers have the opportunity to witness a mental health crisis encounter adapted from an inquest report that stages an officer's use of force in response to an individual in mental health crisis. The officers discuss the scene, identifying the

2 No such assessment tool, to our knowledge, exists expressly for the purposes of de-escalation and mental health crisis response and designed by community stakeholders and consumers who determined what good de-escalation looks and feels like for them.

options and approaches that were available to the officer in the scene and that might have produced a peaceful outcome in which the person's dignity, needs, and safety drive the encounter and the officer's decision-making. The officers then have the opportunity to step into the scene, rehearsing and repeating these alternative strategies. A non-police facilitator, alongside a trio of subject-matter experts (SMEs)—a person with lived experience of mental illness, a mental health clinician, and a de-escalation trainer—have the opportunity to press the "pause button" on the scene and offer suggestions to the officers on alternative approaches and best practices with respect to the specific mental health crisis signs and possible barriers to communication they are witnessing. After the pause the officer has the choice to resume the scene, rewind to a particularly challenging moment, or allow another officer to step in and take the opportunity to practise. The feedback from SMEs to the officer demonstrates in immediate terms *how* knowledge about best practices in mental health crisis response—which, in typical police training contexts, is mainly delivered in a decontextualized lecture format—can be applied in the heat of the encounter, allowing de-escalation competencies to become, moment-to-moment, habituated in the body and integrated into the officer's muscle memory and repertoire of decision-making.

In this essay, we focus our attention on how the scenario-based training program calls attention to the officer's bodily presence when the mere presence of an officer on scene is an escalating force, particularly to Indigenous and Black communities that have experienced disproportionately higher rates of police violence in mental health crisis encounters (Marcoux and Nicholson). We telescope in on the officer's moving body as the site of the "political unconscious"[3] where a commitment to a use-of-force paradigm has been habituated in the body to such a degree that it has become synonymous with officer and

3 By "political unconscious" we draw on Fredric Jameson's arguments in his 1981 book, *The Political Unconscious: Narrative as a Socially Symbolic Act*, in which he examines the political, social, and historical as overlapping interpretive frameworks for the analysis of cultural texts. Here, we extend "cultural texts" to include bodily movement and expressive behaviour, which can be analyzed to reveal the ideological and political "unconscious" that, according to Jameson, permeates them.

public safety, despite evidence that such tactics only aggravate the mental health crisis and increase the risk of injury and harm both to the person in distress and to the officer (Kesic et al.; Kleinig; Watson et al.). We ask whether the Forum Scenario—which invites officers to "rehearse the scene" in front of an audience of civilian specialists and fellow officers—has the potential to produce a form of "muscular alienation," to borrow from Augusto Boal (127), that allows officers to see what their body speaks, defamiliarizing the role of officer as something they inhabit, making it, in turn, subject to alteration and augmentation.

These questions rely on the expansive field of dance ethnography, which, as Deidre Sklar insists, is anchored in the hypothesis that "cultural knowledge is embodied in movement" and that this knowledge is "not just somatic, but mental and emotional as well, encompassing cultural history, beliefs, values and feelings" ("On Dance Ethnography" 6). Bodily movement and gesture are, in other words, encoded communicative and physical acts that carry knowledge and values (Noland xiii)—in this instance, the knowledge and values of police culture premised on a use of force training paradigm. Drawing on this hypothesis, we propose that the Forum Scenario might introduce a gap in the officer's "'maintained' gestural routine" that has been established through training (Noland xiii), engendering a productive "undoing" of bodily behaviours that can then make way for an intentional encoding of other kinds of knowledge that becomes routinized and somatically familiar through "rehearsal learning." If, as Carrie Noland insists, gesture is "a potent means of cultural self-definition" (xvi), then how a police culture defined by a use of force paradigm is instantiated in gestures and movement systems merits close attention.

We undertake this work with full awareness that the dominant methods of responding to individuals in mental health crisis are not sustainable. As a host of community advocates and organizations have observed, one of the consequences of police serving as first responders in mental health crisis events under the mandate of "public safety" is that it criminalizes mental health crisis and perpetuates misleading and stigmatizing perceptions of individuals in mental health crisis as unpredictable and prone to violence.[4] The study is a stopgap measure: an intervention in the standards of police training to contend with the present reality that police will continue to have encounters with at-risk populations in mental health crisis in the absence of dedicated and adequate mental health emergency infrastructure. The study is also responsive to the reality that police will continue to serve as mental health crisis first responders for the foreseeable future not merely because of the sheer volume of calls[5] but also because non-police mental health units cannot respond to a mental health crisis call if there is the potential for harm or if a weapon is present.[6] Moreover, in the present reality, police find themselves as first responders in mental health crisis events because, in countless cases, civilians call police in response to what they perceive to be "suspicious behaviour," not knowing that the person is in mental health crisis.[7] As Alex Vitale argues in *The End of Policing*, "We can never fully eliminate interactions between the police and [people living with mental illness]. There is indeed a need for more training of all officers, and even participation of officers in some crisis-response scenarios. The situation we have today, however, represents a

4 In reality, individuals living with mental illness are more likely to be victimized rather than engage in violence (Burczycka; Desmarais et al.).

5 In the city of Toronto, there are over thirty thousand mental health crisis calls for police assistance each year, and those numbers have risen during the COVID-19 pandemic ("Police-Reported Crime"). Approximately six thousand of these calls are handled by mobile crisis intervention units due not only to limited capacity and restricted hours of availability, but also because these units cannot respond if a weapon is involved (Szklarski).

6 For example, in Eugene, Oregon, CAHOOTS, the civilian-led response that has served as an exemplary model for cities across North America, works alongside police in mental health crisis response, calling on police to "stage" at the ready or take over calls when a weapon or imminent harm is present.

7 Take, for example, the case of Clive Mensah, a thirty-year-old Black man in mental health crisis who was fatally tasered in the backyard of his Toronto-area home by Peel police on 20 November 2019 after reports of a "suspicious male causing a disturbance" (cited in Nassar). As a Black man, Mensah was especially vulnerable to police violence and a misattribution of "suspicious behaviour" because of racial bias.

gross criminalization of mental illness" (167). If police will inevitably continue to respond to mental health crisis calls, merely stepping back and allowing the status quo of inconsistent and widely divergent training standards to persist is untenable. An overhaul of the use-of-force paradigm needs to coincide with robust investment on the part of local, provincial, and federal governments in not-for-profit community supports and mental health crisis emergency infrastructure to divert this responsibility away from police.[8]

This essay proceeds in three parts. Part One introduces a scenario loosely adapted from a Forum Scenario the research team has developed for the study. It is what the team calls a "springboard" scenario: a mental health crisis encounter in which the officer has resorted to a use of force. It ends at the moment the scenario would be paused for group analysis and discussion and officers would be invited to step in to try alternative approaches. Part Two draws on Greg's lived experience and extensive knowledge as a social worker, peer support worker, and study collaborator to recreate on the page the kinds of interventions SMEs would make in the Forum Scenario. Using the "pause" function, Greg unpacks and analyzes the officer's bodily presence from the point of view of his own experiences with police during a mental health crisis, demonstrating how the stop-rewind-replay method brings the officers' awareness to the impacts and effects of their non-verbal communication. In Part Three we examine how this attention to bodily movement might unsettle a use-of-force paradigm, altering the *habitus* of police culture.

---

8 There are over one million interactions between the police and people with mental illness in Canada every year (Boyce et al.) and there are indications that mental health crisis calls requesting assistance from police increased during the COVID-19 pandemic ("Police-Reported Crime").

PART ONE
FORUM SCENARIO SPRINGBOARD—BEN

The scenario you are about to read has been adapted from an actual encounter between an officer and a person in mental health crisis. Our officers in this springboard scenario are actual police officers re-enacting this adapted encounter to spark a discussion. We'll examine the officers' choices, the impacts and effects of their bodily presence and non-verbal communication, and whether different approaches might result in an improved outcome.

Two police officers arrive on scene: a bench in a park near a café with an outdoor patio. The officers are responding to complaints from the manager of the café about a man, BEN*—mid-twenties, Caucasian—who was disturbing customers, yelling at them, and threatening them. The complainant claims* BEN *is intoxicated. The manager insists he has seen* BEN *before, that he sleeps in the park, and that he's always coming around and bothering his customers.*

The police observe BEN *from a distance. He appears agitated, pacing in front of a park bench. He is wearing headphones and listening to music at a high volume. He nods his head occasionally to the rhythm of the music. Something periodically arrests his attention. He stops and cocks his head as though hearing something in the distance. It looks like he is talking to someone who is sitting on his shoulder. He says, "Fuck you, I got this," and resumes pacing. He stops in his tracks again and shouts, "No, they can't. Fuck off."*

The officers approach. Their stride is slow, strong, measured, and their posture is upright. They are in uniform, wearing bullet-proof vests, and their duty belts are equipped with the standard equipment: pistol, taser, OC or "pepper" spray, and baton. The CONTACT OFFICER takes a position about twelve feet away at a thrity-five-degree angle from the park bench. He stands with his right foot slightly in front of the left. He rests his right hand casually on his taser. His left hand rests on his duty belt. The COVER OFFICER stands approximately fourteen feet away and slightly behind the CONTACT OFFICER. The COVER OFFICER also stands with her right foot slightly in front of the left and her right hand also rests casually on her taser.

CONTACT OFFICER: Hello? Hey there.

The music from BEN's headphones is too loud for him to hear the officer's greeting, but he catches sight of them out of the corner of his eye and quickly moves behind the park bench.

Hey, are you Ben?

BEN does not respond. He stands behind the park bench, holding onto it. The CONTACT and COVER OFFICERS make eye contact. The COVER OFFICER adjusts her positioning, moving parallel to the park bench but maintaining her fourteen-foot distance.

My name's Officer Barrett with the Toronto Police. Are you Ben?

BEN does not respond. The officer raises his hand and points his finger at BEN's headphones.

(loudly) Take your headphones off.

BEN does not move or respond.

(yelling) I said take your headphones off.

BEN remains frozen.

The CONTACT OFFICER makes a motion to signal taking off the headphones. BEN complies and takes his headphones off.

Great, thanks. Wow, that music is loud! You're going to blow your eardrums. Can you turn the music down?

BEN remains frozen.

(loudly) The music is blaring. Turn it down.

After a long pause BEN reaches into his pocket for his phone.

The CONTACT OFFICER's right hand, formerly resting casually on the taser, now tightens.

(The slash indicates where the COVER OFFICER's words overlap with the CONTACT OFFICER's, indicating both are issuing commands simultaneously.)

Keep your hands / out of your pockets.

COVER OFFICER: We have to see your hands.

CONTACT OFFICER: Keep your hands . . . / Show me your hands.

COVER OFFICER: Just show us your hands.

The COVER OFFICER begins to move in so that she has a direct line to BEN. She draws her taser and keeps it at a low ready position. She takes very slow and steady steps that gradually move her in toward BEN.

BEN notices the CONTACT OFFICER drawing his taser and begins to panic. He makes a move to bolt. The CONTACT OFFICER runs after him and tackles him, pinning him on his stomach against the ground as the COVER OFFICER grabs his arms, pulls them behind his back with force, and places handcuffs on his wrists.

End scene.

PART TWO
FORUM SCENARIO CONTINUED—STOP-REWIND-REPLAY

NATALIE: So, in this part we're going to imagine we're in the Forum Scenario and the group of eight officers have just witnessed this springboard scenario. We would typically begin by asking the group of officers to break into small pods of two to three, each with an SME, and invite them to discuss the following questions: "What did you observe? Are there things you would have done differently?" You would usually be in one of these pods. What are the first things you would call officers' attention to or invite them to think about?

GREG: If you are someone, or know someone, who has extensive experience dealing with psychosis and/or mental illness, you're likely aware that people with this experience have an amazing ability to read body language. It is a protective measure for people who live with an inherited distrust of others, stemming from negative past experiences, to study people's actions: I can anticipate their next moves by how they talk with their body. In this case and many other real-life cases, officers arrive with biases already in their mind as soon as they determine it is a mental health crisis call. Whether conscious or not, they bring stigmatizing attitudes to the situation and the individual. Whether it is through their training or police culture generally, the officer is given permission to approach with an aura of authority and privilege. Their posture alone conveys this. The fact that the officer begins issuing commands immediately shows impatience and a sense of authority; Ben can't even hear the officer yet but, surely, he can read the body language of someone who is raising their voice or yelling with command. The lowered eyebrows and piercing eyes are matched by the pointed finger and raised arm while the other hand rests on his taser, ready to draw at any moment. Ben does not need to hear the officer's voice to understand the purpose of them being there; the body language says clearly that they are a threat to him.

We also observe the second officer preparing for the worst. Imagine the first officer made a good approach and had built a good rapport with Ben—that would fly out the window knowing there was a second officer who is only focused on apprehension. Someone willing to have a conversation would not take a flanking position so that Ben is cornered by an officer on either side of him. You would want to be in front of someone to use your active listening skills and allow your non-verbal communication and body language to be read more easily. The flank approach is sneaky and covers escape routes. If Ben thinks he has done nothing wrong, then this is a scenario that would only make him more paranoid or fearful of the unknown. In this case, there is no unknown, the second officer makes their intentions clear considering the positioning she moves into, trying to cover from a second angle. Does this situation present a safety concern before even making contact with Ben? That's something the officers need to ask before they even approach.

Ben takes his headphones off; this is a small win for all sides. But the officer intends to push his authority by telling Ben to turn the music down, still. At this point, the officer is still using commands and not treating Ben with respect or as a human that is not feeling well. We also observe that even though Ben attempts to turn down the music, he must reach into his pocket for his phone in order to do that. Yes, an officer must protect themselves in all situations but did he think of the response to the very command he just gave? The simple and common gesture of readiness, having his hand near the taser device, only instills fear and speaks very loudly to all of us when threatened. Ben at this point in the scenario is being threatened with harm, non-verbally. That moment when the officer makes a funny reference to Ben having his eardrums blown and asks him to turn the music down turns out to be a false front hiding their true intentions. The officer is ready to use force to get their way. What is their way? And why is it their way? There is only one outcome from the officer's perspective by drawing the taser and taking steps closer—apprehension by force.

Natalie: Let's imagine that two officers volunteer to step in and try some alternative strategies. Let's say the contact and cover officer get into the same kind of positioning. They replicate the same kind of posture—stride, foot positioning, hand resting on their belts—and they make eye contact, maybe even whisper to each other to coordinate their movements and response. Let's say, we hit the pause button on the scene about thirty seconds in to unpack these things. What do you ask them to consider?

Greg: I would get them talking about their stance. The officers' stances remain at one foot forward, one foot back: a perfect stance for drawing a weapon and being steady to use it quickly. I've learned in my education work for verbal de-escalation techniques that this is referred to as the "safety stance." Ben remains behind the bench from the very beginning because of this stance. It is not a stance that speaks calmly to those it is intended for. It is a position of readiness and it creates a barrier of communication. We see this basic stance in martial arts and it is a ready stance to act out and defend or attack. What I observe in that posture is two officers with a directive to remove Ben from the area to create a sense of calm to the surrounding community and not at any point are they concerned for Ben's safety.

Natalie: What would you ask officers to notice about Ben's bodily behaviours that might suggest he's hearing voices and negotiating competing voices?

Greg: For someone hearing voices, there are some common signs, for instance, a lack of eye contact, common when someone is more focused on what they are hearing rather than what they are seeing. Loud voices take precedence over trusting your eyes because the voices can be so loud that nothing else can get your attention. For most people who experience voices, the voices come from their blind spots. For someone new to these experiences it can be debilitating because you constantly look over your shoulder only to not see anyone there. For Ben to stop mid-pace to look with his ears, this is a sign that the voices are clearly very loud.

It is common to see someone experiencing voices look with their ears—they tend to cock their heads toward an area in that direction with their ears. You may think that the person is looking at the ground but you may notice a blank stare: typically all facial expressions pause so the person can focus their attention on what they are hearing. Some people also react to these voices whether it be a slight giggle, chuckle, or even so far as to talk back to the voices.

A person with extended lived experience of hearing voices can control most of these external signs and body language to hide what they are experiencing and, more often than not, become quiet so as to focus on what they are hearing. You may be mid-conversation and all of a sudden the expression on their face goes blank. You may ask if everything is okay and, although they hear you, there might be brief pauses before they answer. For some of us, it can be embarrassing when people catch us in our moment of listening to a voice. If someone asks if I'm okay, I may say everything is fine; in most cases this is true. It is important not to push the question, "Are you okay?" too far.

In Ben's case, the voices have progressed to either yelling at him, or even commanding him. If someone is experiencing this heightened state of psychosis and is sticking to a specific area, it is quite possible that the voices are the reason. Ben's pacing would signal to me that he is in distress and that is validated even more by him yelling back at the voices. This may be troubling for the surrounding community, sure, but how distressed must Ben be in this state?

You cannot punch the physical voice in your head—some have tried, and some have drastically tried, so how do we physically react to this frustration? We pace, we punch ourselves, we grit our teeth in anger, and sometimes we lay down on the ground in a fetal position. It is intense, it is excessive, it is traumatizing, and it is exhausting. Had I been that officer and realized the area was safe, I would allow Ben that space and time to work on his control of the voices and show him compassion.

For some people experiencing hearing voices, using headphones is a way to cope with these voices. Having loud music can drown out how loud the voices can be and can have a therapeutic effect, especially if the music is calming to the individual. If Ben is hearing voices and drowning out the voices with the music, chances are he does not hear the ambient sounds outside beyond what he's hearing in his head and headphones. Imagine, if the music is this loud and he doesn't hear the police calling him, and suddenly sees them behind him or even in his peripheral vision, then Ben's reaction is nothing short of panic. The officers need to practise patience and take the time to listen and watch Ben prior to approaching. If they do this, they'll quickly realize that Ben is struggling. Wait patiently: wait for Ben to make eye contact, and once eye contact is made, they can use their hand to wave and get Ben's attention.

I'd ask the officers to observe Ben's state when he becomes aware of their presence. He's in a shocked, frozen state. I'd ask them to consider the possibility that Ben has a negative history with police and maybe that's why he is in a frozen state. Think about a trauma-informed approach. Are there past traumas or negative encounters with police that could explain his current response and the fear he is experiencing? Are you still talking to him? Are you both talking at the same time, adding to the chaos of voices in his head? Are the voices saying anything about the officers? Are you giving him the space and time to respond?

If the officer notices the headphones are still loud, even after Ben's taken them off his head, the officers could address that by putting their own finger to their ear and motioning to Ben that they cannot hear him. "Can you hear me, Ben?" "Are you okay, Ben?" Silly questions, I know. But what is amazing is when you show someone a genuine sense of concern, this translates through your body language. "Can you hear me, Ben?" Your hands will motion to your ears, your eyes will squint, your upper torso will lean in so your voice carries slightly farther and your focus will not be on your safety/ready stance. "Are you okay, Ben?" You won't yell this to Ben; you will lower the tone of your voice as if to expect an answer in genuine interest and concern—not out of some ulterior motive to arrest or remove him. When you genuinely care, your voice will change its tone to an authentic concern, your head will tilt slightly to show that you are concerned, you might crouch down and grasp your hands as a way to ease their worries and fear. Addressing someone's emotions and validating how they are feeling is a key component of de-escalation.

Natalie: Okay, so let's imagine that two other officers volunteer to step in to take over and resume the scene. But they take up a positioning that assumes they've already established rapport and mutual trust with Ben and stand about ten feet away from them. We would likely play the scene out for a bit, allowing the officers to take in Ben's reaction to this. But we'd likely hit the pause button to unpack this and talk about time and distance.

Greg: From a safety perspective, is ten feet a safe distance away? That is not for me to decide on behalf of officers who risk their lives during their jobs week in and week out. However, Ben is not a serious threat and, in this scenario, we are outside with loads of space. More importantly, it's a louder environment. If the person you have been called to talk to is someone who is hearing voices, being outside is a huge communication barrier for them, therefore body language plays a larger role in making connections: it will be hard for a person to distinguish the officers' voices from those they are hearing in their head.

Could the officers both be twenty feet back in this scenario? Yes. The farther away the officers, the safer everyone will feel. At twenty feet away and farther, the officers would not need to approach with their safety/ready stance. That distance will also allow them to use their approach to ensure they are prioritizing the comfort of the person in a mental health crisis. The officers can make sure to slowly approach Ben and casually walk closer. How can the officers think about minimizing their presence knowing that the uniform alone is going to be a trigger? How can the officers make themselves smaller? Can they lower their shoulders, lean forward in a way that signals they want to listen, lowering their posture and height in turn? How can they signal gently with their hands to Ben that they'd like to talk, knowing that he can't hear them through the headphones and the voices he is wrestling with? Is there a way to raise a hand out in front as if to say, "Woah, it's okay—I'm here to say hello and I'm here to help." It's important for the officer to stay attuned to their own body language, knowing when and how to best approach with ease, modelling calm. Of course, someone in a state of psychosis may have a diminished capacity to "read" body language and movements that aim to model calm, but the important point to make here is that thinking about body language—how it can escalate and de-escalate a situation—is critical. For some folks in psychosis who are in a protective, fearful state, specific senses such as sight may become heightened and telescope on the possible threat of who is in the immediate vicinity. So, having that ability to be self-reflective about how the body is communicating and adapt, moment to moment, based on how the person in mental health crisis is responding is key. Above all, those in psychosis will have a diminished capacity to react in expected ways; they may need more time to process heightened sensory input and information. So officers have to learn to sit in long pauses and exercise patience: providing the space and time for people in psychosis to respond safely is very important.

Natalie: If the officers decide they'd like to resume the scene after this brief discussion, what would you ask them to try in relation to their posture?

Greg: Something I am always speaking to officers about is being mindful of their hands and where they sit. Many officers have shared that when they are standing around for a long period of time that they need to put their hands somewhere and that putting them in their pockets is too difficult. So they typically rest their hands on their duty belt. But these belts house their use-of-force weapons and aggressive tools, so they must be mindful of how this appears to someone who is fearful of police. More often than not, their hands end up holding onto their bulletproof vests, which is a little less intimidating. If the officers are mindful of their stance, posture, and where they are placing their hands in the scenario, their approach will be much less intimidating to Ben. They need to try to keep an open-body posture and keep their hands away from weapons. If they do this, Ben will feel much less threatened, making it much easier for him to understand and process the officers' requests.

If the officers remain genuinely concerned for Ben's safety, the body language will follow suit. Transparency, above all, is key. If Ben reaching into his pocket to turn the music down makes the officers nervous, the contact officer could explain the dangers that they both could face and tell Ben how to remove the phone safely for all of their sakes. There is nothing wrong with being transparent. The officers can even explain why they need to have their hands near their tasers until they know everything is safe instead of pretending that it's a casual gesture that the person in crisis doesn't notice. Ben might be uncomfortable but at least he will know the officer's intention. This includes the mechanics and actions of the cover officer and the need for safety.

NATALIE: A refrain we hear often from officers going through this stop-rewind-replay rehearsal approach is that "hindsight is 20/20"—that it's unrealistic to replay the scene to "fix" choices with the foresight of knowing what could happen/had already happened. But these "fixes" are about identifying and *practising* the foundational principles that make de-escalation possible and that can be applied in most cases. And it's about rehearsing them until they become second nature, replacing a reflexive recourse to use-of-force tactics.

GREG: Sure, hindsight is 20/20, and I think most of us would like a second chance at many of the things we have tried to do and possibly failed at. It comes down to training and it speaks volume to the lack of mental health knowledge in policing.[9] Most recently I asked a group of recruits, recent graduates from police college who had just joined a police force in southern Ontario and completed their in-service training, if they had any mental health classes in their courses. The answer was simply "no." Fifteen soon-to-be officers had absolutely no idea about the population that they are paid to protect aside from a three-hour class where they learn about diagnoses, which makes no difference to any officer considering the diagnosis only increases bias.

9 The significant work to be done in creating sustained, consistent, standardized, and evaluated mental health training for police officers in Ontario is evidenced by a host of reports, including those mentioned at the top of this essay by Paul Dubé, Frank Iacobucci, and Terry Coleman and Dorothy Cotton, as well as a number of inquest recommendations dating back to 2011.

Where are the courses taught by people who are not police: the social workers, the human-rights workers, the mental health workers, the peer workers who have a lifetime of lived experiences? These are the people who can teach our police and first responders the true and needed knowledge to empower them to be more compassionate and proactive protectors. Getting a good look at mental health crisis scenarios under the guidance of mental health experts, prior to being on patrol, would lessen an officer's chances of ever saying hindsight is 20/20.

PART THREE
DEHABITUATING A USE-OF-FORCE PARADIGM

This examination of what police training habituates, and can potentially dehabituate, in the bodies of police draws on a genealogy of dance ethnography that, since the 1980s, turned to the social and philosophical theory of such thinkers as Pierre Bourdieu, Michel Foucault, and Maurice Merleau-Ponty to undertake "cultural analyses of bodies in motion" (Reed 520). In particular, it lies at the interstices of two dominant tendencies that have characterized dance studies since the turn of the twentieth century. According to Sklar, these two tendencies consist of, on the one hand, studies that examine how the body somatically organizes knowledge and, on the other, a focus on how social and political meanings become sedimented and embodied within movement systems ("Remembering Kinesthesia" 92). As a movement system, the use-of-force training paradigm is a powerful illustration of the ways in which these two tendencies come together in a complementary fashion that captures how political structures become enfolded into bodily behaviours and ways of knowing, part of a repertoire of intuitive judgment that comes to "feel right," somatically naturalized as what the officer does in a successful execution of the role in accordance with the law. In Marxist philosopher Louis Althusser's language, the successful embrace and execution of these bodily practices allows the officer to be successfully interpellated as an officer and come to recognize themselves as an officer.

The implications of this movement system within working definitions of police use of force is significant; use of force is defined as the tactics used to "gain control of a subject using no more force than is reasonably necessary, having regard firstly to officer safety and secondly to minimizing harm to the subject" (*Use of Force* 3). The prioritization of the officer's own safety and the right to use force "on reasonable grounds" is enshrined in Section 25 of the Canadian Criminal Code, entrenching an "us versus them" outlook. This outlook is reinforced in use-of-force block-training exercises, in which officers are repeatedly subjected to innocuous interactions with the public that turn deadly in a split second, requiring drills that stress-inoculate officers and cultivate a "warrior mindset," allowing them to maintain the fine motor skills required for weapons handling and hands-on tactics while under extreme stress. The movement system established in block training centres on controlling the subject, as per use-of-force doctrine,[10] rather than communicating with them, and this orientation primes officers to view uncooperative or non-compliant people in distress as more threatening than they are, leading to unnecessary uses of force (Li et al.).

This interlacing of the somatic and political in the movement systems of police training also helps to explain why efforts to dismantle a use-of-force paradigm at the level of discourse and intellectual argument will invariably run up against the impassable "thin blue line" of police culture. The use-of-force doctrine shapes what sociologist Pierre Bourdieu refers to as the body's *hexis*, "the motor function, in the form of a pattern of postures that is both individual and systematic . . . linked to a whole system of techniques involving the body and tools, and charged with a host of social meanings and values" (87). The body's *hexis* is an extension of the *habitus* of police culture, as a "system of lasting, transposable dispositions which, integrating past experiences, functions at every moment as a matrix of perceptions, appreciations, and actions" (82–83). While the officer may have the illusion of autonomous

10 By a use-of-force "doctrine," we allude to the ways in which the use of force is doctrinal in the sense that it represents a set of beliefs that inform police training and police culture more broadly.

action and independent decision-making, this is a heavily "regulated improvisation," to borrow Bourdieu's phrase (79), governed by the collective practice of the *habitus*, which is produced and reified in use-of-force training. The use of force is made synonymous with officer safety in the context of an always already looming threat to that safety. It is, in short, an ideological orientation that shapes the body's *hexis*: its posture, its motor functioning, its reflexive recourse to weapons handling, as well as its somatic feelings and perceptions. Moreover, the "homogeneity of the habitus" is what makes these bodily practices "immediately intelligible and foreseeable" but also rote and "taken for granted" (Bourdieu 80)—part of a process of sedimentation into patterns of movement and perception that are ordinary and routinely maintained.

The deeply intertwined relationship between movement practices and ideology helps to explain how social structures are perpetuated at the level of the body (Sklar, "Remembering Kinesthesia" 91). It is also powerfully illustrative of the ways in which ideology does not rest in the minds of subjects but is, rather, fundamentally material, residing in what the body *does*—its movement systems and practices. For Althusser, in his 1970 essay "Ideology and Ideological State Apparatuses," this materialist view of ideology helped to explain how the labour power and relations of production required to sustain ideological systems like capitalism could be reproduced. Rereading this essay through the lens of dance ethnography allows for a deepened appreciation of the implications of Althusser's claim that ideology—as "the imaginary relationship of individuals to their real conditions of existence"—is material (82). That is, it exists in governing institutions that precede and shape the individual's *practices*—what the individual does, including bodily actions, rituals, and behaviours. These are practices to which the subject is habituated, performed outside conscious awareness and inseparable from the ways in which one spontaneously lives out one's daily existence. They become invisible, inextricable from what Althusser calls "world outlooks" that are inhabited but remain obscured. Althusser's insistence that ideology manifests itself in practices elucidates how a use-of-force paradigm becomes a self-sustaining ideological system at the level of the body, underscoring why a close scrutiny of what is being actively entrained in bodies is so critical and what an analysis through an interdisciplinary lens of dance ethnography, movement analysis, and performance studies might unveil.

But this view of ideology as material and operating through bodily practices also points to what can be undone and dehabituated in these practices. With a "special motive," scenario-based training environments can be productive sites for what the late sociologist and ethnomethodologist Harold Garfinkel would call "breaching experiments": establishing familiar, commonplace scenes with a "life-as-usual" character only to gradually estrange participants from them, allowing otherwise invisible background expectancies to come into view.[11] By starting with the "springboard" scenario, staging a use-of-force encounter between an officer and an individual in mental health crisis, the Forum Scenario opens with a scene that is, unfortunately, all too familiar. But the high-fidelity repetition of the familiar only sets the stage for patterns of recognition to be de-realized and the course of entrained decision-making to be disrupted. The "non-fictional" familiarity of this scene enables the officer to accept its realism and sustain engagement even as its tacit givens are de-realized and interrogated with each iteration. Through the Forum Scenario's stop-rewind-replay function, officers unravel the scene as they rehearse, allowing them to test alternative options that lead to a progressive deepening of new forms of bodily knowledge. The iterative "open rehearsal" process engages both bodily doing and observational learning through body-to-body witnessing; officers see themselves being seen and how they are being seen, heightening a sense of mutual accountability.

Through this iterative process, the Forum Scenario offers an opportunity to regularize de-escalation tactics that become integrated bodily and mentally—part of a movement system that expands the repertoire of available patterns of action stored in the memory and allowing expert intuition, premised on de-escalation strategies, to develop. As researchers of decision-making and judgment have argued, skilled intuition relies on "the

11 "Procedurally," Garfinkel explains, "it is my preference to start with familiar scenes and ask what can be done to make trouble" (37). Estranging participants from these familiar scenes should, according to Garfinkel, "tell us something about how the structures of everyday activities are ordinarily and routinely produced and maintained" (38).

recognition of patterns stored in memory" (Kahneman and Klein 516). The development of a movement system that intentionally encodes de-escalation competencies allows alternate patterns of recognition to be stored in the memory, modifying the body's *hexis* toward new sets of skilled intuitions to draw upon in the heat of a mental health crisis encounter. As Sklar insists, the "hold of the habitus is not absolute": it is possible to transcend its grip through new forms of bodily practice, proprioception, and awareness ("Remembering Kinesthesia" 91). In short, it is through the body's *hexis* that the *habitus* of police culture might be altered, a proposition that holds fast to the promise of performance to advance a social praxis through bodily doing and action. If ideology is material and lies in the successful embrace of practices that interpellate subjects, then bodily practices are the starting point to unsettle entrenched ideological positions and precipitate profound systemic changes within police culture.

WORKS CITED

Althusser, Louis. "Ideology and Ideological State Apparatuses (Notes Towards an Investigation)." *Lenin and Philosophy and Other Essays*, translated by Ben Brewster, Monthly Review P, 1971, pp. 79–97. mforbes.sites.gettysburg.edu /cims226/wp-content/uploads/2018/09/Week-3b-Louis-Althusser.pdf.

Boal, Augusto. *Theatre of the Oppressed.* Translated by Charles A. McBride and Maria-Odilia Leal McBride, Theatre Communications Group, 1979.

Bourdieu, Pierre. *Outline of a Theory of Practice.* Cambridge UP, 1977.

Boyce, Jillian, Cristine Rotenberg, and Maisie Karam. *Mental Health and Contact With Police in Canada, 2012. Statistics Canada*, 2015, www150.statcan.gc.ca/n1/pub/85-002-x/2015001/article/14176-eng.htm.

Burczycka, Marta. *Violent Victimization of Canadians with Mental Health-Related Disabilities, 2014. Statistics Canada*, 18 Oct. 2018, www150.statcan.gc.ca/n1/pub/85-002-x/2018001/article/54977-eng.htm.

Coleman, Terry, and Dorothy Cotton. *TEMPO: Police Interactions: A Report Towards Improving Interactions Between Police and People Living with Mental Health Problems. Mental Health Commission of Canada*, Jun. 2014, mentalhealthcommission.ca/wp-content/uploads/2021/05/TEMPO-Police-Interactions-082014.pdf.

Desmarais, Sarah L., Richard A. Van Dorn, Kiersten L. Johnson, Kevin J. Grimm, Kevin S. Douglas, and Marvin S. Swartz. "Community Violence Perpetration and Victimization Among Adults with Mental Illnesses." *American Journal of Public Health*, 12 Nov. 2014. 10.2105/AJPH.2013.301680.

Dubé, Paul. *A Matter of Life and Death: Investigation Into the Direction Provided by the Ministry of Community Safety and Correctional Services to Ontario's Police Services for De-Escalation of Conflict Situations. Ombudsman Ontario*, Jun. 2016, ombudsman.on.ca/Files/sitemedia/Documents/OntarioOmbudsmanDeescalationEN_1.pdf.

Garfinkel, Harold. *Studies in Ethnomethodology*. Prentice-Hall, 1967.

Iacobucci, Frank. *Police Encounters with People in Crisis: An Independent Review Conducted by the Honourable Frank Iacobucci for Chief of Police William Blair, Toronto Police Service. Commission of Inquiry Respecting the Death of Donald Dunphy*, Jul. 2014, ciddd.ca/documents/phasetwo/police_encounters_with_people_in_crisis.pdf.

Jameson, Fredric. *The Political Unconscious: Narrative as a Socially Symbolic Act*. Cornell UP, 1981.

Kahneman, Daniel, and Gary Klein. "Conditions for Intuitive Expertise: A Failure to Disagree." *American Psychologist*, vol. 64, no. 6, Sep. 2009, pp. 515–26.

Kesic, Dragana, Stuart D.M. Thomas, and James P.R. Ogloff. "Estimated Rates of Mental Disorders in, and Situational Characteristics of, Incidents of Nonfatal Use of Force by Police." *Social Psychiatry and Psychiatric Epidemiology*, vol. 48, no. 2, Feb. 2013, pp. 225–32. 10.1007/s00127-012-0543-4.

Kleinig, John. "Legitimate and Illegitimate Uses of Police Force." *Criminal Justice Ethics*, vol. 33, no. 2, 2014, pp. 83–103. 10.1080/0731129X.2014.941539.

Li, Danyao, Sean Nicholson-Crotty, and Jill Nicholson-Crotty. "Creating Guardians or Warriors? Examining the Effects of Non-Stress Training on Policing Outcomes." *American Review of Public Administration*, vol. 51, no. 1, 11 Nov. 2020, pp. 3–16. 10.1177/0275074020970178.

Marcoux, Jacques, and Katie Nicholson. "Deadly Force: Fatal Encounters with Police in Canada: 2000–2017." *CBC News*, 4 Apr. 2018, newsinteractives.cbc.ca/longform-custom/deadly-force.

Nassar, Shanifa. "A Young Black Man was Fatally Tasered in his Own Backyard—Now his Family is Demanding Answers." *CBC News*, 21 Jul. 2020, cbc.ca/news/canada/toronto/clive-mensah-black-taser-police-1.5655022.

Noland, Carrie. Introduction. *Migrations of Gesture*, edited by Carrie Noland and Sally Ann Ness, U of Minnesota P, 2008, pp. ix–xxviii.

"Police-Reported Crime Incidents Down During the Early Months of the Pandemic, While Domestic Disturbance Calls Increase." *Statistics Canada*, 1 Sep. 2020, www150.statcan.gc.ca/n1/daily-quotidien/200901/dq200901a-eng.htm.

Reed, Susan A. "The Politics and Poetics of Dance." *Annual Review of Anthropology*, vol. 27, 1998, pp. 503–32. 10.1146/annurev.anthro.27.1.503.

Sklar, Deidre. "On Dance Ethnography." *Dance Research Journal*, vol. 23, no. 1, spring 1991, pp. 6–10.

———. "Remembering Kinesthesia: An Inquiry into Embodied Cultural Knowledge." *Migrations of Gesture*, edited by Carrie Noland and Sally Ann Ness, U of Minnesota P, 2008, pp. 85–111.

Szklarski, Cassandra. "With Spotlight on Police Failures, How Can the System Better Respond to Mental-Health Crises?" *CTV News*, 15 Jun. 2020, ctvnews.ca/canada/with-spotlight-on-policing-failures-how-can-the-system-better-respond-to-mental-health-crises-1.4985077.

Use of Force Training Manual. Commission of Inquiry Respecting the Death of Donald Dunphy, Royal Newfoundland Constabulary, Exhibit P-0624, 17 Feb. 2017, ciddd.ca/documents/exhibits/P-0624.pdf.

Vitale, Alex. *The End of Policing*. Verso, 2017.

Watson, Amy C., Beth Angell, Melissa Schaefer Morabito, and Noel Robinson. "Defying Negative Expectations: Dimensions of Fair and Respectful Treatment by Police Officers as Perceived by People with Mental Illness." *Administration and Policy in Mental Health and Mental Health Services Research*, vol. 35, no. 6, Nov. 2008, pp. 449–57. 10.1007/s10488-008-0188-5.

BREAKING AND BALLROOM: A MATCH SET IN THE OLYMPICS

SEROUJ APRAHAMIAN

Beginning in the 1990s, the world's leading competitive ballroom dance organizations decided to relabel their activities as "dancesport" in the hopes of entering the Olympic Games. They reasoned that since most people thought of ballroom as a recreational activity—with its "Standard" partner-based dances such as the waltz, tango, and foxtrot, as well as its "Latin" category of forms such as the samba, cha-cha, rumba, pasodoble, and jive—changing the name of the genre would draw more attention to its athleticism and regimentation, qualities they felt were needed to get into the Olympics. Thus, in April 1998, the Canadian branch of the leading global ballroom governing body changed its name from the Canadian Amateur Ballroom Dancers Association to the Canadian Amateur DanceSport Association (today known simply as Canada DanceSport).

Around the same time, breaking was experiencing a resurgence throughout North America after a period of dormancy following its overexposure and commercialization in the mid-1980s. Many of the key figures involved in this resurgence emphasized the need to counteract the mainstream media's depictions of the dance as a fad or spectacle, symbolized most prominently by the community's campaign against the term "breakdancing." As Steffan "Mr. Wiggles" Clemente of the Rock Steady Crew, one of the architects of this campaign, put it, "If we kept walking around calling ourselves 'breakdancers,' they'd be like, 'Ah, y'all them kids from the '80s, man that shit's played out.' But when we started calling ourselves b-boys, it was like, 'What, this some new shit?'" (*Freshest Kids* 57:02–57:13). In addition to giving the dance a renewed image, this renaming effort sought to pay homage to the form's cultural roots, as practitioners always called their dance breaking and its practitioners b-boys and b-girls, not the media misnomers of breakdancing or breakdancers.

In December 2016, these parallel attempts to resignify the meaning of each dance style converged in a manner few could have predicted: the International Olympic Committee (IOC) announced that, for the first time ever, dancesport would be introduced into its athletic programming—but through the discipline of *breaking*, not ballroom (International Olympic Committee, *Buenos Aires 2018*). The trial run of the dance at the 2018 Youth Olympic Games (YOG) in Buenos Aires, Argentina, was soon followed by the full inclusion of breaking in the 2024 Summer Olympic program in Paris, France. Even though b-girls and b-boys had never petitioned to be in the Olympics, nor did they have any connection to the dancesport (ballroom) world, the IOC was now merging these two styles together as part of its own rebranding campaign aimed at attracting a younger, more urban demographic. In other words, with a series of arbitrary decisions aimed at crafting a more "hip" image, the Olympics deemed breaking to be a dancesport and assigned the World DanceSport Federation (WDSF) administrative power over its operations.

In this essay, I explore some of the underlying issues surrounding this historic development within the context of Canada, where both the breaking and ballroom communities play a prominent role in their respective international scenes. In the process of surveying how these two far-removed dance styles were brought together by the IOC, I ask four questions regarding the social and ideological impact of this convergence: How have Canadian b-boys and b-girls responded to being placed under the governance of the WDSF? How have the national breaking and dancesport communities interacted with one another since the Olympics announcement was made? What are the possible consequences of this decision on the future aesthetic, cultural, and socio-economic development of both dances? Finally, how have issues of power and identity been negotiated as part of this process?

I contend that breaking's adoption as the first ever dancesport at the Olympics is fraught with ideological and social contestation. This relates not only to the concern that the Olympics might negatively affect breaking's cultural values and aesthetics, with many fearing that it will steer the dance more toward athletics rather than artistic expression (Li and Vexler), but also, perhaps more importantly, the impact this move will have on the autonomy of the breaking scene, much of which is concentrated today on competitions. Having largely been nurtured through independent, grassroots efforts since the 1990s, leading actors and events within this competitive circuit are now being brought under the centralized authority of the WDSF. As will be discussed below, this has serious implications for the future direction of the dance, as the generally free-form approach of breaking stands in stark contrast to the institutionalization and stricture of the competitive ballroom industry. However, the prospect of Olympics accession—and the perception that financial opportunities will accrue from it—has tempered overt conflict over these differences among key actors within both the Canadian breaking and dancesport communities. Instead, a tacit state of co-operation has developed where both parties are seeking to coexist, while at the same time using their respective cultural, contractual, and commercial power to determine the direction of breaking at the Olympics. As such, this fragile arrangement represents a modern-day struggle over the economic and embodied values of a dance, and the conceptualizations shaping each side's claim to authority over it.

At the outset, I want to make clear that this is a topic that I have been directly involved in since December 2016, when I helped reveal that it was the WDSF that held contractual power over breaking at the Olympics—a fact that had been overlooked in media and public discourse up until that point. Instead, most discussions of breaking's accession focused on the IOC's decision to adopt the form, making no mention of the competitive ballroom industry's official governance role. Therefore, much of this chapter reflects my own personal observations of what has happened since that time. In addition, as a breaking practitioner who has been living in Toronto since late 2015, I have an intimate understanding of the competitive breaking community in Canada, which I have also supplemented through first-hand interviews with b-boys and b-girls involved in the Olympics process, as well as with the head of the WDSF's Canadian affiliate, Canada DanceSport (CDS) President Sandy

Brittain. I have combined such oral testimony with textual analysis of news articles and social-media posts in order to bolster my conclusions. As will be seen below, I have privileged quotations from the latter source material as much as possible to emphasize the extent to which the discussion in this chapter is publicly available information that readers can access, verify, and interpret for themselves.

THE OPENING ROUND

To understand how and why breaking was paired with ballroom, we must begin by examining the IOC and the business model underlying its operations. The most important point to note in this regard is that about 75% of the IOC's income is generated from selling media rights to broadcasters, with NBC being the main benefactor within this arrangement and a contractual partner of the IOC until at least 2032. However, since about 2012, audiences around the world have been turning away from the games, with younger viewers especially becoming disinterested in the IOC's traditional activities. For example, only an average of 15.5 million people watched the 2020 Summer Games in Tokyo, Japan, resulting in more than a 50% decline in ratings from the London Summer Olympics in 2012 (Adgate). The 2022 Winter Games in China were similarly disappointing, with a 43% drop in NBC's ratings from the 2018 games (Wetzel). Those few viewers who are tuning in have also become increasingly senior over time, with the median age of Olympic audiences today being in the low- to mid-fifties (Adgate). Needless to say, this is of major concern to outlets such as NBC and, in turn, the IOC. Unless the Olympics begins reaching the millennials it is rapidly losing, it risks being deprived of the television sponsors at the heart of its operations.

The IOC leadership has responded to this "crisis of relevance" (Liew) by adding a record number of new, youth-oriented activities to its roster, including skateboarding, surfing, sport climbing, and, most recently, breaking. That this latter discipline debuted at the 2018 YOG in Buenos Aires exemplifies just how much the IOC is driven by a desire for younger viewers. This point is further illustrated in the official proposal for breaking's YOG accession, which features such recurrent statements as: "DanceSport/Breakdance has a wide audience reach among Youth," breaking "allows young people to recognize trendy means of expression," "the inclusion of DanceSport/Breakdance . . . will strongly support the IOC's desire to attract youth," and so on (International Olympic Committee, *Buenos Aires 2018*). The president of CDS, Sandy Brittain, also made clear to me that "the IOC decided that breaking would appeal to the youth of the world and that is their goal, to try to get more youth interested in the Olympics." Like other dancesport officials around the world, she was disappointed to see that Standard and Latin ballroom would still not be included in the Olympic program but conceded that she "can see where the IOC was coming from in that . . . in the Standard, it seems to be our senior categories that are the biggest thing." In other words, the IOC deemed ballroom to be unappealing to the millennial audience they were seeking to reach, whereas breaking was seen as a perfect fit. As a result, the IOC urged the WDSF to pitch breaking to the YOG organizing committee—despite having no connection to the dance whatsoever—and in December 2016, after two decades of vying for the Olympics, the ballroom industry was finally allowed to get its foot into the door of the games.

But this raises a further question: Why did the WDSF want to join the Olympics in the first place? Why did they change the name of their discipline from ballroom to dancesport in the 1990s and lobby so vociferously for over two decades to become part of this athletic competition? The most immediate answer is, again, television revenue. A portion of the broadcast income that the IOC generates is distributed to the federations governing sports in the Olympics, as are the corporate sponsorship packages that often accompany the full inclusion of sports. By offering television visibility, the WDSF also believed that the Olympics would enhance ballroom's popularity and generate even further revenue.

In addition to this profit motive, however, the WDSF was eager to enhance its social standing by gaining Olympic approval. As dance scholar Juliet McMains details throughout her book *Glamour Addiction*, the competitive ballroom industry is heavily rooted in notions of social refinement and upward mobility, as everything from classes, competitions, costumes, and cosmetics in the dance are marketed according to Western standards of perfectionism. In fact, the history of ballroom is itself rooted in taking the social dances of various communities throughout Europe and the Americas and transforming them into highly codified practices that are deemed to be more disciplined and developed. These notions are embodied through strict rules placed upon practitioners aimed at "objectively" measuring and controlling their performances. Gaining Olympic authorization would further validate this penchant toward standardization and show that ballroom was a rigorous and professional—and, thus, superior—form of dance. In this sense, adopting the language of sports was not an aberration from ballroom dance history but, rather, a logical extension of it.

Nevertheless, despite the many years of effort the WDSF put into meeting the IOC's criteria and modelling itself off sports such as figure skating, the IOC ultimately denied their accession and, instead, steered them toward breaking. Like other community-based, youth-oriented activities now being included in the games (see Thorpe and Wheaton), breaking places a premium on creativity, with practitioners encouraged to embody the dance in their own unique way after having learned its basic structure and vocabulary. Breaking's connection to the beginnings of hip-hop culture are also heavily emphasized, with b-girls and b-boys expected not only to have proficiency in certain movements but also to understand the history and principles behind them, as well as associated forms of expression such as DJing, rapping, and aerosol art. In this sense, there is a heavy emphasis on culture and creativity in the dance that conflicts with the standardization of both the sporting and ballroom worlds. Indeed, it is precisely this emphasis on creativity that has made breaking popular among young people. For instance, even when breaking competitions are held, most promoters in the Canadian community also emphasize what are called "cyphers": impromptu dance circles where practitioners are free to dance without any formal guidelines or rules. In this way, tournament-style competitions are coupled with cyphers and are, thus, not considered athletic events but rather loosely structured platforms for dancers to engage with one another and express themselves.

I will discuss how the IOC's favouring of breaking has affected the WDSF's self-conception in more detail below, but, for now, suffice it to say that the ballroom industry's drive for profit ultimately prevailed over its lack of connection to the breaking community and its contrasting cultural values. In fact the WDSF began immediately claiming that breaking was one of its many disciplines, referring to b-girls and b-boys as "our youngest athletes," and arguing, without any convincing evidence, that they had a long history of organizing breaking competitions ("WDSF Announces").[1] "Millions of dancers around the world will be delighted over this Olympic embrace" proclaimed then-WDSF president Lukas Hinder in a congratulatory speech following breaking's sudden YOG accession. "It certainly is the fulfilment of a long-held dream and it will allow us to showcase the full breadth of DanceSport to the world at large" ("What a Day!").

Meanwhile, given that no breakers were consulted by the WDSF or the IOC regarding this decision, b-boys and b-girls learned about the dance's Olympic adoption the same way the public did: through news headlines. Accordingly, they took to social media to express a mixture of indifference, cautious optimism, and confusion. "I've been asked my opinion on Breaking being in the Olympics," wrote Richard "Crazy Legs" Colón, one of the best-known breakers in the world. "I have no response at the moment, because I don't know the details." Another outspoken public figure, Karl "Dyzee" Alba from the Supernaturalz Crew in Toronto, made a vlog weighing the pros and cons of the announcement, concluding that breaking in the Youth Olympics would secure a net benefit for the dance. "The majority of b-boys who know me, know that my dream is that all b-boys have the opportunity to make a great living from b-boying and that b-boying will be loved and respected worldwide," he explained. "B-boying in the Olympics can open up that door" (Dyzee Diaries, "The Truth About Bboyin"). Although he acknowledged that this step would likely cloud popular understanding of the dance's history and culture, with practitioners now having to fight against the notion that breaking is a sport, the premise that the Olympics would bring greater notoriety and, thus,

1 See also Yu.

financial opportunity to a precarious dance practice seemed to override all other concerns.

What was being overlooked in these initial posts by prominent breakers, however, was the fact that the WDSF was given administrative power over breaking at the Olympics. Having noticed the word "dancesport" in several of the articles referring to breaking's Olympic accession, and knowing that the term signified ballroom dancing, I began researching the background to the IOC's decision and quickly learned that the WDSF was behind the move. Of course, this raised immediate concerns about breaking not only being misrepresented on a global stage but also being exploited by an entity that had no prior connection to the dance. Since nobody in the community was discussing how the IOC gave ballroom dancers governing power over breaking, I began producing articles, videos, social-media posts, and petitions detailing who the WDSF is and how their governance of the dance could have adverse consequences ("Get the WDSF's Hands Off Hip-Hop"). These efforts succeeded in generating a great deal of community awareness and pushback against the IOC's adoption of breaking under the auspices of the WDSF.

In response to the public pressure that was mounted through these efforts, practitioners and promoters began calling for Olympics breaking to be led by people from within the community, as opposed to the ballroom industry. At the same time, the approach most event organizers and practitioners took, as the WDSF and IOC began reaching out to them, was to engage co-operatively with Olympics decision-makers, afraid that too much overt criticism would jeopardize the revenue and legitimacy they felt this global event would offer. "Our view is that it will be more productive to give the WDSF a bit of time to get organized and to interview volunteers from the breaking community than to concern ourselves at this very moment with who may ultimately control Olympic-level breaking," read a public statement from the Pro Breaking Tour, a leading competition circuit in North America. Its Canadian affiliate, the You Be Ill organization (formerly known as the Universal B-Boy League), was even more forthcoming, with its founder, Geoff Reyes, describing WDSF officials as "great minds" who took "a risk and actually bet on breaking," concluding that "if it takes a vehicle like the Olympics to get people's attention and take Breaking seriously, then I'm all for it" ("Breaking in the Olympics!"). In April 2017, Reyes invited the president of WDSF's Canadian branch, Sandy Brittain, to his annual Rock Harder event in Toronto, with the aim of building a closer relationship with the organization. Thus, just as the IOC adapted to the marketing interests of its television sponsors, and the WDSF conformed to the Olympics's youth-focused agenda, leading breakers around the world willingly accepted the WDSF's authority over their dance, with the hope that it would usher in new financial opportunities. When the Youth Olympics were eventually held in October 2018, they were overseen by a committee of such leading b-boys and b-girls who consulted for the WDSF under the heading of "Breaking for Gold."

Canadian breaking was represented at the Youth Games by Mathieu "D-Matt" Du Ruisseau from Montreal, who came in seventh in the b-boy category, and Emma Misak from Surrey, BC, who won a silver medal in the b-girls division. However, rather than being supported by the IOC, WDSF, or the Canadian Olympic Committee, these two dancers had to pay their own way to the Youth Olympics's qualifying events in the United States and Japan, as well as the finals in Buenos Aires. In fact, both Misak and Du Ruisseau started GoFundMe pages to raise money for their travel (Holmes; Sono), which is unusual in the breaking community, with promoters generally expected to fly out those who win their qualifying events. Of course, this lack of funding was even more bizarre given the dominant narrative that Olympic inclusion would lead to greater financial rewards for b-girls and b-boys alike. Like many other Olympic athletes (Business Insider), these two Canadian competitors encountered the reality of being amateur participants in the games, with the flow of resources and financial opportunity promised to them failing to materialize. And while the event in Buenos Aires was generally well-received in terms of its presentation of breaking's format and cultural context, questions remained regarding the Olympics's allocation of resources and decision-making power over the dance moving forward.

Fig. 1. B-girl Flo from Vancouver, BC, executing a freeze at the Ontario Dancesport Regional Qualifier held in Toronto on 29 April 2023. Photo © Jerick Collantes.

PARIS 2024

Having proclaimed breaking a success at the Youth Olympic Games in Buenos Aires, where it is said to have attracted ninety thousand spectators a day (Rossingh), the IOC quickly added breaking to its 2024 Summer Games in Paris as well. In the Olympic report advocating for this next step, breaking was said to have over one million young participants in France alone and over six million followers on social media (International Olympic Committee, *Olympic Games Paris 2024*). Putting aside the accuracy of these figures, it was clear that breaking's youth appeal remained the driving force behind its accession.

Meanwhile, as breaking's Olympic inclusion moved forward, Canada's dancesport leaders began familiarizing themselves with their breaking counterparts. "We started going out of our way to find the best consultants in Canada for breaking," explained Brittain, adding that they formed a special subcommittee of b-boy and b-girl volunteers to oversee the dance's incorporation. This committee included Geoff Reyes of You Be Ill, who, as mentioned above, had been inviting the WDSF to his breaking competitions since 2017. "The way that [Brittain] tells the story is, 'Yeah, I came and it was very dark, loud, and it smelled like weed' [laughs]," explains Reyes when recalling how he first met the president of Canada DanceSport at his annual breaking event (Tales of the Cypher 37:00–38:40). This anecdote, which was relayed on a podcast and repeated by Reyes to me in our interview, points to the general culture clash that was occurring as these two divergent dance forms came into contact. Interestingly, like other scholars of the dancesport industry, author Caroline Joan S. Picart notes that competitive ballroom dancers generally stray away from popular social dances spaces, which are perceived to be bastions of seedy and unsophisticated behaviour. "Studio [ballroom] dancing is associated with discipline and technique," she writes. "In comparison, 'street' or 'club' dancing is associated with spontaneity of expression and movement (along with smoke and alcohol)" (21). McMains comes to this same conclusion, arguing that the competitive ballroom industry props up its image of sophistication by claiming superiority over the social dances it has historically appropriated (*Glamour Addiction*). As in the aristocratic circles in which ballroom developed (McMains, "Brownface"), notions of order, cohesion, and precision are embodied in these dances through regimentation and signified through notions of proper etiquette and decorum. Thus, it should come as no surprise that dancesport officials associated breaking—a freeform, youth-oriented dance style that originated among working-class African American teenagers in the Bronx, New York—with darkness, noise, and disrepute.

With this depiction in mind, it is important to look at how dancesport officials have interpreted the IOC's bypassing of ballroom in favour of breaking, and how they have approached their governance over this unfamiliar and culturally antithetical dance style. Interestingly, rather than value the alternative principles enshrined in breaking and reflect on their own possible shortcomings, the WDSF's officials have used their traditionalist values as a pretext for bringing b-boys and b-girls into their fold. Echoing the "civilizing missions" of Europe in the colonial period (Outevsky), they have convinced themselves that their authority and expertise is needed to regulate an otherwise fragmented and ill-mannered community. "Breaking, until they came to Canada DanceSport, was an unorganized kind of discipline," Brittain told me in our interview. "It didn't have a national body or a world body and so, by becoming part of dancesport, it has given them an avenue to get more organized." This same saviour mentality has been echoed by WDSF's representatives around the world, such as former communications director Roland Hilfiker, who told *VICE News* that "breaking's [participation] in the Olympic games will open up new horizons for what was to a certain extent a subculture up until now—not a subculture, but a limited-scale type thing" (Yu). Jean-Laurent Bourquin, the former CEO of the WDSF, similarly told the *Washington Post* that breaking "needed to be codified with universal rules, judging and protocols," and only the dancesport industry was capable of such a task (Maese). These statements signal how dancesport officials have rechannelled their values of standardization and regulation into a condescending management role geared toward making breaking, in the words of Brittain, "an actual sport, not just a street dance."

Canada DanceSport's breaking subcommittee, which formed into a non-profit called Breaking Canada, has been the main vehicle through which this "professionalization" process has been occurring. For instance, in August 2021, Reyes substituted his annual Rock Harder competition with a CDS National Qualifier in Toronto, where participants had to register and pay a membership fee to their provincial CDS affiliate. However, this was not a qualifier for the Olympics but, rather, for the WDSF annual World Championship event in China, which was, in turn, a qualifier for the WDSF's World Games in Alabama. In other words, these competitions are a part of the dancesport industry's standard series of events, which are now being grafted onto the breaking community to register members and assign them official rankings. Just as Canadian ballroom practitioners compete in a national qualifier that selects four dancers to go the WDSF's respective World Championships, World Games, and so on, breakers are now being subsumed within this system in line with the WDSF's declaration that the dance is one of their disciplines and must be streamlined accordingly.

Another component of this streamlining process relates to judging, with Breaking Canada now recruiting seasoned b-girls and b-boys to go through WDSF adjudicator training. Participants have to pay a fee to take part in this training and pass an exam to purchase a WDSF judging licence, which then must be maintained through a biennial renewal. Of course, the assumption of participants is that they will someday be paid as judges for WDSF events, and perhaps even for the Olympics. In addition, as is also common in competitive ballroom, breaking judges are being officially categorized as "retired" and barred from entering *any* further competitions themselves. This is quite a divergence from the dance's usually more informal method of competition evaluation and mentorship, where judges are not authorities who learn in a classroom and separate themselves symbolically from competitors. Rather, they are considered active participants in the dance who assess performances based on their embodied knowledge, do a showcase during the competition to demonstrate their competence, and may even be called out to compete when practitioners disagree with their decisions. Certainly, no breaking judges have ever had to "retire" from competitions to carry out their duties. Unfortunately, breaking's more horizontal approach is rapidly giving way to the stricture and rigidity of the dancesport industry. If this pattern continues, similar steps in the realm of certifications for event promotion, studio instruction, musical copyright, and competition tier systems are likely to follow suit.

Of course, many Canadian b-boys and b-girls are wary of the potential erosion of breaking's social, artistic, and cultural integrity that may result from this process, and those working with Canada DanceSport often justify their involvement in terms of trying to protect the dance. They have put in hours of work consulting the dancesport industry, largely as free volunteers, in the hopes of seeing the dance represented properly on the Olympics stage. In fact, this was one of the reasons that the original members of the CDS's breaking subcommittee formed the non-profit Breaking Canada. In the words of Victor "Vicious" Sono, a leading member of the group and a prominent figure in the Montreal breaking scene, "Breaking Canada was like an idea to protect ourselves, like, whatever the federation is asking us to do. To show that, okay, breaking has some kind of platform with our dancers, and to be able to maintain the art." Niels "Storm" Robitzky, a well-known b-boy from Germany who was one of the architects of the judging system currently being used by the WDSF, also made clear that "we value our creativity in breaking. Standards would choke that" (Breaking Canada 57:00–57:06). The system he helped prepare emphasizes categories and values from within the breaking community that are to be applied through a spectrum-based comparison of performance, rather than a rigid calculation of scores. This system is promoted in terms of fighting for the cultural integrity and freedom of the dance, with Robitzky even stating during a panel discussion at the CDS National Qualifier that "people need to realize that this is our dance, this is our community, we have our cultural values, and they need to do it like that. Otherwise, it wouldn't be the same thing and it won't even work with the IOC" (Breaking Canada 1:54:55–1:55:12).

And it is here, on the opposing poles of breaking and ballroom mapped along the Olympics field, that the competitive direction of these dance styles is being contested. Although it certainly seems that the IOC is intent on harnessing breaking's "lifestyle-oriented," "creative," and "high performance" appeal,[2] how this will work under the regimented, rule-bound, and profit-oriented system of the WDSF and its Canadian affiliate, the CDS, remains to be seen. The steps and pronouncements of the latter seem to suggest that the highly regimented and controlled system of the dancesport industry will increasingly be imposed on the breaking community. At the same time, the WDSF is eager not to upset the IOC, whose interest in attracting young viewers is dependent on breakers buying into the process and helping present the dance's distinctive qualities. Were b-boys and b-girls to oppose how breaking was being presented at the Olympics, the latter's goals of rebranding itself for younger viewers would be greatly damaged and, in turn, the WDSF's reputation as a viable federation would be tarnished. In the short run, this will likely mean that Canadian breakers will continue to be brought in as consultants for the

2 These quotes are taken from the official proposal to add breaking to the Olympics by the Paris 2024 Organizing Committee for the Olympic and Paralympic Games. See Dyzee Diaries, "The Final Proposal."

WDSF and will attempt to use their cultural capital to determine how breaking is presented at the Olympics.

However, in the long run, it is the WDSF who have contractual power over the dance, and they are increasingly throwing their own events that are not directly connected to the Olympics, where breakers are being required to succumb to their authority by joining local WDSF affiliates, paying membership fees, going through accreditation training, purchasing adjudication licences, gaining event permissions, and deferring to dancesport officials for final decisions on the Olympics. As Brittain explained to me in our interview, Breaking Canada "is basically under Canada DanceSport. They pay an associate membership to us and they have to follow our different rules." Reyes also admitted that his non-profit "acts as the agent for Canada DanceSport," with the CDS signing all of the cheques and agreements related to breaking, and breakers providing the knowledge and public persona needed to push the process forward. How much b-girls and b-boys will compromise under the weight of the dancesport industry's contractual and financial power, and how much the WDSF will revert to its historic legacy of standardizing and sterilizing social dances, will determine the trajectory of competitive breaking in Canada for the foreseeable future.

FROM "BREAKDANCE" TO "DANCESPORT"

When b-boys and b-girls began to push back against the media misnomer "breakdancing" in the 1990s, it was about more than a matter of terminological preference. It was about demanding respect for the dance and allowing its practitioners to determine its destiny. Given the inexperience of those practitioners who found themselves in the middle of breaking's 1980s exposure, little was done to educate the public about the values, history, and terminology of the dance. Instead, companies and promoters that were willing to hire breakers were the ones who determined how the form would be presented, often highlighting its most acrobatic features. The expressive aspects of the dance, as well as its cultural heritage and aesthetic codes, became obscured through this process and, as dance scholar Sally Banes concluded in 1984,

Fig. 2. Canadian competitors Illz and Phil Wizard wait for their names to be called in the next round of the WDSF World Breaking Championship, held in Seoul, South Korea, 21 October 2022, where Phil Wizard went on to take gold. Photo © Jerick Collantes.

"The media hype of break dancing . . . changed both its form and its meaning." Of course, many involved in the dance at the time were not happy with such misrepresentation, but they mostly went along with it in the name of earning money and exposure. Only later did they realize that allowing others to define the dance and extract value from it without respecting its practitioners resulted in the denigration of breaking. Indeed, the campaign to do away with the term breakdancing in the 1990s was precisely about reclaiming the power to represent the dance on its own terms.

In many ways, the competitive ballroom dance industry has also sought to determine how the public perceives its practices. The decision to bid for the Olympics was predicated on the notion that the language of sports aligned with the WDSF's goal of distancing itself from the social dance roots where its practices originated. Gaining the IOC's seal of approval would mean ballroom dancing would be legitimatized as a "serious" discipline, not a frivolous pastime. When the IOC decided to deny their accession in favour of breaking, the WDSF reoriented this self-conception into one of professional governance. Just as they had regimented European folk dances into aristocratic ballroom practices in the 1800s and, later, reformatted African American and Latin American social dances such as the foxtrot, tango, swing, rumba, samba, and so on, the dancesport industry was now using its self-conception of discipline and professionalization to justify its takeover of breaking. Indeed, that the WDSF did not consult anybody from the breaking community before gaining Olympic inclusion demonstrates their willingness to claim ownership over the form and regulate it as they see fit.

Nevertheless, many breakers have accepted this custodial role of the dancesport industry in the hopes that the Olympics will ultimately lead to greater financial opportunity and mainstream exposure for b-boys and b-girls. Unlike other youth-oriented activities such as skateboarding, whose leading figures publicly campaigned against—and ultimately succeeded in stopping—the Olympics's attempt to give the International Federation of Roller Sports governance power over their sport (Smith), or the parkour community's vocal opposition to Olympics inclusion of their discipline under the auspices of the International Gymnastics Federation (Bull; Associated Press), most breakers in Canada and around the world have felt their only choice is to work within the framework imposed on them by the IOC. In a manner reminiscent of the 1980s, they have gone along with the "dancesportification" of their art form, under the assumption that the Olympics is something lucrative for their community—despite the fact that the Olympics itself is losing revenue and relevance, and looking *toward* practices such as breaking precisely because it is in difficult straits.

At the same time, unlike during the height of breaking's commercialization in the 1980s, b-girls and b-boys today have been more proactive in using their agency to affect how the dance is represented on a global stage. Indeed, most practitioners have justified their involvement in the Olympics process under such a premise. Although they lack contractual and economic power in this arrangement, the cultural capital they wield is not insignificant, as the involvement of bona fide breakers is necessary for the IOC and WDSF to succeed in attracting the young viewers they seek. Given the limited opportunities for making a living through breaking, leading promoters and practitioners have lent their credibility to the Olympics with the hope that they can navigate its cultural representation and ultimately yield some economic benefits for the community. Nevertheless, if the dance's debut in the 2024 Paris Games proves to be a success, the dancesport industry will likely accelerate its consolidation of breaking competitions around the world and further revert to its penchant toward streamlining and standardizing the dance. How all of this pans out after Paris 2024 will shape how b-boys and b-girls interact with the dancesport industry and greatly impact how competitive breaking is embodied in the future. As such, the debut of dancesport at the Olympics is not just a historically unique merger of two different dance styles at an athletic festival, it is a revealing case study into how issues of power, representation, and discourse continue to shape struggles over cultural values, resources, and expressions in the modern era.

WORKS CITED

Adgate, Brad. "Tokyo Olympics Ratings Plummeted—But NBC Dominated Primetime." *Forbes*, 10 Aug. 2021, forbes.com/sites/bradadgate/2021/08/10/viewing-to-the-tokyo-olympics-follows-a-familiar-pattern/?sh=44731c6064ae.

Aprahamian, Serouj. "Get the WDSF's Hands Off Hip-Hop." *Change*, 1 Jan. 2017, change.org/p/international-olympics-committee-get-the-wdsf-s-hands-off-hip-hop.

Associated Press. "Parkour Group Urges IOC to Reject Their Sport from Olympics." *Toronto Star*, 1 Dec. 2020, thestar.com/sports/olympics/2020/12/01/parkour-group-urges-ioc-to-reject-their-sport-from-olympics.html.

Banes, Sally. "Breaking Changing." *Village Voice*, 12 Jun. 1984, p. 82.

Breaking Canada. "The Symposium: Dancing Around Pandemic." *Facebook*, 13 Aug. 2021, facebook.com/breakingcanada/videos/893763398211532.

Brittain, Sandy. Personal interview with Serouj Aprahamian. 3 Aug. 2021.

Bull, Andy. "'#weareNOTgymnastics': Parkour Fights to Retain its Soul." *Guardian*, 5 Dec. 2018, theguardian.com/sport/blog/2018/dec/05/parkour-fight-soul-gymnastics.

Business Insider. "Why Olympians are so Broke | Big Business." *YouTube*, 4 Aug. 2021, youtu.be/ZatBRfMnxUE.

Colón, Rich. "Recently I've Been Asked . . . " *Facebook*, 9 Dec. 2016, facebook.com/OfficialCrazyLegs/posts/1747001718959890.

Dyzee Diaries. "The Final Proposal & IOC Vote for Breakin (Bboyin) in the 2024 Paris Olympics." *YouTube*, 27 Jun. 2019, youtu.be/-tU6pDYivEw.

———. "'The Truth About Bboyin in the Olympics' | Bboy Vlog | Ep 9." *YouTube*, 21 Dec. 2016, youtu.be/JypG2vWzAfs.

The Freshest Kids: A History of the B-Boy. Directed by Israel, Image Entertainment, 2002.

Holmes, Tracy. "Olympic Silver for Surrey Breakdancer." *Surrey Now-Leader*, 12 Oct. 2018, surreynowleader.com/news/olympic-silver-for-surrey-breakdancer/.

International Olympic Committee. *Buenos Aires 2018 Youth Olympic Games: Proposal for Additional Sports. Olympic World Library*, 6 Dec. 2016, library.olympics.com/Default/digital-viewer/c-186569.

———. *Olympic Games Paris 2024: Paris 2024 OCOG Proposal on New Sports. Olympic World Library*, Jun. 2019, library.olympics.com/Default/digital-viewer/c-207712.

Li, Rong Zhi, and Yonatan Asher Vexler. "Breaking for Gold: Another Crossroads in the Divergent History of This Dance." *The International Journal of the History of Sport*, vol. 36, no. 4–5, 2019, pp. 430–48. 10.1080/09523367.2019.1615896.

Liew, Jonathan. "Crisis is Engulfing the Postponed Tokyo 2020 Games—But Does the World Still Need the Olympics?" *New Statesman*, 10 Feb. 2021, newstatesman.com/politics/2021/02/crisis-engulfing-postponed-tokyo-2020-games-does-world-still-need-olympics.

Maese, Rick. "How Break Dancing Made the Leap From '80s Pop Culture to the Olympic Stage." *Washington Post*, 9 Feb. 2021, washingtonpost.com/sports/2021/02/09/break-dancing-olympic-sport-paris-2024/.

McMains, Juliet. "Brownface: Representations of Latin-ness in Dancesport." *Dance Research Journal*, vol. 33, no. 2, winter 2001, pp. 54–71. 10.2307/1477804.

———. *Glamour Addiction: Inside the Ballroom Dance Industry*. Wesleyan UP, 2006.

Outevsky, David. "What's in a Name?" *World Dance Council Education Department*, Feb. 2013, wdced.com/2013/02/written-by-david-outevsky-whats-in-a-name.

Picart, Caroline Joan S. *From Ballroom to DanceSport: Aesthetics, Athletics, and Body Culture*. State U of New York P, 2006.

Pro Breaking Tour. "UDEF Perspective on the 2018 Youth Olympic Games." *Facebook*, 11 Jan. 2017, facebook.com/probreakingtour/posts/1160749847377068.

Reyes, Geoff. "Breaking in the Olympics!" *You Be Ill*, 28 Jun. 2019, youbeill.com/blog/breaking-in-the-olympics.

———. Personal interview with Serouj Aprahamian. 6 Jul. 2021.

Rossingh, Danielle. "Breakdancing at the 2024 Paris Olympics? Here's Why it Makes Perfect Sense." *Forbes*, 21 Feb. 2019, forbes.com/sites/daniellerossingh/2019/02/21/breakdancing-at-the-2024-paris-olympics-heres-why-it-makes-perfect-sense/?sh=6627aec86d0b.

Smith, Brett. "How Olympic Skateboarding Almost Didn't Happen." *VICE*, 14 Sep. 2016, vice.com/en/article/53xd88/how-olympic-skateboarding-almost-didnt-happen.

Sono, Victor "Vicious." Personal interview with Serouj Aprahamian. 19 Jul. 2021.

Strife.tv. "Is Breaking a Dance Sport? Breakdancing in the Olympics Controversy | STRIFE TV." *YouTube*, 24 Feb. 2017, youtu.be/JtQttZVVcB4.

Tales of the Cypher—BreakingPodcast. "Tales of the Cypher Podcast—EP 68 (English)—Geoff Reyes—UBL/Breaking Canada." *YouTube*, 9 Aug. 2021, youtu.be/1h6TnGLTP9Q.

Thorpe, Holly, and Belinda Wheaton. "The Olympic Games, Agenda 2020 and Action Sports: The Promise, Politics and Performance of Orginisational Change." *International Journal of Sport Policy and Politics*, vol. 11, no. 3, 2019, pp. 465–83.

"WDSF Announces the 2019 World Breaking Championship." *World DanceSport Federation*, 23 Jan. 2019, worlddancesport.org/Media/Press/Release/201901_WDSF_Announces_the_2019_World_Breaking_Championship-2877.

Wetzel, Dan. "Olympics Opening Ceremony Draws Record-Low Ratings: Why Aren't Americans Tuning In?" *Yahoo! Sports*, 5 Feb. 2022, sports.yahoo.com/olympics-opening-ceremony-draws-abysmal-ratings-why-arent-americans-tuning-in-011318548.html.

"What a Day!" *World DanceSport Federation*, 7 Dec. 2016, worlddancesport.org/News/WDSF/What_A_Day-2252.

Yu, Brendan Francis. "The Battle for Breaking on the Olympic Stage." *VICE*, 7 Apr. 2017, vice.com/en/article/4xzq33/the-battle-for-breaking-on-the-olympic-stage.

CO-CREATING A DECOLONIAL LENS THROUGH WHICH TO VIEW NORTHWEST COAST FIRST NATIONS DANCE GROUP PERFORMANCES

MIQUE'L DANGELI

Sm Łoodm 'Nüüsm di waayu. Ts'ymse'nu. La̱xsgyiik di pdeeg̱u. Gispaxlo'ots di wil 'nat'ału. Tak'waan di wil 'waatgu. Laxyuubm Lək̓ʷəŋən ada WSÁNEĆ *di wil dzog̱u. Assistant Professor das Indigenous Arts a ts'm Art History ada Visual Studies da University of Victoria di hałesa'nu. Sm t'oyaxsu da sigidm hanaa'na̱x, smgyigyet, ada tx'anii gyet da Lək̓ʷəŋən* and WSÁNEĆ *int haboolda na laxyuubt asda 'wag̱ayt la'ooy. Luk'wil ayaatlga'nu wila 'wootgu gwa̱'a̱. G̱ani si'aamł waalu ndm gwiniits'a łoomsk da na gyigyet, na la̱xyuubt, ada na k̲'ala akst. T'oyaxsut 'nüüsm!*

I started this essay by adhering to ayaawk (my people's protocol) of introducing myself by the matrilineal line that defines my identity as a Tsimshian woman of the Eagle Clan from the community of Metlakatla, Alaska. In our language, Sm'algya̱x, I also shared that I am Assistant Professor of Indigenous Arts in the Department of Art History and Visual Studies at the University of Victoria. I closed in my language by following our ayaawk to acknowledge and thank the Lək̓ʷəŋən and WSÁNEĆ Chiefs, Matriarchs, Elders, and all their people for the honour of being a guest in their traditional, ancestral, and unceded territories. My positionality as an art historian, dance scholar, and artist is critically informed by both my responsibility as a Ts'msyen guest in unceded Coast Salish territories—including that of the Musqueam, Squamish, Tsleil-Waututh—and deeply rooted in my lifelong traditional training as a dancer, choreographer, and leader of the Git Hayetsk. I am blessed to have learned my language, protocol, and the history of our songs and dances from my Elders and cultural leaders in Alaska and British Columbia and have earned the responsibility of performing ceremony, teaching our language and dance, and being an ambassador for our people and community in public performances and cultural exchanges with Indigenous and non-Indigenous communities both nationally and internationally. These experiences inspired me to deepen and strengthen my knowledge of Indigenous dance along the Northwest Coast through my doctoral thesis, *Dancing Sovereignty: Politics and Protocol in Northwest Coast First Nations Dance* (2015) and subsequent publications.[1] I coined the concept of dancing sovereignty as a theoretical framework from which to critically engage with the ways in which sovereignty is embodied in Northwest Coast First Nations dance practices through protocol —bodies of law which form Indigenous legal systems. My study examines the processes through which protocol is asserted, negotiated, and enacted by First Nations dance artists throughout their selection and performance of ancestral songs (meaning those that they have inherited rights to), the creation and performance of new songs and dances, and their collaborative processes when working with non-Indigenous dance artists or other Indigenous artists

1 Dancing sovereignty, just as visual sovereignty, functions as a term that describes both the ways in which Indigenous artists assert sovereignty through their work and how these assertions are an integral part of their process of creation. My analysis of individual practices of dancing sovereignty focuses on the ways in which protocol is asserted, negotiated, and enacted—as a practice of transmotion—by dance artists in their song compositions, choreography, collaboration, and dance group performances. Gerald Vizenor uses the term transmotion to refer to Anishinaabe practices of sovereignty rooted in physical and metaphorical movements through time and ancestral territory. For him, transmotion is conveyed through the motions and meanings of oral histories, subsistence, and visual art. My approach extends his conceptualization to include dance in order to investigate practices of sovereignty specific to Northwest Coast First Nations dance artists, their epistemologies, and territories. See Dangeli, *Dancing Sovereignty: Protocol and Politics in Northwest Coast First Nations Dance*; Rickard et al.; Rickard; Dowell; Raheja; and Vizenor.

of different Nations, as well as in response to performative contexts.[2] Now my book project, it's the first extensive analysis of newly created performances—songs, dances, and collaborations—by First Nations dance group leaders, composers, and choreographers on the Northwest Coast.

My journey as a dance artist began early in life.[3] Around the age of ten I began travelling throughout North America to perform with Tsimshian dance groups from my community. I continue to do so today on an international level with the Git Hayetsk Dancers. For the past twenty years I have co-led Git Hayetsk in partnership with my husband—artist, carver, composer, and singer Mike Dangeli. We are an internationally renowned intergenerational First Nations dance group specializing in mask dances. Many of the songs and dances we perform are older ones that have been handed down to us through our families. Through this inherited repertoire, we sing and dance the history

2 Over the five-year period of my doctoral research, I studied the performances of Tsatsu Stalqayu (Stó:lō, Squamish, Musqueam, and Lil'wat Nations), Chinook SongCatchers (Nisga'a and Squamish Nations), Children of Takaya (Tsleil-Waututh Nation), Spakwus Slolem (Squamish Nation), Urban Kwakwaka'wakw Dance Group and Dancers of Damelahamid (Gitx̱san and Cree Nations), Dakhká Khwáan Dancers (Tagish and Tlingit Nations), Le-La-La Dancers (Kwakwa̱ka̱'wakw Nation), and G̱wa'waina Dancers (Kwakwa̱ka̱'wakw Nation). Central to my research is the work of Squamish dance artist S7aplek (Bob Baker), leader of the Spakwus Slolem Dancers; Gitx̱san dance artist Gildedowet (Margaret Grenier), artistic director of the Dancers of Damelahamid; and Kwakwa̱ka̱'wakw dance artist Wa̱x̱awidi (Chief William Wasden), leader of the G̱wa'wina Dancers. I'm grateful to them for their ongoing permission and support of my research.

3 Growing up in Metlakatla, Alaska, I was taught by leaders in my community to be a dancer, caretaker of songs and dances, and person of responsibility at Potlatches and totem pole raisings. From upper primary and through secondary school (1987–1998), I travelled with Tsimshian dance groups, Git Lax Lik'staa Dancers, and the Fourth Generation Dancers to share songs and dances at ceremonies, cultural exchanges, and other events across the US and Canada. Performing with dance groups in cultural exchanges with Indigenous and non-Indigenous people throughout North America has been a central part of my life ever since. While attending the University of Washington as an undergrad, I was a member of two Tsimshian dance groups based in Seattle: Tsimshian Haayuuk and Git Hoan, who I travelled and performed with extensively. Upon graduating from UW and moving back to Metlakatla in 2002, I had the privilege of leading the Git Lax Lik'staa Dancers for two years.

of our ancestors with a critical awareness that all of these songs and dances were once new. As future ancestors, we carry forward our peoples' practice by creating new songs, dances, masks, and regalia to record and reflect on our experiences as First Nations people today. Our descendants will remember us, in the way we remember our ancestors now, through the continuum that is our embodied archive of songs and dances. The members of our dance group come from the Tsimshian, Nisga'a, Gitxsan, Haida, Haisla, Tlingit, Tahltan, Sechelt, and Musqueam Nations. Our traditional territories are now referred to as the Southeast Alaskan Panhandle, the West Coast of British Columbia, and Western Washington. Teaching Indigenous dancers from these diverse Nations in my work with Git Hayetsk, learning from their practices, and from other Indigenous dancers with whom we've shared the stage has given me a depth of knowledge and lived experience with Indigenous dance practices locally and globally.

During our Git Hayetsk performances, one of our main objectives is to generate a greater understanding of Northwest Coast First Nations people, our cultural practices, histories, and art forms among diverse audiences, as well as challenging preconceived notions of Indigeneity. Decades prior to the Truth and Reconciliation Commission of Canada's 94 Calls to Action, we were utilizing our performances, as many dance groups have done throughout the history of this region, as a platform to initiate critical discussions on issues that now are considered foundational to decolonization, indigenization, and reconciliation. Mike and I—and most recently our middle son, Nick Dangeli̩—also carry out this work through public-speaking engagements in North America and abroad. In the summer of 2023, Nick and I lectured, performed, and taught as international guest artists at Marrugeku's two-week-long dance lab, Dancing on Contested Lands, in Gadigal Country (known by its colonial name as Sydney, Australia). Earlier that year, Mike and I co-presented a keynote on Northwest Coast First Nations dance practices, with a focus on the creation of Git Hayetsk's ridicule dance, for the Canadian Association for Theatre Research's (CATR) annual conference at Dalhousie University. At the local level in Vancouver, I have worked toward the goal of decolonizing the wider public understanding of Northwest Coast First Nations dance by engaging in conversations on Indigenous performance on multiple panels organized by Full Circle: First Nations Performance, the Coastal First Nations Dance Festival, and the PuSh International Performing Arts Festival. This essay is derived from my presentation, "Co-creating a Decolonial Lens Through Which to View Northwest Coast First Nations Dance Group Performances," for the 2022 Dance Studies Associations (DSA) conference pre-symposium in Vancouver, which was organized by Peter Dickinson. I invite DSA participants, and now you the reader, to co-create a decolonial lens through which to view Northwest Coast First Nations dance practices, collaborations, and performances, focusing on the history of cultural genocide through the Potlatch Ban in Canada, our resistance, and resurgence. My DSA presentation and now this essay is also a continuation of an ongoing critical dialogue generated by discrimination that I and other First Nation dance artists from the Northwest Coast faced due to a lack of understanding about the complexities of our practices. While conducting my doctoral research, it was strikingly common for the Indigenous dance artists that I interviewed to share the ways in which they are constantly confronted by preconceived notions suggesting that their dance practices are thought to be a tradition in the most oversimplified sense. Most often these dismissive comments happen in conversations with members of audiences, dance artists of all genres, academics, presenters, and arts administrators. The stereotype that Northwest Coast First Nations dance performances are merely unchanged routines of ancient songs and dances passed down over generations discredits the work of Indigenous dance artists from this area who are actively producing performances of both ancestral songs—performances of which were made illegal for sixty-seven years by the Canadian government—and newly created works through practices that have overcome both cultural and physical genocide. These performances are critically engaged with the present while carrying forward ancestral knowledge in ways that are strategically engaged to press political issues. To provide a critical framework to engage with these complexities in the work of individual Northwest Coast First Nations dance artists and their dance groups, I will cover four fundamentals vital to co-creating a decolonial lens to view their performances.

1. THE NORTHWEST COAST IS THE ONE OF THE MOST DIVERSE REGIONS OF INDIGENOUS PEOPLE IN WHAT IS REFERRED TO AS NORTH AMERICA

I wish it would go without saying that we're not all alike (and that goes for more than just our physical appearances), but more often than not we have to say it! The cultural and linguistic diversity in this region is extreme. It is one of the most diverse regions of Indigenous people in what colonialism has deemed North America. Northwest Coast First Nations refers specifically to the Indigenous peoples whose territories are now known as Western Washington, the West Coast of British Columbia, and the Southeast Alaskan Panhandle. There are seventy First Nations and approximately fifty-nine Indigenous languages on the Northwest Coast. This does not include the huge number of Bands under the wider category of First Nations, nor does it include the vast number of dialects of each Indigenous language. The diversity in cultural practices, as well as shared or similar beliefs and practices, is not only at the heart of but also accounts for the strength of the work of Northwest Coast First Nations dance artists and their dance groups.

2. "DANCE GROUPS," NOT DANCE TROUPES OR COMPANIES, ARE CENTRAL TO THE EXPRESSION OF IDENTITY AND INDIGENOUS RIGHTS ON THE NORTHWEST COAST

The term "dance group," not dance troupe or company, is used in the everyday vernacular of Northwest Coast First Nations people to refer to collectives of singers, drummers, and dancers who perform songs and dances owned by their Nations, families, and communities. Currently, there are upward of three hundred dance groups in both rural and urban communities along the Northwest Coast, with new ones forming every year. Around forty dance groups are based here in the Lower Mainland. Dance groups are not state-sponsored or state-sanctioned. Their membership and activities are entirely self-determined, governed, and funded. Membership of each dance group is delineated in a variety of ways. Some dance groups limit their membership to a people who are of one First Nation, family, or community, and others are composed of one or more of each of these categories. Dance groups are intergenerational. The ages of their membership ranges from newborns to Elders. This intergenerationality is central to Indigenous pedagogical practices (ways of teaching) that allow for embodied knowledge to be transferred and maintained by people of all generations. For example, Squamish dance group Spakwus Slolem, based in North Vancouver and led by composer and choreographer S7aplek (Bob Baker), is an example of a dance group whose members are all of one Nation and from different, but related, families.

Ownership of songs and dances performed by dance groups are passed down hereditarily and/or given, what we refer to as "gifted," between individuals, communities, and Nations.[4] Rights to songs and dances, and the ways in which they are performed, are governed by what First Nations people refer to as "protocol"—bodies of laws that form Indigenous legal systems. These rights are expressed in terms of ownership and permission through oratory delivered by dance group leaders at the time of their dance group's performance. Dance group leaders, or leaders for short, have responsibilities similar to that of artistic directors in most dance companies. They manage the dance group membership, practices (known in other dance genres as rehearsal), and performances, and oversee their adherence to protocol.

The relationship between protocol and Northwest Coast First Nations dance practices is immensely complex. One of the main focuses of my dissertation

---

4 Among Northwest Coast First Nations people, the phrase "gifting a song" is commonly used to refer to the act of granting another person the right to its use. As is discussed in the introduction to my thesis and in the first chapter, songs and dances are property. The rights to perform songs are inherited through family lines or gifted by a person who has the rights to grant permission. Ownership of songs and dances can be held individually, collectively, or both. It is a shared protocol that the ownership and/or permission is stated in the oratory before the song is performed. When the song is an inherited privilege, ownership is most often articulated in terms of belonging (i.e., "this song belongs to . . . "). These types of songs are sometimes referred to as "ancestral songs." When the right to perform a song is received through gifting, however, the introduction of its ownership and permission is usually articulated along the lines of "this song belongs to ____; it was gifted to ___ from ___." The composer is also acknowledged in the introduction as an important part of the song's history.

research was the ways in which protocol is asserted, negotiated, and enacted by Northwest Coast First Nations dance artists in their processes of creation, collaboration, and performance. I won't spend too much time on it here, as I will focus on it in greater detail in other articles.[5] The main point I wish to make here is that for Northwest Coast First Nations people, songs and dances are not only an integral expression of our identities, an embodied archive of our languages, histories, relationships to and ownership of land and waterways, but it is also our legal system. A common analogy made about the ways that protocol governs the ownership of songs and dances is to compare it to the copyright system in Western law. I feel, however, that identity theft or identity fraud is more accurate, as the act of singing a song or performing a dance that does not belong to you is a claim—through Indigenous legal means—to another's identity and the territorial rights and ceremonial privileges that are owned by that hereditary line. This is one of the many reasons why appropriation hurts our communities so deeply. Generations of our people along the Northwest Coast have worked diligently and made painful sacrifices to ensure the survival of these songs, dances, and oratory. Some even endure imprisonment under the Potlatch Ban.

3. NORTHWEST COAST FIRST NATIONS SONGS, DANCES, AND CEREMONIES WERE OUTLAWED IN CANADA FROM 1884–1951, AND FOR SIXTY-SEVEN YEARS, IT WAS ILLEGAL TO BE WHO WE TRULY ARE

Northwest Coast First Nations dance practices cannot be separated from their criminalization in Canada through what is referred as the Potlatch Ban.[6] In 1884 the Canadian government revised the Indian Act to ban Potlatches as well as other First Nations ceremonies throughout the country. This included

5 See Dangeli, "Dancing Chiax, Dancing Sovereignty" and "Dancing Sovereignty: Reclaiming the Grease Trail Through Protocol, Movement, and Song."

6 For first-hand testimony on this topic, I highly recommend Beyond Human Power (2019), a powerful film on the effects of the Potlatch Ban on Northwest Coast First Nation dance today by Tlingit/Tahltan First Nations filmmaker Gordon Loverin.

the performance of all associated songs and dances. Put succinctly, Potlatch are Indigenous legal traditions where hereditary privileges of Northwest Coast First Nations people, their associated histories, and their kinship are asserted through oratory, songs, dances, and, in some cases, totem-pole raisings, and affirmed through feasting and the distribution of gifts to the witnesses. Missionaries, government agents, and other colonial figures viewed Potlatching and all associated ceremonies as a hindrance to assimilating First Nations people into Euro Canadian society. First Nations people were jailed and had their ceremonial belongings (masks, regalia, and all else related to the Potlatch) confiscated and put into museum collections, of which very little has been repatriated. Despite assimilation efforts made through the Potlatch Ban, alongside the horrific one-hundred-and-fifty-year history of child internment camps known as Indian Residential Schools committing cultural and physical genocide, many First Nations communities continued to Potlatch in secret throughout the nineteenth and early twentieth centuries. Parents and caregivers faced imprisonment if they kept their children from attending Indian Residential Schools. With entire communities devoid of their children, passing on knowledges of these songs, dances, and ceremonies posed extreme challenges, the ramifications of which are still very much felt today, shaping cultural resurgence methods of each community and Nation.

As early as the 1940s, the formation of and performances by dance groups in British Columbia critically engaged with and resisted the Potlatch Ban. Artist and political activist George Clutesi (Nuuchahnulth Nation, 1905–1988) led a dance group in the 1940s to encourage First Nations youth to be proud of their heritage and to promote the accomplishments of First Nations people in a way that would garner the attention and respect of non-First Nations people (Hawker 122–23). Art historian Ronald W. Hawker observes that Clutesi's dance group performances broke the terms of the Indian Act, which prohibited First Nations people from dancing in locations off their own reserve (Hawker 122–23). The section of the Indian Act to which Hawker refers specified that First Nations people had to obtain the permission of an Indian agent to participate in any "show, exhibition, performance, stampede, or pageant" outside their reserve or be held liable to a fine or imprisonment (Venne 230).

Political activist and actor Chief Dan George (Tsleil-Waututh Nation, 1899–1981) was also knowingly, and defiantly, in breach of the Potlatch Ban when he began his family's dance group, the Children of Takaya, in the 1940s. His son, Chief Leonard George, grew up as a dancer and singer in Children of Takaya. Chief Leonard George shared with me that he remembered that in order "to make their performances legal," since the Potlatch Ban was still in effect, they "performed bluegrass music as well as Tsleil-Waututh songs and dances" (George). Children of Takaya are one of the earliest dance groups that I have been able to trace in British Columbia. Performing under the leadership of Chief Leonard George's son, Gabriel George, their membership today is still primarily composed of Chief Dan George's grandchildren and great-grandchildren.

Under Chief Dan George's leadership, Children of Tayaka was known to have performed inside Indian Residential Schools for the students. S7aplek (Bob Baker), leader of the Squamish dance group Spakwus Slolem, said to me in an interview that watching Chief Dan George's dance group perform when he was a student at St. Paul's Indian Residential School was what inspired him to start his own group. Spakwus Slolem is one of the leading dance groups in Vancouver's lower mainland.

The formation of dance groups became widespread among Northwest Coast First Nations people from the 1960s on. The increase in dance groups in Canada may be connected to the lifting of the Potlatch Ban in 1951. While the United States government did not institute laws criminalizing Potlatching, government agents, missionaries, teachers, and others placed intense pressure on Indigenous people in Alaska and Washington, as elsewhere, to refrain from participating in their cultural practices and assimilate into Euro American culture. Much like the Indian Residential Schools in Canada, Indian Boarding Schools in the United States, as well as many other colonial mechanisms of cultural and physical genocide, brutally reinforced these efforts. Since the 1950s, the widespread formation of dance groups in both rural and urban areas along the Northwest Coast has been a powerful social and political movement of cultural resurgence for Indigenous people in this region.

Taking into account what I have discussed in sections two and three of this essay, I'm compelled to share a conversation I recently had with an official of a prominent government-funded chain of recreation centres in British Columbia. This person requested to meet with me out of their program's concern that Indigenous people were not responding to their invitation to teach Northwest Coast First Nations dance to people of all backgrounds at their facilities. They were quite frustrated about the consistent refusal to what they considered a generous invitation mainly because it was a key tenant to their reconciliation programming. They posed a question that I get quite often: "Why don't your people share your practices by teaching others to do them?" A simple answer, without repeating the information covered in previous sections, is because it is who we are. We have inherited the right to perform these songs and dances from our ancestors. We teach them to other Indigenous people who also have this inherited right or who have been gifted their use through their family and other relationships. To teach them to non-Indigenous people is to approve and bolster their appropriation. It's only been legal for us to sing our songs, perform our dances, potlatch, and hold other ceremonies for the past seventy-three years. Rather than asking us to teach non-First Nations people our songs and dances as a part of so-called "reconciliation," create and offer opportunities to right these historical wrongs and provide us with the support (space, funding, etc.) to strengthen our own practices as we work to recover what was lost in our cultural genocide.

4. THEY MIGHT LOOK LIKE OLD SONGS AND DANCES TO YOU, BUT THEY ARE NEW TO US

I'm going to keep this point simple: just because we are in our regalia (ceremonial clothing) and singing in our language doesn't mean that what we are performing is ancient. The history of our cultural genocide doesn't allow for such a luxury. In many First Nations communities, no songs or dances survived. The majority of songs that were recorded on wax cylinders by early folklorists, ethnographers, and anthropologists have been made inaccessible by museums through their colonial notions of copyright. New ones had to be created in order to hold ceremonies once again. Northwest Coast First

Nations dance artists are composing new songs and choreographing new dances nearly every day. Along the coast, hundreds of new songs and dances are being brought to life (performed for the first time in front of witnesses) by First Nations people at Potlatches and other ceremonies every year.

In conclusion, I felt compelled to present what I shared here as a paper at the 2022 DSA conference, and to now publish it in this book, out of tremendous concern that in this so-called time of truth and reconciliation there's a tendency to disengage with the fact that there are a great many devasting truths that Canada has yet to acknowledge, let alone reconcile, in the country's historical and ongoing settler colonialism. Your participation in the co-creation of this truthful decolonial lens I have offered is the diverse perspectives that you bring to enhance it in your own way and in how you decide to use to view and engage with Northwest Coast First Nations dance, in collaboration with Indigenous dance artists from this area, and in your own process of decolonizing your courses and pedagogy.

WORKS CITED

Dangeli, Mique'l. "Dancing Chiax, Dancing Sovereignty: Performing Protocol in Unceded Territories." *Dance Research Journal*, vol. 48, no. 1, 2016, pp. 75–90.

———. *Dancing Sovereignty: Protocol and Politics in Northwest Coast First Nations Dance*. 2015. UBC, Ph.D. dissertation.

———. "Dancing Sovereignty: Reclaiming the Grease Trail Through Protocol, Movement, and Song." *The Routledge Companion to Indigenous Art Histories in the United States and Canada*, edited by Heather Igloliorte and Heather Taunton, Routledge, 2023, pp. 30–42.

Dowell, Kristin L. *Sovereign Screens: Aboriginal Media on the Canadian West Coast*. U of Nebraska P, 2013.

George, Chief Leonard. Personal communication with Mique'l Dangeli. 25 Sep. 2013.

Hawker, Ronald William. *Tales of Ghosts: First Nations Art in British Columbia, 1922–61*. UBC P, 2003.

Lovern, Gordon, director. *Beyond Human Power*. Wolf Spirit Films, 2019.

Raheja, Michelle H. *Reservation Reelism: Redfacing, Visual Sovereignty, and Representations of Native Americans in Film*. U of Nebraska P, 2010.

Rickard, Jolene. "Visualizing Sovereignty in the Time of Biometric Sensors." *South Atlantic Quarterly*, vol. 110, no. 2, Spring 2011, pp. 465–86.

Rickard, Jolene, George Longfish, Zig Jackson, Pamela Shields Carroll, Ron Carraher, and Hulleah Tsinhnahjinnie. "Sovereignty: A Line in the Sand." *Strong Hearts: Native American Visions and Voices*, special issue of *Aperture*, no. 139, 1995, pp. 50–59.

"This Day In History: July 1, 1967." *Vancouver Sun*, 2 Jul. 2015, web.archive.org/web/20200220072900/http://www.vancouversun.com/This+history+July+1967/6876736/story.html.

Venne, Sharon Helen. *Indian Acts and Amendments 1868–1975: An Indexed Collection*. U of Saskatchewan Native Law Centre, 1981.

Vizenor, Gerald. *Fugitive Poses: Native American Indian Scenes of Absence and Presence*. U of Nebraska P, 1998.

RESPONSIVE WITNESSING: A CONVERSATION

EMILY JOHNSON, KARYN RECOLLET, JOSEPH M. PIERCE, AND CAMILLE GEORGESON-USHER[1]

The following is a conversation between Emily Johnson, Karyn Recollet, Joseph M. Pierce, and Camille Georgeson-Usher moderated by Ginger Dunnill in response to Johnson's collaborative dance work *The Ways We Love and the Ways We Love Better—Monumental Movement Toward Being Future Being(s)*, which is based on and around Jeffrey Gibson's sculpture *Because Once You Enter My House It Becomes Our House.*[2] The dance was presented at Socrates Sculpture Park, Long Island City, NY, on 16 September 2020; this conversation took place in partnership with Digital Hub and STTLMNT.

Johnson's *The Ways We Love . . .* is a site-specific dance work that stages pathways for regeneration, renewal, and transformation. The performance begins with a gathering at the shore of the East River estuary with words from artist/activist Nataneh River, and then moves to ascend Gibson's monument. Incorporating storytelling, invocation, movement, and light, *The Ways We Love . . .* illuminates

1 Thank you to Rohan Kulkarni for editing the Zoom-generated transcription and for the addition of the gestures made (bracketed) during the recording that were deemed relevant to create full meaning in companionship with the spoken word.

2 A documentary film of Emily Johnson's *The Ways We Love*, made by Cut/Cut/Cut (Chelsea Knight and Itziar Barrio), can be seen at catalystdance.com/the-ways-we-love-and-the-ways-we-love-better. Jeffrey Gibson's *Because Once You Enter My House It Becomes Our House* was on view as part of the MONUMENTS NOW exhibition at Socrates Sculpture Park, New York, from summer 2020 to March 2021. See Gibson.

> Indigenous presence and the histories held in the parkland, which is situated in Lenapehoking—homeland of the Lenapeyok people. The performance culminates with the planting of tobacco, and the project continued in spring 2021 with the planting of Sehsapsing corn seeds—a tribute to the future and a commitment to Lenape return.

Ginger Dunnill: Thank you so much, everyone, for joining us. And I'd like to introduce Emily Johnson to step into the responsive witnessing portion of our program. And I'll just let Emily take it from here.

Emily Johnson: Thanks, everyone. I'm just going to ask Camille and Karyn and Joseph to say "hi," and we can start to chat and introduce yourselves as you want to, and when you want to. Thank you all for witnessing thus far.

Camille Usher: Love that we're all waiting for whoever wants to go first. I suppose I can start just by introducing myself. I'm Camille Georgeson-Usher—I also go by Camille Usher. I am currently in Toronto, where it was raining this morning, and maybe you got our rain that came to you later. Now it's very sunny. It's very nice that it's turned around and I'm excited to go outside later. I'm originally from Galiano Island, BC. And my family is a mix of many Coast Salish Nations from around that territory. My grandmother is from the Northwest Territories, particularly from Fort Good Hope, and then moved down south and fell in love with a fisherman. And so that's how I came to be. I have something that I wrote from what we watched, but I'm going to wait until the others introduce themselves.

Karyn Recollet: I'm really happy to be a witness, and I'm honoured to be sharing space with you. My name is Karyn Recollet and I am a Cree person thinking through my relationship with/through diaspora right now. And thinking about how that feels in my body to talk about myself as a Cree diasporic human. I am living in Courtice, Ontario, which is about an hour away from Toronto. I am also just wanting to hold space right now for that amazing offering. And I'm really looking forward to being able to reciprocate and

Fig. 1. Emily Johnson's *The Ways We Love . . .* Photo © Scott Lynch.

give back in terms of the kinds of offerings that I can make in response to your pretty fantastic work, Emily.

Joseph Pierce: And I'm Joseph Pierce. I'm a citizen of the Cherokee Nation. And I am currently living in Brooklyn, which is the ancestral homeland of the Canarsie and Lenape people. But I'm originally from South Texas. I grew up in Corpus Christi, which is in South Texas, and I'm a writer and an academic and I was grateful to have been at the performance when it happened, and I'm grateful to be able to be with everyone here today to talk about it.

Emily: I have no agenda at all for this discussion. We, the four of us, speak together in many different configurations around ideas and desires for gathering for better futures, for Indigenous futures. We talk about protocols, sometimes we talk against protocols . . . And one thing that really struck me as I was watching this time was when Nataneh talks about standing against . . . like, standing against the city and sitting against this city and sleeping against the city and dreaming against the city; it really struck me in a different way this time listening to that and hearing—hearing those words, particularly sleeping against this city, that we are always, always, always in every cell and every moment against colonialism. And how, in these ways where, you know, Joseph is watering the plants at the end with his hands and yeah, that just struck me in a new way today.

Joseph: It was not chance that Emily asked me to hold the bucket of water that came from the East River. And the water that we use to water the tobacco seedlings, the tobacco plant at the end, has a long history too, right? Because that water is a living relative—the water is so capacious and able to hold memory and medicine and air, and reciprocity. When we hold—this is something that I just sort of thought about now—when we hold the water that holds our generational vibrations, interspecies/interstellar insulatory, vibrations of light and matter, we produce care, so much care, because this is what our ancestors did. So to do this brings us into being, into relation because they knew and their knowing has carried over across thresholds of movement and of memory. And that relation, that gesture brings us into being with the future dream and ancestral time. And I think that that's what this work does for me; it brings into relation the futurity of our ancestors and of us being potential or becoming future ancestors in a way that really gets at the heart of what it means to be a good relative, what it means to be in relation in an ethical and reciprocal way. And that really struck me too this time, you know, how kind and generous that work is.

Karyn: Yeah, I also feel, just in kind of picking up that, that moment, we talk a lot about rock matter and that I never get this word that you share with us, Joseph—is it vesicles?

Joseph: The rock word? Vesicles right. Vesicles.

Karyn: The vesicles, yes. And just in this conversation, in this work, it's actually kind of coming together for me now—the vesicles are actually the water vessels. And I didn't know that until I thought of hands and water, and planting, and spilling over. And in this kind of thinking through the relationships with the work to Gibson's work I am placing the obelisk and the monument, or rather monument "otherwise" and the planting together. I've been reading a lot of [American science-fiction writer] N.K. Jemisin's work lately, particularly *The Fifth Season*, which is part of their Broken Earth Trilogy. And I've been thinking about obelisks and monuments a lot. And as Emily, our conversations have been orbiting around the speculative architecture and thinking about the rising of all the monuments, the unearthing of them. *(makes hand gestures through the following sentences to animate her words)* So I'm also kind of thinking through these alternative kinds of landing practices that we do. Thinking through the relationship between Indigenous thinking and thought, and Black radical traditions of being in relation with the speculative. And I'm wondering if, as we fall into relation with each other, we are more ascending rather than falling. And perhaps the shapes of those gatherings around this obelisk become a way of thinking about a gesture of becomingness—alternative forms of gathering around these obelisks as alternative architectures that may not be monuments but monuments "otherwise"? What if our ways of thinking about relationships mirrored those more-than-human relatives to consider an orientation that builds upon what is underneath, like the dinosaur bones, you know, the bone fragments of ancestors coming together, and actually coming up again as future ancestors in that way. So that kind of reminded me of those vesicles *(creates in a V shape with her hands)* that hold so much potential and possibility for alternative movement practices of being in relation.

Camille: Karyn, I love that you re-inspired me to read N.K. Jemisin, because I've been going non-stop. I have read *The City We Became*, and one thing I was writing, as I was watching this piece today, was the idea of the body in relation to the city and how, in the book, the body becomes the tentacles that build the city's ligaments, and you can see the arms when you're reading it and the arms are the river. As she raises her arms, the rivers rise too, and so I just really love that. And I'm also simultaneously rereading a lot of Octavia Butler, and I'm really in this kind of future city-building mindset. And so every morning I go out and I run around Toronto, jogging, not just like randomly running. But it's kind of my time that I reimagine the city as I'm moving my body around it. And so I'll just read what I was writing while [the performance] was happening. It's not very long, but it's kind of around this imagining the future

Fig. 2. Stacy Lynn Smith and Ashley Pierre-Louis in *The Ways We Love . . .* featuring Jeffrey Gibson's sculpture *Because Once You Enter My House It Becomes Our House*, Socrates Sculpture Park, 2020. Photo © Scott Lynch.

city that I think you were doing so beautifully, Emily. Okay, so this is what I wrote. And I'm not going to edit myself, so bear with me. Okay?

> *(reading out loud)* You allowed me to imagine a future city years from now that has been struggling so hard to breathe, but it finally sighs in relief. I see plants you put in the ground, the seeds you will plant next year, the size of skyscrapers, eating the buildings, and eating the buildings whole with their green tentacles as the plants overgrow what we have felt. I heard a humming from human and animal coexistence where the animals were finally louder than us again, where we could hear the trees speaking to us again. I felt a vibration that presented itself from the collective mobility of our bodies in whatever way we needed to move that rattled the rest of the carcasses of the long-expired cars. This city forces us to be slow with one another, to travel less quickly, and to allow ourselves to allow breath back into the city's lungs.

Fig. 3. Stacy Lynn Smith, Ashley Pierre-Louis, and (upper) ensemble members in *The Ways We Love . . .* featuring Jeffrey Gibson's *Because Once You Enter My House. . .* Socrates Sculpture Park, 2020. Photo © Scott Lynch.

And then I was just kind of writing about breathing and how our breath absorbs the tension of the cities. And when a city is having a hard time breathing, we too have a hard time breathing. And that's where I ended, so I'll stop there.

Emily: Just from breath . . . you know, this particular performance offering was made in the midst of covid here in New York City, and Karyn and I started a writing practice at the start of this, when we all had to shelter at home. Mostly because Karyn was worried about me, living here in New York City. We started to Zoom very regularly and started to write together in a process that is ongoing. During those conversations we were really talking a lot about breath—about the difficulty to breathe and the exchange of breath with our more-than-human kin, particularly with trees. There's one tree that I can see outside my window that I built a very strong relationship with over the many months that I was mostly sitting here. The moment of that performance—we had these performers and dancers that were so amazing. We had one rehearsal time because we were trying to limit our time together and, of course, adhering to protocols of safety and such. The first time that we gathered in our rehearsal, we were in a circle, all six feet apart, wearing masks, and we just started to stretch together. And it was almost like the first deep breath I think I'd taken in months, just being in a circle together with people again, people who had been aching to do that, who had been aching to dance and be together and there was . . . there was like a bit of relief. Somehow I think I felt in my chest toward the end of that performance offering when I'm saying the names, there are those of us who are still dancing around the ziggurat while others have descended the ziggurat and joined the audience to go and plant. It is an effort, how you so beautifully described, like reimagining the city through replanting, rematriating, and through rebreathing. But we are speaking of people who can no longer breathe. I'm saying names of people who can no longer breathe. And as I spoke with the dancers in that last section that you don't see so much, but you hear me breathing and saying the names; we're not conjuring those people, but we are conjuring the joy of them, with them, and for them. And in our exertion of beath, we are trying to extend and share that breath beyond this physical life that we have—to their life that has been taken. All of those names are names of people who have been taken. All of them in the ongoing genocide of missing and murdered Indigenous women, trans and Two Spirit and so we . . . yeah, breathe. That's what came to mind, just as you were talking about breath.

Joseph: Karyn and I have laughed and had some joy over this word that I have been toying with, which is the vesicle which is like a bubble of air—specifically, a bubble of air that is lodged in a rock. And when a rock emerges from a molten to a solid state, the vesicles are the little tiny bubbles in the rock that create space. So that process of creation is very literally the breath of life, and the rocks all around us—particularly volcanic rocks—are imbued with this breath. And I think that there's a lot we can learn from that. That there are pockets of air, pockets of shelter, or pockets of breath that are there for us. And maybe, to think along with the futurity that we've been invoking, the city tends to hide breath or tends to take your breath away. And yet we know from our stories that there are always pockets of breath, because the rocks, when they were made, were made with pockets of breath. Always. I think that's like a lesson that we need in these months. And I think that that's also like a survival strategy.

Karyn: It's interesting that as we're focusing on this breath, I'm considering the ways in which we find and express love—like the most intense, felt love as that which seems to be always the kind that takes our breath away. For me, that's more than an expression in that I'm thinking, maybe, it's not taking our breath away, maybe it's just that our breath is forming those vesicles, that our breath is actually breathing in those orbs, or those spheres. *(makes a gesture for orbs)* And maybe it seems like something is being taken away, but it's really not. It's breathing how we were always meant to breathe: in relation. Perhaps we were always meant to breathe with abandon, and also meant to be able to breathe through a burn (as in this moment) because we had these physical kinds of gestures that helped us do that. And so maybe I can offer a series of speculative provocations—I'll call them that because they'll sound pretty provocative—and probably a bit speculative. Okay, so I'm thinking about the monument as sigil, as some sort of a landing glyph. *(Gracie appears on camera.)* This is my gorgeous star being, Gracie. And I'm thinking about the technologies of falling into relation as witnesses to Emily's offerings—with canoe, with kayak, with a vesicle of wood that suspends itself as a space of possibility- and futurity-making in the vesicle of the ocean of the water.

I ask, "What are the falls as we land into place?" Maybe these gestures are not just falls, but the embodied experience of gradients, scales, levels *(gestures levels with both hands)*, of atmospherics that we experience mirrored in the obelisk, mound, ziggurat's different layers—like layers in the atmospheric both above, below, and tentacularly *(expands her arms out sideways)*. There are all these different multitudinous atmospherics that we experience before we come into this world in this physical form, and even after when we move on into other forms. So thinking about falling in the grammars of landing into relation, at first I thought it sounded like this pedestrian kind of processioning—kind of marching, almost. But then I was thinking that these processions were not militaristic, that they sound like marching because we are learning to breathe within a burn; we step hard because we have to awaken these obelisks that are in the ground, in the dirt. We have to be in relation with all the subterranean beings, like the worm songs are probably water, right? These grammars of landing probably place into sonic, vibratory form these patterns. And it's no coincidence that these marches, that these processions, activate abolitionist choreographies in this moment in time, and that these movements are connecting devices to the future. So we have to awaken these obelisks in the ground, in the dirt . . . the speculative architectures that are technologies of return or homing devices, which because of dislocation because of the Sixties and Millennial Scoops, we can't go home in the traditional sense of going home, especially when we live in diaspora. So marching is like picking up the sonics of our future being through our relationships with the rock, with more-than-human relations. Maybe they're like side shuffles in moments, like stomp dances. And these are the different forms of landing, the speculative marches they'll never understand. They'll never connect that way. So maybe this is a space of an undoing of breath or a procession of breath, of undoing sounds like being out of breath. Because, as I mentioned, all the most intense loves are exhausting. Like we are breathless. When we are feeling that abandon, not abandon of the continued exilic movement of father's abandonment, but the abandon that feels expansive *(expands her arms up and out)*—in breathing with abandon and abundance. I'm thinking that this catching of our breath is really vesicle breathing, showing us how to breathe through a burn. Our histories, our ongoing legacies, our genealogies prepare us for this moment in showing us how to breathe through a burn. We are living in post-apocalyptical times, right—as in experiences of residential schools, forced exiles, so we think about this. So, maybe, in relation with dirt and with soil, these obelisks are arising now (as in Gibson's wonderful creation) to teach us this, to do breath like we do bioluminescence, where we suss each other out in the darkness, where we can sleep there; we can dream there; spaces where we can push ourselves to the limits so that we can vesicle breathe again. We can be in those spaces of refuge and invite others and call each other into those spaces with us. So as we are planting, we are also panting; we require these spaces to do that.

CAMILLE: One thing that I've been thinking a lot about recently that I've noticed in this last year that I haven't noticed ever is that I need help with breathing from other people. And I've noticed that it's very hard to do on my own now. And maybe I'm pulling that a little bit from the city, but also from this idea of collective future building, of collective future cities, I suppose, where we do need to help each other breathe. I love this conversation about rocks because rocks symbolize so much for us. I think they hold the history as well as the future. Because they are built of our atmosphere and they are built of the matter that we can't see anymore—they hold that matter. And I know that in our conversations we've all kind of moved around the idea of the matter that we are connected by, so dark matter and chaos, and, you know, different kinds of matter that connect all of us. And I wonder about how we are breathing in that matter as well, how that further connects us through this kind of invisible energy matter. I'm going to stop there and think more about rocks and breathing.

JOSEPH: I had just gotten my hands tattooed a couple of weeks before the performance, just three lines on my fingers, mirroring old traditional Cherokee tattoos. Within the last scene [of the film], when Emily asked me to water the plants, the water was running over my fingers, through my fingers, through these three lines where, in the Cherokee way, we have an upper world and a middle world and a lower world. And so watering the plants was actually trickling the water from all three of these worlds. From the upper, to the middle, to the lower toward the roots of the plants. In a sense, there's a worlding practice going on there; we could say this is chance but it's obviously not chance. There's no way.

CAMILLE: I also feel when I'm coming back to rocks . . . the way I'm in relation to them is very intimate. And it's a very intimate, I suppose, sensual idea of how they're created, and how we live in relation to them. I suppose in the broader sense of what we're talking about there is this sense of intimacy and this world-building practice in caring for these plants, of watering plants. You have to be more intimate, and you have to breathe what they're breathing, because you're there in relation with them. I'm thinking a lot about intimacy and how this almost active slowness while we're being together, even if it's in the digital, is revolutionary. To be slow and to be able to breathe a little bit slower with plants, without plants, with rocks, or even here on Zoom, these spaces foster intimacy.

Emily: There's a new way I'm thinking, just from this conversation, about intimacy, breathing, and endurance, and, Camille, you are a long-distance runner and I have also always been an endurance-based athlete and then dancer and I've never really questioned why I love, why I desire that feeling of breathlessness that Karyn talked about: that push and that need to pull in so deeply and exhale so deeply. This relationship with the vesicles and the breathing through the burn and that intimacy is calling me to think about that endurance in a new way. You said something, Joseph, that I think about creating future pockets of air, and I'm thinking of that.

Karyn: That is so beautiful, creating future pockets of air. It's almost like futurity bundles for those future ancestors that are in our processions, that are coming and have been in our present. I can offer something that I've been thinking about in this relation, because we are talking about rock, and I've been thinking a lot about adoption lately. In my own experience of adoption, I was born in Prince Albert, Saskatchewan, and then adopted out, brought east, and I was pretty much raised in southern Ontario. I think about the generosity of the form of a conversation, almost like whenever we can kind of get together with our beautiful witnesses, it feels like a different kind of relational praxis that we're engaging in. And I think, Camille, you really spoke beautifully about a slow kind of stretched out thinking that we can carry a vesicle for—we have this kind of intimacy anyway. And I think we all kind of desire that and maybe even a little more so during COVID—this intimacy of a conversation, an engagement. This is a time to really think about intimacy and embrace intimacy in ways that perhaps other moments in time might not have made possible. I wonder, for instance, if adoptees are drawn to thinking about relations with rock and more-than-human kin, because we've had to construct this future imaginary of kin with what we

Fig. 4. Emily Johnson in *The Ways We Love* . . . featuring Jeffrey Gibson's *Because Once You Enter My House*. . . Socrates Sculpture Park, 2020. Photo © Scott Lynch.

had on hand. So when I was growing up, I had this huge rock that I used to make all these stories about—because in my imaginary it became a big boat, a platform, a refuge—it became all of these things. And I used to sit there with my rubber boots and just like practise rowing and pretend I was on these big excursions. So I had, you know, I had this big rock: I had meteorite, I had moss, I had lichen, I had fire, I had star. This sort of sensual worlding, where kin was memory, and where memory was kin. And so it was super accentuated by smell, touch, feel that for me to touch the more ephemeral skin of my ancestors could be completely possible because I had my rock there; I had my rock kin, or landing technology, despite not having the language at that time to really speak it or identify this relation in that way. So I think that this connection with rock, stars, and the rupture that accompanies their process, their formation, and their activations provides connection to a language for diasporic landings.

So I'm really moved by the grammars of the gesturing in this piece [referring to the film], to think through, what does that kind of pull look like? What does it look like to breathe through a burn? What is that sort of inwardness?

And that pull. It almost made me feel like that was the vesicle, that was the space of, you know, that sort of breathlessness—like you can actually see what it looks like, almost as a folding, like a blanket, like a star blanket. I ask, "What is that space that is created as we fold into each other?" This folding into each other creates an atmosphere that maybe suspends time, place, and space and changes it into something else—into the potential of an otherwise. So our bodies are those vesicles and I think that that language is really interesting—the language that this piece presents in terms of—and language is probably not the right word, but the grammars, the choreographies, the gestures. I'm interested in seeing how that kind of speculative choreography creates these kinds of architectures that allow us to be in relation with each other—and really get behind each other and what we need.

Emily: I always joke that Karyn has taught me to look up because I'm so ground-focused in my work and in my being. I think, Karyn, as you were just describing movement, speculative choreography, and the shapes—it may be in relation to what you were speaking of before—but I think about the activations of waking up. What is waking up or pulling up the obelisk from deep within the ground via the stomp, via the stomping? For me that stomping that we do *(stomps up and down)* is partly, yes, that wake up of below, the underneath, but it's also a pulling up, so when I stomp down I actually think of the pull up *(extends one arm up)* after the down. And the stomp, it's a pull up. And now, for the first time, I'm also thinking rock-based from the ground up to rock-based in the celestial, like all the way—like in that stomp, you actually pull all the way up.

Joseph: I think it's important for us to name our diasporic kinships and the ways in which we relate to our ancestors. My father was also adopted by a white family and so my relationship with Indigeneity is also fractured and ruptured. In my case, I'm a generation removed from the event, the rupture of adoption, but, nevertheless, I still feel and have an intimacy with those effects. But one of the things that I have learned from this work, our conversations, and from learning Cherokee stories—because I've had to learn them—is about how we survive these ruptures. And now that I'm thinking about it, in the original story of how Cherokees were given the gift of fire, all of the animals tried to go get the fire but none of them can. And the one who is able to get fire is the water spider, and the water spider is able to spin a basket, a vesicle, a little pocket, and the fire, the ember, goes inside the basket. And that's how the water spider is able to walk back across the water and bring the fire to the people. And so that's how the sacred fire that burns in the middle of the stomp grounds was brought to Cherokee people. Like a vesicle, it's also a womb and that's another etymological term for that. Ultimately, all of these things relate not just to ancestral futurities, but also to grounding practices that are never just about grounding, but also about reaching across the breach of time and space toward the stars.

EMILY: That is so beautiful, Joseph. And as the video was playing, I was nervously pacing and walking around my apartment just gathering little things that reminded me of different times that we've had together, and one of them was behind a photo that I picked up. Nothing is chance, right? I wrote this tiny little note to myself and a future star being on Karyn's prompt, back in 2017, when we were doing a different project here (in Lenapehoking). We were outdoors on Randalls Island in the East River. And I wrote, "Star being, it's as if it's not the future, but it is the future at the same time." That's me trying to call a star being into my life. And as you're talking now, I just keep thinking of the water moving over your fingers. And then there are the relations of the water spider, the basket, and fire that makes me think about your hands and the way we are describing intimacy. We've talked about this before, but it's very strong in my mind right now—that water of the East River that also has been part of so many ceremonies *(gestures with her arms flowing inward)*, one, of course, that we intimately know led by our dear friend and person that you are so intimate with, [cross-disciplinary artist, writer, and curator] SJ Norman. The East River has brought water and blood and ash from across so much distance, and, to bring water here, as we merge with this water—that was the water that went through those three worlds of your hands and spilled onto the ground. That is so . . . that's everything, and it just makes me want to hold your hands, caress your hands.

Fig. 5. Audience members planting in *The Ways We Love . . .* featuring Jeffrey Gibson's *Because Once You Enter My House . . .* Socrates Sculpture Park, 2020. Photo © Scott Lynch.

JOSEPH: The ceremonies are so important. My dear friend and collaborator SJ Norman and I were working on a project called *Knowledge of Wounds*, which was preceded by a work that he did called *Cicatrix 1 (that which is taken/that which remains)*. And at the end of this work, SJ had a vessel, a container with his blood, that was offered to the East River. The next year we had a fire as part of *Knowledge of Wounds*, and the ashes from the fire were also offered to the East River. And so the following year, or later that year, that was the water with the ash and the blood that was trickling over my fingers to water the plants that had been planted at the end of this ceremony—which is what it was—the dance ceremony that is multi-scalar in a way, the continuities that are created when we recognize them. Just as when we recognize that this water is also the water that held ash and blood and prayer. That is how we recognize our ongoing relationships. That's how we recognize the continuity of our beings. That's how we resist erasure and oblivion—because the land remembers, the water remembers, and the stars remember.

Thank you.

WORKS CITED

Gibson, Jeffrey. *Because Once You Enter My House It Becomes Our House*. 2020, MONUMENTS NOW exhibition, Socrates Sculpture Park, Long Island City, NY. Monumental sculpture. socratessculpturepark.org/artist/jeffrey-gibson/.

Jemisin, N.K. *The City We Became*. Orbit, 2020.

———. *The Fifth Season*. Orbit, 2015.

Johnson, Emily. *Then a Cunning Voice and a Night We Spend Gazing at Stars*. 19–20 Aug. 2017, Randalls Island, New York, NY. Dance performance.

———. *The Ways We Love and the Ways We Love Better—Monumental Movement Toward Being Future Being(s)*. 16 Sep. 2020, Socrates Sculpture Park, Long Island City, NY. Dance performance.

Norman, SJ. *Cicatrix 1 (that which is taken/that which remains)*. 8 Jan. 2019, Performance Space, New York, NY. Performance.

Norman, SJ, and Joseph M. Pierce. Knowledge of Wounds. 20 Jun. 2021–21 Jun. 2022, Performance Space, New York, NY. Digital event series.

Socrates Sculpture Park. "Emily Johnson's Collaboration with Jeffrey Gibson at Socrates." *YouTube*, 17 Feb. 2021, youtube.com/watch?v=nJAmqdMnFCk&ab_channel=SocratesSculpturePark.

GROUND(ING) TRAVEL: MOVEMENTS TO RESIST SO-CALLED "BETTERMENT" IN DANCE AND DANCE STUDIES

EVADNE KELLY

Since 2018 I have been working with large teams of artists, scholars, and activists to lead and co-create an award-winning project series that exposes and counters oppression in Ontario education (see intothelight.ca). My research on white settler-colonial supremacy discourses in medical and educative spaces in Ontario has addressed my own place within such systems as a white, cisgender settler scholar and performer, but it has not directly addressed my ideas and practices as a Western theatrical dancer (see Kelly, Manning, Boye, Rice, Owen, Stonefish, and Stonefish and Kelly, Rice, and Stonefish). As a lifelong dance artist and dance studies scholar invested in "unsettling the settler within" (Regan), however, here I shift my attention to focus on that very relationship. The white settler-colonial discourses I focus on are collectively known as so-called "race betterment." Such ideas and practices include eugenics (the mistaken notion that you can improve the human race through controlled heredity) and euthenics (an assimilationist notion that you can improve the human race by controlling the environment). Both capitalize on ableist and racist notions of evolution oriented toward singular and narrow definitions of fitness, unilinear progress, efficiency, and Eurocentric value-laden notions of vitality and personhood.[1] Europeans have used dehu-

1 Both Herbert Spencer and John S. Mill, for example, held ideas about what it means to be human that favoured values around intellectual capacity coupled with individual autonomy. Mill also made the case that those who were deemed to have a "lower grade" existence were less-than-human, as he equated them with pigs who are satisfied with less

manizing betterment discourses in conjunction with terra nullius (the idea that Turtle Island was uninhabited) and the Doctrine of Discovery to unjustly claim sovereign ownership of the land (Royal Commission on Aboriginal Peoples; Truth and Reconciliation Commission of Canada 4–5). How do Western theatrical dance forms in Canada—as expressive enactments of ideas, values, and beliefs about bodily movements through space and time—participate in, move through, and resist such ideas of terra nullius, occupation, and takeover, especially as those ideas reside in bodies? In the space-time of this essay, I bring my increased understanding of white settler-colonial race betterment, which seeks to control, shape, and/or eliminate certain bodies and their movements, into conversations about my dance training and practice in Western theatrical dance forms. These forms afford a nuanced exploration of bodily control as, in some cases, a life-negating assertion of power over and, in other cases, as a life-affirming source of physical and spiritual knowledge, attunement, agency, expression, transformation, relationship, and pleasure. I ask how betterment discourses and practices influence my kinesthetic identity. How do I occupy and move through space-time? What kind of engagement with time and space does my movement practice suggest? What does it feel like to move across this ground? And how might I know and travel this ground differently than I do now?

The road map of this reflection is not straight. It weaves together lived experience of dance with institutional archival evidence, neither of which are untouched by colonial betterment narratives. As Diana Taylor illustrates in *The Archive and the Repertoire*, archives themselves are a site for normative control through how their materials are selected, classified, and presented (or hidden from view). The silences I have encountered in the eugenics archives are profound. As a result, I engage with documents and artifacts through my

---

in life. Quoting Mill, "It is better to be a human being dissatisfied than a pig satisfied; better to be Socrates dissatisfied than a fool satisfied. And if the fool, or the pig, are of a different opinion, it is because they only know their own side of the question. The other party to the comparison knows both sides" (121). Mill believed that human beings possess human dignity in proportion to their higher faculties. Those he deemed to lack capacity and a sensitivity to the world were also deemed to be less-than-human and possess less dignity.

relationship with dance to amplify the stories that master what betterment narratives seek to silence.

This weaving dance is not neutral. Dance, loosely defined as body (human and non-human) movement through space and time, is social and political. As I have written elsewhere, I experience "dance as intensities, energies, and emotions [. . .] expressed kinesthetically in the visceral sensibilities, movements, rhythms, and sounds emerging in-between bodies" (*Dancing Spirit* 15).[2] For social justice and decolonizing scholars Carla Rice, Susan D. Dion, Hannah Fowlie, and Andrea Breen, such intensities, emotions, or affects might offer pathways out of white settler ignorance through narratives that address "accountabilities as beneficiaries of settler colonization" (19). How can engagements with archives and my lived experience become part of my dance or journey out of white settler ignorance and into accountability as someone who has benefited from colonialism (the policies and practices of seeking political control over another territory, occupying the territory with settlers, and exploiting it economically), which utilizes race betterment discourses.

In moving along this pathway out of ignorance, I articulate how white settler betterment discourses sustain themselves in bodies and show how dance becomes a method for bolstering, resisting, moving through, and unsettling these discourses. I explore the experiences of three white settler cisgender women (including myself) who face a crisis as they grapple with conflicting embodiments of betterment in the face of debility, disability, and death within their dancer-identified bodies. The archive sheds light on the ways eugenics and euthenics are harmful in how they negate full participation and vitality. These three lived experiences inform my reflections on "ground(ing) travel" toward knowing and moving differently. As grounding allows electrons to flow, ground(ing) travel allows me to articulate the energy, feeling, thought, and movement that I carry and that flow through my body according to the

2 Recent proponents of affect theory, influenced by Baruch Spinoza, show the political dimensions of affect as a process of exchange between bodies (see Ahmed, *The Cultural Politics*) and performances of nationalism (see Muñoz, "Ephemera as Evidence" and "Feeling Brown"). Bodies have an "affective angle" (Ahmed, "Happy Objects" 36) or affective standpoint comprised of one's own unique personal and cultural context and past experiences.

pathways and orientations afforded by the knowledge I have gathered. As I move, my body grounds some messages and transforms others. Through the concept of "ground(ing) travel," I shift away from the Western theatrical training that encouraged me to perceive my body's movement in generic, politically neutral spaces. Instead, I embrace a more critical and nuanced understanding of place (Tuck and McKenzie 20). By bracketing the -ing suffix, I draw attention to my white settler experiences of movement in relation to specific place-based processes of colonization, settler colonization, and decolonial prioritization of Indigenous land and life and how the ground emerges in these relationships (Tuck and Yang; Tuck and McKenzie). This journey offers a ground(ing) methodology—an exploration of body movements that seeks to foster full expressive participation with an attunement towards the ways we move in relation to place and understanding and consciously not (re)producing the harm of white settler-colonial betterment. Even more, this is a ground(ing) aimed at unsettling and transforming settler-colonial ideas and practices.

RACE BETTERMENT IDEAS AND METHODS

My research has looked closely at nuanced, gestured, covert, and unevenly experienced meanings of embodied performances and imagined progress in southern Ontario as a starting place to think about the impacts of early Canadian nationalism, subject formation, and First Nations/settler relations within educational institutions. I have explored these impacts as central to decolonizing Canadian educational institutions in the present and future. Harmful "betterment" methodologies continue to target First Nations, Black, racialized, disabled, poor, and 2SLGTBQ+ peoples for brutality, dehumanization, and elimination for the benefit of white, non-disabled, propertied settlers. Two such methods include eugenics and euthenics. These terms are relevant to my movement out of ignorance, as they refer to dominant ideas and practices that continue to play a role in attempts to control bodily movements and determining who gets to live in ways that have bolstered white settler supremacy on Turtle Island. Late-nineteenth-century and early-twentieth-century environmentalists drew their ideas about evolution from French naturalist Jean-Baptiste Lamarck to assert that the environment shaped physical, intellectual, and behavioural traits that future generations would inherit. They also believed they could intentionally manipulate or reform environments to accelerate a process of supposed race betterment (McLaren).

As race betterment discourses, both environmentalist and eugenic thinking and practice in Ontario had as their cornerstone a concern about white racial degeneracy. Analysis of these terms and their usage also shows a pattern of underlying thought imbued with value-laden judgments about human life. First, agents of race betterment classified some human lives as superior to others, deeming them less evolved (along a unilinear evolutionary path of progress and betterment) and sometimes even less-than-human. Second, both led to deterministic interpretations of biology: the health and behaviour of individuals and groups were bound by inherited (eugenics) or acquired (environmentalism) biology. Finally, despite different methodologies, they both led to the attempted annihilation of particular groups of people in Ontario, specifically those who did not fit white settler, Anglo-Saxon, propertied, middle-class, and non-disabled norms.

The language used by Ontario eugenicists and euthenists has drawn from notions of evolution involving Herbert Spencer's theory of the "survival of the fittest."[3] Spencer's approach has been used to justify British imperialism, colonialism, and the brutal treatment of those targeted by betterment discourses. Knowing such discourses across Turtle Island are part of a colonial and settler-colonial project, how then is my understanding of dance and

---

3 For example, in a series of radio addresses called *The Future of the Race* sponsored by the Eugenics Society of Canada, Canadian eugenicists discuss their erroneous belief that future heredity problems would result from allowing the "feeble in mind or body" to survive and propagate. They opposed state-sponsored care and support because they believed it interfered with natural processes of selection, which would eliminate the so-called feeble—a broad category that included poor, racialized, disabled, and many more who did not fit white, Anglo-Saxon, settler-colonial world views. This, according to medical doctor William Hutton, "is an unforgivable sin, for it is an *offence* against future generations" (36).

movement, which is implicated in and impacted by these damaging beliefs, also part of a settler-colonial project?

Terms Ontario eugenicists and environmentalists engaged with to describe and judge human beings within narrative frames of progress, usefulness, worth, fitness, and efficiency are important, as they uphold discriminatory perspectives at the intersection of ableism, classism, sexism, and racism (Kelly et al.). According to Susan Burch, who focuses on North American institutionalization as a settler-supported process of colonialization, through the lenses of normality, fitness, and competency, "settler ableism actively serves and reflects broader colonial principles and aspirations. Beliefs in superiority and practices of domination—inherent aspects of settler colonialism—regularly invoke ableist logics" (9–10). Settler-colonialism also wove its way into Western theatrical dance forms of ballet and modern dance.

Dance forms can challenge and reinforce colonialism, euthenics, and eugenics. In his book on modern-dance pioneer Ted Shawn, Paul Scolieri discusses sexuality scientist Havelock Ellis's theory of dance as a form of "unconscious eugenics" (147). For Ellis, dance was a method for achieving spiritual and sexual fitness and an "unconscious reenactment [. . .] for individual and racial survival" (148). Dance practices have also been tools of euthenics, embodying ideals of acquired fitness through physical training and use of the body. Scolieri notes that Shawn viewed dance as a means of "(re) producing ideal bodies" (87), which he sought to exemplify with his own white settler, non-disabled body as the ideal of fitness. These perspectives show how dance forms can embody, reflect, and perpetuate narrow ideas about life and human expression. In my early experiences with Western theatrical dance, I encountered such narrow perspectives. At the same time, why have I found that the same forms of dance have affirmed and supported vitality, pleasure, heightened sensitivity in relationship, greater awareness of my body, and have been a source of agency, power, expression, transformation, and ecstasy? Why has my white settler body, whose size and shape barely pass through the narrow confines of dance institution fitness ideals, been allowed in? I find my pathway through these questions by exploring the uneven, nuanced, and covert ways in which colonial notions of betterment are embodied.

WHAT DO WANDERING SPINES KNOW?

Between 1 May 2018 and1 June 2019, I did extensive research at the University of Guelph Library's Archival and Special Collections on one of the school's founding colleges, the Macdonald Institute—a domestic science normal school.[4] I read through archival documents dated between 1904 to 1948, with a particular focus on the 1930s. Course calendars, a eugenics reference library, course outlines, slides, exams, student course work, letters of reference, and lecture notes showed that the Macdonald Institute and the Ontario Agricultural College taught eugenics and euthenics for over thirty years, from 1914 to 1948.

The goals of the eugenics course are clear: a 1935–1936 eugenics exam question asks, "What steps would you recommend to improve the Canadian race?" ("Examination papers"). In this context, the term "Canadian race" refers to Euro-colonial, white, middle-class, Anglo-Saxon, non-disabled settlers and their efforts to justify and normalize their dominance and privilege. Course materials show that teachers taught controlled reproduction through sterilization, birth control, assimilation, restrictive marriage laws, immigration policies, social hygiene, physical exercise, health, nutrition, and curative therapies as methods of Canadian race betterment (see Kelly and Rice, "Universities Must Open Their Archives and Share Their Oppressive Pasts"; Kelly, Manning, Boye, Rice, Owen, Stonefish, and Stonefish; Kelly, Boye, and Rice; Kelly, Rice, and Stonefish; and Kelly and Rice, "Pathways to Disrupt Eugenics in Higher Education").

More recently, between October 2020 and July 2021, the president's office of a large Toronto hospital hired me to research their history of race betterment. This research further confirmed the role of white settler institutions in establishing systems that sought to shape, control, and eliminate the "unfit" through health, welfare, and care circuits. Even more clarifying was the realization that I had now researched the process of training women in race

4 My research into the history of the Macdonald Institute was generously funded by Bodies in Translation: Activist Art, Technology, and Access to Life, a SSHRC Partnership Grant co-directed by Carla Rice and Eliza Chandler.

betterment and the outcome of that training as it played out in practice in the hospital setting. Again, I could see the systemic process through which methods of race betterment pathologized and then disappeared those who did not fit the white settler norm—the so-called "unfit."

But as I worked my way through the archives of these institutions, I also became aware of those white settlers who were implicated in and negatively impacted by race betterment. For example, in the Macdonald Institute archive, I came across a folder full of reference letters. The Director of Macdonald Institute, Olive Cruikshank, wrote the following in her letters for one white settler student entering the workforce. The letters show the uneven ways in which white settler-colonial betterment is at work.

> February 11th, 1938 [Anonymous student], is a reliable student. She has a keen, fairly analytical mind and expresses herself quite well, although she may be rather too anxious to state her opinions. She has a wide, real interest in human nature, is cooperative and willing. Unfortunately [anonymous student] has a high shoulder which detracts from her appearance.
>
> March 18th, 1938 Miss [anonymous student], of Niagara-on-the-Lake, Ontario [. . .] has been quite an alert student. She has, unfortunately, a misformed shoulder which detracts from her appearance, which is otherwise satisfactory.
>
> March 29th, 1938 [Anonymous student], Niagara-on-the-Lake, has a delightful personality. She is so alert, bright, cheerful and willing to co-operate, that one soon forgets the deformity of her back.
>
> July 3rd, 1939 [Anonymous student], Niagara-on-the-Lake, who is relieving [anonymous] in St. John's Convalescent Hospital in Toronto, has had pupil work in St. Joseph's Hospital, London. She is a capable young woman, but her deformity does detract considerably from her otherwise pleasing personality.

The more I read through the letters, the more I understood how the Institute deployed harmful betterment ideas and practices in ways that would profoundly and negatively affect the full participation of some students as agents of the future. The letters signal how those with institutional authority judged bodies for their fitness as measures of vitality, capacity, and full personhood. The letters are evidence of safeguarding white settler-colonial supremacy through gatekeeping who has a future during and after attending the Macdonald Institute. Those in positions of authority prevented those students they judged to be unfit or subnormal from full participation in the workforce. One student's treatment exemplifies how the Institute reduced her subjectivity and personhood through concerns over the appearance of her spine—judged as a hindrance, a problem, a *deformity* (indicating defective, flawed, malformed) that detracted from her vitality. Would this student need to be cured of her so-called deformity, or physically improved somehow to have the same opportunities as other students to participate fully in life? As I read these letters, I couldn't help wondering how this student felt about her spine.

I am a dancer with a curvy spine. My relationship to my spine is complexly shaped by pathologizing, stigmatizing, shaming, and individualizing betterment discourses. At nine years of age, my dance teachers found my spine's spiralling, winding, and curving orientation a deformity, something to fix, cure, hide, and suppress. As I grew (and my body loved to grow), so did my curves. Within a year, my doctor presented me with a tricky choice: I could wear a brace for many years and give up dancing altogether, or I could wear electrodes on my back and receive electric stimulation through the night for many years. I was fortunate to get the electrodes—dance is my anchor in the world. For the next five years of my dreaming life, I experienced intense electricity moving through my muscles. Every two minutes throughout the night I endured thirty seconds of the machine taking control of my body and contorting it back to straight. Electric currents fought their way through my muscles to find the ground. Intense contractions and muscle stimulation turned to sharp pain as the cords aged and my skin developed an allergic reaction to the tape that held the electrodes in place. Nevertheless, this was the best option to prevent me from curving out of control. The electricity offered a controlled movement to control movement, control my shape, and, as I understood it, make me normal and improve my life.

My experience of electric therapy was an encounter with euthenics, and my full participation in dance hinged on it. It imparted on me the idea that I am somehow less than whole—not entirely formed, not quite developed. But my body never learned to be straight—maybe it never wanted to. This experience has forever made me uneasy about the motivations of body therapies and cures that aim to control, shape, and eliminate the "unfit."

As a young dancing adult, I remember auditioning for a modern dance summer school at a world-renowned New York dance studio—the home of my favourite dance company. I had been dreaming about this moment for a long time. First, we were given a number. Next, we were told to pin it onto the front and back of our form-fitting dancewear. I danced my heart out, going past the limits of what I knew. I felt so good about my dancing, and I couldn't have demonstrated my love of it more. But I soon realized what they were looking for when they turned off the music, placed us in rows, and asked us to roll down through our spines one at a time. One of the judges came over to me and inspected my spine as I rolled down. I knew then it was all over. Whether or not it was my winding spine, my dancing, or my large body that prevented me from success that day, I can't know for sure. But the practice of measuring had a profound effect in its messaging. My body was being assessed for its fitness that day and that seemed to take precedence over my dancing. My full personhood as a dancer was denied.

I received many messages as a young mover. Some targeted my size: "You just need to lose five to ten pounds"; "Your pelvis is too big, move your pelvis more"; "You can play the part of the man because you're big"; "You go in the back because you're big"; "That dancer over there will get hired more than you because she has a small frame." Other messages targeted my spine: "Just lower your right shoulder an inch, then you'll look even"; "Keep your pelvis still to stabilize your spine"; "Avoid rotation"; "Avoid giving into your scoliosis"; "If you make it, your career will be short because of your spine. It will cause extra wear and tear on all your joints. Is that really what you want?"

At the time of this writing, I am forty-nine years old and still dancing! I was fortunate to find a path in a modern dance company with dance mentors who gave different messages: "Travel and expand in space"; "Move dynamically"; "You're a big mover"; "Move from the inside out"; "Connect to your breath"; "Feel the ground"; "Listen closely with your body to feel"; "Open your senses." These mentors wanted me to be a full participant and a whole expressive person. It was their ethos, flowing from Martha Graham, that

> There is a vitality, a life force, an energy, a quickening that is translated through you into action, and because there is only one of you in all time, this expression is unique. And if you block it, it will never exist through any other medium and it will be lost. The world will not have it. It is not your business to determine how good it is nor how valuable nor how it compares with other expressions. It is your business to keep it yours clearly and directly, to keep the channel open. (De Mille 264)

This message saved me in many ways. As a result, I am slowly learning to enjoy and experience my size and my curvy spine as a gift: a source of vitality, full participation, and meaningful action.

EMBODIED BATTLES WITH ABLEIST FORMS OF ELIMINATION

Despite the life-affirming messages I have received from my unique dance mentors, for many years I felt compelled to keep searching for a cure to my wandering spine. Finally, I found Pilates, and it became my new euthenics. Joseph Pilates developed the movement rehabilitation method in the early decades of the twentieth century. While the history of its development is complex, it is important to note here that he worked closely with ballet dancers; the physical culture of the times, which idolized the physically fit white, non-disabled body and participated in the manufacture of a "morally and socially superior political and social body," was also a likely influence (Holmes 59). In many ways, Pilates has balanced my body from the many hours of intense dance company rehearsal work. But Pilates is also not neutral in the work it does on the body. As dance scholar Sarah Holmes notes, political and social ideas are embedded in Pilates (Holmes 59–65). Pilates can uphold profoundly exclusionary Eurocentric, racist, and ableist embodiments of hierarchy, progress, efficiency, and fitness. Throughout her book, *Digging the Africanist Presence in American Performance: Dance and Other Contexts*, Brenda Dixon Gottschild shows how there is a Eurocentric orientation to verticality in the spine that resists movements of the hips. I was fortunate to work at a Pilates studio that also wove in additional somatic methods that fostered more fluidity and imagery. We worked with all sorts of soft rollie tools to create movement experiences that felt good and allowed for more movement in places people felt stuck. Yet betterment discourses still wove their way in.

One day I was doing some one-on-one bodywork with a woman who was once a soloist for a ballet company. She offered a profound understanding of the ableist attitudes entwined within ballet circuits and its relationship to personhood. She had developed a rare progressive and life-threatening condition that affects movement control and coordination. She would arrive in the Pilates studio appearing exhausted and stiff. Together we explored movements that she expressed felt good in her body. One day she shared with me that she was contemplating Medical Assistance in Dying (MAiD) because she felt like a burden.[5] I wondered if her vitality was under threat because the qualities and characteristics that tethered her to a sense of humanity and personhood were now different.

Her changing relationship with her dancer's body seemed to have had a powerfully debilitating effect on her sense of identity. Lenore Manderson and Susan Peake write, "Social membership demands autonomy and control of the physical body" (qtd. in Anderson 65). Whether or not this is true, the ideals of personhood are often articulated as self-reliance, invulnerability, autonomy, and capability. Western theatrical dancer identities are in some ways an acceleration of these ideals. They are dependent on one's mastery, skill,

5 See Canada, House of Commons, Bill C-7 for the Canadian government's institutionalization of MAiD.

body appearance, energy, and magnetism (Anderson 64). Non-autonomous relations that allow for full participation are often undervalued, unrecognized, and even stigmatized. In addition, non-autonomy is viewed as a costly burden on society. This may help to explain why rapid and extreme changes to my Pilates partner's experience of bodily control, agency, and pleasure in movement seemed to trigger a profound grief. I wondered if her experience of feeling like a burden also triggered internalized ableism, which then seemed to put her whole existence into question. Either way, she expressed a deep love for the feeling of dancing. She simply loved moving, and she needed a new repertoire. I did all I could to help her locate movements that felt good and prolonged those moments with her.

My fellow dancer's experience links to the fact that many people have criticized MAiD as a return to eugenic ideas and practices that will disproportionally target First Nations, Black, racialized, poor, 2SLGTBQ+, and disabled communities. These communities share concerns about coercive health practices in the context of systematic barriers to life. For some in the disability community, institutional care is carried out in such degrading ways that death appears like a better option (Canada, House of Commons, "Dr. Catherine Frazee" and "Dr. Heidi Janz"; Canada, Senate). In her article "XI. Death, Debility and Disability," feminist bioethics scholar Margrit Shildrick discusses the unevenness of vulnerability in her work on assisted dying. Shildrick is careful to situate the complexity of her arguments about assisted dying within a neoliberal and eugenic context whereby disabled people are under more significant pressure to consider assisted dying and, as a result, have greater vulnerability. She applies Lauren Berlant's cruel optimism, which is described by Shildrick as the ongoing endurance of worn-out bodies for the promise of something better (157). While there is a danger in this description of undermining ongoing individual and community agency, activism, and praxis along with the hopes and pleasures that can come with efforts to make life better, Shildrick points out that the cruel optimism of the majority relies on the scapegoating of those viewed as a "drain on society's resources" and holding back progress to something better (157). In Shildrick's words, "People with disabilities will be targeted for death" (158) because, in a culture of ableism, non-disabled people are quick to assume they have less to live for. Many critical scholars of the body call for a shift away from narrow and damaging liberal enlightenment notions of autonomous personhood and call for new understandings that "desire messy dependency," intentional interdependence in care collectives (Nishida) and "distributed competence," whereby autonomy plays out in a distributed, relational, extended, and interactional encounter (Goodley and Runswick-Cole 10).

I understand my experiences in the Pilates studio as connected to ongoing legacies of eugenics and euthenics in Ontario.[6] Agents of settler-colonial betterment have embedded ableist value-laden ideas about bodies—how they appear, behave, and move—within notions of personhood. But how are people expected to move? How must people sense through their eyes, ears, and moving bodies to be considered "fit"? What is movement efficiency? When are bodies efficient/inefficient? Who and what does movement efficiency serve? According to a 1937 eugenics and recreation conference report by Weaver Pangburn held in the Macdonald Institute Reference Library, eugenic physical-movement educators wanted their students to embody specific values. Quoting Pangburn,

> We reviewed the major values in organized recreation that have importance for eugenics. Among them were: (a) the development of courage, physical strength, nervous strength, early experience in community life and adjustments, experience in leadership, experience in self-control, good health habits, physical efficiency and recreational skills [. . .]. (10–11)

We can understand more by exploring the 1939 notes of one student who studied eugenics as part of her more extensive program in domestic science at the Macdonald Institute. The student's notes show us how course instructors were to examine physical behaviour during student "demonstrations":

6 Especially as they relate to Herbert Spencer's evolutionary theory of use known as the "survival of the fittest."

> a) Appearance—neat, immaculate hands and hair, colourless nail polish, not too much makeup; b) Voice—pleasing, quiet, not shrill but clear voice which carries to back of room; c) Mannerisms—avoid mannerisms. Be exacting about everything. Try to express as much self control as possible; e) Posture—stand erect, good posture is absolutely essential; do not lean on table; never put your hands above your shoulders; never turn your back to the audience; stand on both feet." (Macdonald Institute Student)

Such physical demonstrations, or performances, of efficiency and fitness are familiar to me in my experiences with Western theatrical dance.

EMBODIED BATTLES WITH BETTERMENT PROGRESS NARRATIVES

Recently, I was providing some end-of-life care for one of my dance mentors. Her dance life wove together with her identity as a white settler feminist. For the two decades I knew her, I understood her to have faith that her own actions and the actions of those around her were making the world better along a unilinear course of healing and social-justice progress. She taught me to celebrate my size and see it as a source of power in the world, not something to hide. She taught me to get bigger, take up space, expand in all directions physically, energetically, emotionally, perceptively. She taught me to embody intensity. She was intense and demanded the same level of full spiritual, emotional, physical, nutritional, artistic, and intellectual engagement from those around her. In my interactions with her, there was no arriving, only striving and emergence. I recall her articulating her belief that spiritual, political, and psychological change and empowerment come from the body and the mind working together. Body and mind together were change in the act of becoming, and that was dance (Anonymous). She was dynamic in the studio, and I felt her disappointment when I did not generate those qualities. At times she expressed feelings of frustration and benevolent sentiments that I could not follow. At other times it felt like full engagement had turned to full self-regulation and control. But I knew what she was looking for in me, and I slowly and steadily found my way into moving as emergence.

But as I witnessed her grapple with her body quickly and unexpectedly changing from disease, I started to understand new and harmful layers of her embodied practice of striving and emergence. Her striving seemed related to Berlant's "cruel optimism" whereby bodies keep enduring in the face of adversity by the promise of something better. A fatal illness was taking hold. The physical pain she experienced seemed severe, but I believe she also experienced immense torment from her inability to overcome illness and return to a memory of her younger, more physically fit self. There seemed to be a sadness and hopelessness in the contradictions that battled in her body—in her emerging self. I now wonder if deeply internalized ableist betterment narratives were a part of that battle. In her final months, I witnessed her struggling with the changes in her body—changes that were not progressing toward healing or getting better, but changes that were not in her control. Seemingly crushed and lied to by herself through disassociation and disbelief, she could not inhabit her true form because it did not line up with her life's work to achieve progress and to overcome the daily threats to her health. This was tragic but also crucial for me to witness—these were her final lessons for me.

My mentor's ongoing efforts to overcome the feelings, sensations, and changes that come with aging and illness exemplify the deeply ingrained culture of ableism that has woven its way into Western theatrical dance (Anderson). The links between dance and ableism are not surprising since the body is central to race betterment discourses. My mentor was strongly opposed to forms of oppression (including eugenics), but her sense of vitality seemed to hinge on her autonomy, capability, self-reliance, and progress toward physical improvement. Despite her own beliefs about healing and justice, destructive, value-laden surveillance and control of her body and its fitness seemed to battle inside her, perhaps even unconsciously, as a significant threat to her vitality and personhood.

Looking at these struggles with physical control and change I have perceived in myself, in my Pilates confidant, and in my dance mentor, I think back to Ellis's theory of dance as a form of "unconscious eugenics" (Scolieri 147).

These struggles are not an innate desire for improvement. Instead, they are the embodied manifestation of destructive material and discursive betterment ideas and practices learned and woven into our everyday lives, perhaps even through dance, becoming bone-deep, "in(sinew)ated with power relations" that permeate the body, its practice, and its performance (Foster 9).

But what about my mentor's life-affirming message to travel through space, occupy space, eat up space, travel more, and expand? As a large person, these cues given by my teachers have created opportunities for me to feel whole as a dance artist. If dance is a philosophical treatise on relationships between bodies, time, and space, what kind of engagement with bodies, time, and space does my own dance training suggest? Despite my attunement to bodies, sounds, energies, rhythms, and spaces when I dance, I recognize that Western theatrical dance is a human-centric project for human self-interest within a capitalist structure that goes deeper than the proscenium frame. It is generally not a practice of reciprocal relations with the land whereby more is given than taken (Simpson). Instead, it is a practice that tends to use the ground to dance instead of dancing with and for the ground. Here I grapple with my love of that kind of expansive embodied travel through space, and I reflect on new experiences of ground(ing) travel that unsettle my training within Western traditions of theatrical dance. Through the guidance and wisdom of mentors I have worked with recently, I lean in and listen to the ethical approach to responsive relations they story. This is especially important now as the Truth and Reconciliation Commission of Canada and the Huronia Regional Centre class action lawsuit have exposed all the institutional mechanisms and processes of settler-colonial betterment and their resulting inequitable effects.

EMBODYING GROUND(ING) TRAVEL DIFFERENTLY

As a dance artist and scholar, I think of my next moves through the Truth and Reconciliation Commission of Canada's (TRC) 94 Calls to Action and the Huronia Regional Centre class action lawsuit. I listen to the calls for action and transformation with my full body and understand them as the most crucial dance I have learned so far. They inspire questions: As a mover, what do I bring into existence? What mentors and training do I seek? What and how can I learn from my moving experiences? How do rhythms dance in my body? Where do these rhythms come from? When does a rhythm become violent? What are the felt rhythms that enable relationality/prevent relationality? When we don't want to endure damaging betterment ideas and practices, how do we find/feel/pay attention to different rhythms and make new rhythms? These are questions I continue to explore in my ongoing relationship with dance.

Being a participant of theatre and performance researcher and worker Jill Carter's (Anishinaabe/Ashkenazi) Native Performance Culture and the Rhythm of (Re)Conciliation: Remembering Ourselves in Deep Time project in 2020 and 2021 allowed me to re-educate myself on the land in and around Ontario. Carter encouraged us to attend many Indigenous-led events. At one event, urban Cree scholar/artist/writer Karyn Recollet presented a Landing Acknowledgement. She noted how British colonialism reduced active, living beings into passive things. Land, for example, became a generic thing that people could discover, use, claim, and own. She brought a sense of emergence into the meeting space by weaving an active web between her positionality and the event itself. Her active landing into the specific place and time of our gathering reminded me that the British colonial and Methodist missionary practice of translating actions into nominal things also occurred in British colonial Fiji, where my mother was born. As I continue to track the effects of British colonialism in relation to my own family and its travels around the globe, I am actively rethinking my landing relationships and my travelling in specific places and times, especially as a dancer.

In Carter's Deep Time group, we had been doing creative work responding to the TRC's Calls to Action, which culminated in *Streaming Life: Storying the 94* (Geller). Our work helped me reflect on grounding travel in relation to discourses used to justify European dominance over First Nations, Inuit, and Métis, including terra nullius and the Doctrine of Discovery. What do the lies of terra nullius and the Doctrine of Discovery feel like in my own body? Is my love of expansive travelling through space part of the life-negating lie? Or a more vital form of travel that centres difference?

Reflecting on my fraught embodied knowledge of the world, I have been working with the words "ground(ing) travel" to think about how I move through not just abstracted and generic notions of space and time but specific places and times.[7] I stay close to ground(ing) feelings and movements despite the controlling tempos of capital-progress time—the human promise of secure, stable, predictable gains that begins with the fantasy of an ideal and then tries to accomplish the impossible formation of that ideal through the production of stable identities, territories, structures, and objects. If progress-time intends to separate bodies hierarchically by reasoned, measured control over time and space, then ground(ing) travel is a non-human-centric, unreasoned, undisciplined time and space. It is thinking/feeling differently against the process of capital progress.

Yet, like the euthenic electric therapy that tried to cure me of my winding and wandering spine as the currents fought their way through my muscles to get to ground, ground(ing) travel is not a neutral form of travel. On the contrary, it is, despite my intentions, a winding and deeply fraught journey to ground(ing)—movements toward understanding and unsettling my implication in the white setter colonial project.

This writing has created a pathway for me to reflect on and transform my dance practice through what Cree scholar Willie Ermine calls an "ethical space of engagement," which thinks through discursive, political, social, and spatial relationships and collisions between First Nations and Western settler thought worlds. Ground(ing) travel as a mixed ethical space of engagement helps me to encounter the cracks, fissures, contradictions, and inconsistencies within Western society and knowledge, and helps me to catch a glimpse of my own settler-colonial mindset and practices (Ermine). According to Ermine, to enter an ethical space of engagement, settlers need to actively seek out the return gaze of First Nations peoples to see their own culture anew and to pull apart their embedded assumptions of power. Ground(ing) travel moves me toward feeling and living with an open desire for change and emergence within

7 As an example of this approach to the use of politically neutral and generic space, theatre director Peter Brook wrote in his book *The Empty Space*, "I can take any empty space and call it a bare stage" (11).

a liminal unknown rhythm-space that affords possibilities for unsettling and transforming settler-colonial betterment ideas and practices.

In this book *Power Moves*, I seek to highlight and honour the power moves of the student who sought support as she entered the workforce and imagined her future, of my Pilates partner's disturbing movements that mobilized warnings of MAiD, of my dance mentor's moves toward big and expansive felt-sensed emergence. Their movements inspire my own. With my writing, I aim to ignite a call to action, encouraging a transformation in the white settler mentalities that attempt to interfere with and erase our differences. Under the guise of health and well-being, the legacies of eugenics and euthenics persist within dance practice, education, and research, as well as within the institutions that support them. Yet there is also an ongoing legacy of strong resistance. As I continue my journey in dance—through performance, creation, research, teaching, and writing—I am committed to listening to those who have experienced the harmful effects of so-called "betterment" and allowing their wisdom to guide my transformation and centring of difference.

WORKS CITED

Ahmed, Sara. *The Cultural Politics of Emotion*. Edinburgh UP, 2004.

———. "Happy Objects." *The Affect Theory Reader*, edited by Greg Seigworth and Melissa Gregg, Duke UP, 2010, pp. 29–51.

Anderson, Bailey. "Overcoming and Denial: Disability and Modern Dance in the United States." *Dance Research Journal*, vol. 52, no. 3, Dec. 2020, pp. 58–75. 10.1017/S0149767720000364.

Anonymous. Radio interview. *Evi-Dance*, CIUT 89.5, U of Toronto Community Radio, 5 May 2002.

Berlant, Lauren. *Cruel Optimism*. Duke UP, 2011.

Brook, Peter. *The Empty Space: A Book About the Theatre: Deadly, Holy, Rough, Immediate*. Penguin, 2008.

Burch, Susan. *Committed: Remembering Native Kinship In and Beyond Institutions*. U of North Carolina P, 2021.

Canada, House of Commons. Bill C-7 (Royal Assent). *Parliament Canada*, 17 Mar. 2021, parl.ca/DocumentViewer/en/43-2/bill/C-7/royal-assent.

———. "Dr. Catherine Frazee (Professor Emerita, School of Disability Studies, Ryerson University, As an Individual)." Standing Committee on Justice and Human Rights (JUST), 43rd Parliament, session 2, no. 6, 10 Nov. 2020, 12:08. *Our Commons*, ourcommons.ca/DocumentViewer/en/43-2/JUST/meeting-6/evidence.

———. "Dr. Heidi Janz." Standing Committee on Justice and Legal Affairs (JUST), 43rd Parliament, session 2, no. 6, 10 Nov. 2020, 12:19. *Our Commons*, ourcommons.ca/DocumentViewer/en/43-2/JUST/meeting-6/evidence.

Canada, Senate. "Jonathan Marchand, Chair, Coop ASSIST—Quebec Cooperative for Independent Living." Standing Committee on Legal and Constitutional Affairs, 43rd Parliament, session 2, 1 Feb. 2021. *Senate Canada*, sencanada.ca/en/Content/Sen/Committee/432/LCJC/10ev-55128-e.

Cruikshank, Olive. Letter of recommendation to M.M. Evans, A. Wright, R.M. Currie, and B.L. Bridges. U of Guelph Library Archival and Special Collections, RE1MACA0017, Box 13, Files 1938 and 1939.

De Mille, Agnes. *Martha: The Life and Work of Martha Graham*. Random House, 1991.

Ermine, Willie. "The Ethical Space of Engagement." *Indigenous Law Journal*, vol. 6, no. 1, 2007, pp. 193–203.

"Examination papers." U of Guelph Library Archival and Special Collections, RE1MACA0004, Box 3, Folder 1936–37, 1937–38.

Foster, Susan Leigh. Introduction. *Worlding Dance*, edited by Foster, Palgrave Macmillan, 2009, pp. 1–13. palgrave.com/us/book/9780230205949.

Geller, Philip. "A Proposed Guide to Witnessing: Dialoguing with *Streaming Life: Storying the 94* As a Site for Call-and-Response." *Canadian Theatre Review*, vol. 192, fall 2022, pp. 74–77. 10.3138/ctr.192.016.

Goodley, Daniel, and Katherine Runswick-Cole. "Becoming Dishuman: Thinking About the Human Through Dis/Ability." *Discourse: Studies in the Cultural Politics of Education*, vol. 37, no. 1, Jan. 2016, pp. 1–15. 10.1080/01596306.2014.930021.

Gottschild, Brenda Dixon. *Digging the Africanist Presence in American Performance: Dance and Other Contexts*. Praeger, 1998.

Hutton, W.L. "The Future of the Race." *The Future of the Race: A Series of Radio Addresses*. Sponsored by the Eugenics Society of Canada. University of Waterloo Special Collections & Archives, Parent's Information Bureau Fonds, 1938, pp. 35–38.

Holmes, Sarah W. "The Pilates Pelvis: Racial Implications of the Immobile Hips." *Dance Research Journal*, vol. 46, no. 2, Aug. 2014, pp. 57–72. 10.1017/S014976771400028X.

Kelly, Evadne. *Dancing Spirit, Love, and War: Performing the Translocal Realities of Contemporary Fiji*. U of Wisconsin P, 2019. 10.2307/j.ctvhrd016.

Kelly, Evadne, Seika Boye, and Carla Rice. "Projecting Eugenics and Performing Knowledges." *Narrative Art and the Politics of Health*, edited by Nail Brooks and Sarah Blanchette, Anthem, 2021, pp. 37–62.

Kelly, Evadne, and Carla Rice. "Pathways to Disrupt Eugenics in Higher Education." *Sites of Conscience: Place, Memory, and the Project of Deinstitutionalization*, edited by Elisabeth Punzi and Linda Steele, UBC P, 2024.

———. "Universities Must Open Their Archives and Share Their Oppressive Pasts." *The Conversation*, 16 Jan. 2020, theconversation.com/universities-must-open-their-archives-and-share-their-oppressive-pasts-125539.

Kelly, Evadne, Carla Rice, and Mona Stonefish. "Towards Decolonial Choreographies of Co-Resistance." *Social Sciences*, vol. 12, no. 4, Mar. 2023. 10.3390/socsci12040204.

Kelly, Evadne, Dolleen Tisawii'ashii Manning, Seika Boye, Carla Rice, Dawn Owen, Sky Stonefish, and Mona Stonefish. "Elements of a Counter-Exhibition: Excavating and Countering a Canadian History and Legacy of Eugenics." *Journal of the History of the Behavioral Sciences*, vol. 57, no. 1, Jan. 2021. 10.1002/jhbs.22081.

Macdonald Institute Student (1937–1939). "Dietetics Demonstrations." U of Guelph Library Archival and Special Collections, RE1MACA0017, RE1 MAC A0184, Box 1.

McLaren, Angus. *Our Own Master Race: Eugenics in Canada, 1885–1945*. McClelland & Stewart, 1990.

Mill, John Stuart. *On Liberty and Utilitarianism*. Knopf, 1992.

Muñoz, José Esteban. "Ephemera as Evidence: Introductory Notes to Queer Acts." *Women and Performance*, vol. 8, no. 2, 1996, pp. 5–16. 10.1080/07407709608571228.

———. "Feeling Brown: Ethnicity and Affect in Ricardo Bracho's *The Sweetest Hangover (and Other STDs)*." *Theatre Journal*, vol. 52, no. 1, 2000, pp. 67–79. 10.1353/tj.2000.0020.

Nishida, Akemi. "Rethinking Interdependence: Desiring Messy Dependency." Gender and Women's Studies Colloquium, U of Wisconsin-Madison, WI, 12 Aug. 2019. gws.wisc.edu/event/gender-and-womens-studies-colloquium-2019-02-28/.

Pangburn, Weaver W. "Recreation and Eugenics." *Journal of Heredity*, vol. 30, no. 9, Sep. 1939, pp. 407–11. 10.1093/oxfordjournals.jhered.a104778.

Regan, Paulette. *Unsettling the Settler Within: Indian Residential Schools, Truth Telling, and Reconciliation in Canada*. UBC P, 2010.

Rice, Carla, Susan D. Dion, Hannah Fowlie, and Andrea Breen. "Identifying and Working through Settler Ignorance." *Critical Studies in Education*, vol. 63, no. 1, 2020, pp. 15–30. 10.1080/17508487.2020.1830818.

Royal Commission on Aboriginal Peoples. *Report of the Royal Commission on Aboriginal Peoples. Library and Archives Canada*, Oct. 1996, bac-lac.gc.ca/eng/discover/aboriginal-heritage/royal-commission-aboriginal-peoples/Pages/final-report.aspx.

Scolieri, Paul A. *Ted Shawn: His Life, Writings, and Dances*. Oxford UP, 2020.

Shildrick, Margrit. "XI. Death, Debility and Disability." *Feminism & Psychology*, vol. 25, no. 1, 4 Feb. 2015, pp. 155–60. 10.1177/0959353514562816.

Simpson, Leanne Betasamosake. *As We Have Always Done: Indigenous Freedom Through Radical Resistance*. U of Minnesota P, 2017.

Taylor, Diana. *The Archive and the Repertoire: Performing Cultural Memory in the Americas*. Duke UP, 2003.

Truth and Reconciliation Commission of Canada. *Truth and Reconciliation Commission of Canada: Calls to Action. National Centre for Truth and Reconciliation*, 2015, ehprnh2mw03.exactdn.com/wp-content/uploads/2021/01/Calls_to_Action_English2.pdf.

Tuck, Eve, and Marcia McKenzie. *Place in Research: Theory, Methodology, and Methods*. Routledge, 2015.

Tuck, Eve, and K. Wayne Yang. "Decolonization Is Not a Metaphor." *Decolonization: Indigeneity, Education & Society*, vol. 1, no. 1, Sept. 2012, pp. 1–40.

HISTORIES INSIDE OUR BODIES: THE TALKING TREATIES PROJECT'S MOVEMENTS AND MATERIALS

GABRIEL LEVINE

> What I understand to be power is that you're able to hold up a tree, literally, by holding hands with your neighbour. It's our duty to hold up the people next to us and to teach, if we can. I teach knowing that I don't know everything, and I am one of many. I'm always so afraid to put things down in writing. We know how that can go wrong. (Ange Loft, "Remember Like We Do" 27)

This writing grows out of four years of following the Talking Treaties project, led by interdisciplinary artist Ange Loft, through multiple workshops and presentations, an art installation, and two iterations (in 2017 and 2018) of a big outdoor pageant at historic Fort York called the *Talking Treaties Spectacle*. Loft, who is Kanien'kehá:ka from Kahnawake Mohawk Territory, has pursued this project in Toronto under the umbrella of Jumblies Theatre + Arts, a community-engaged art organization whose multi-year collaborative projects often culminate in large-scale spectacles that feature performers from a range of disciplines and abilities ("About Jumblies"). The aim of the Talking Treaties project is to bring forward the history of Indigenous treaty-making on this land and to affirm the necessity of that history and those treaties to the Indigenous and non-Indigenous people who live here. Loft and her collaborators (including the writer and historian Victoria Freeman) began the project by conducting dozens of interviews, including with members of the treaty-holders, the Mississaugas of the Credit, and then wove the words gathered in the "talking" part of the project into community-engaged art and performance. The project combines many things I value: the large-scale movement of people in site-specific pageantry; community-engaged art, music, and dance; puppetry and performing objects; and the reactivation of histories that seek to undo the colonial violence of the present. As a guest living on this land, a white Toronto-based academic and artist, I wrestle with writing about this work. As Loft points out, colonial powers have long used written documents to supersede the weave of embodied relations established by Indigenous treaty-making practices. Here, I take up the relational and embodied practices of treaty, both in the Talking Treaties project and in the history it extends, in the hope that my writing will not recapitulate an exploitative and extractive colonial history.

As I've followed the project over the years, I've realized that Loft and her collaborators are doing something crucial and a little dizzying. The Talking Treaties project, as I'll explore, is more than a historical investigation, a set of educational tools, and a series of playful performances and installations about histories of treaty-making on this land. It consciously *enacts* and *embodies* those histories, building a corporeal-material performance language that continues the work that treaty-making has been doing among Indigenous people for generations upon generations. Treaty, in the Haudenosaunee and Anishinaabe traditions that Loft extends, is a collective embodied practice—combining words, actions, movements, material things, sounds, places, and mnemonic devices—that fosters ongoing, living relationships.[1] It is a way of building relationships over the long term, with understandings of respect and reciprocity that are far different from the written deeds and deceptive "agreements" that colonial powers have coerced from Indigenous nations (Stark). Over the past decade, treaties have been increasingly mentioned and discussed in educational curricula, land acknowledgements, and public discourse (see "Treaties"). But there is a gap between the knowledge of treaty history and action in the present. We can learn histories, look at images, and listen to testimonies, but as Loft has said, "How do we feel like we know these

1 On treaty as a "living relationship," see Stark; on embodiment and collective practice, see Levine 11–18 and Spatz 70–86.

understandings really inside our bodies?" (Polishing the Chain). The Talking Treaties work attempts to do just that, inviting Indigenous and non-Indigenous people to move through charged historical spaces, where relational understandings can sediment in our bodies in often playful and surprising ways.

EMBODIED UNDERSTANDINGS

I have been deeply affected by my engagement with the Talking Treaties work, not least because for me, as for most non-Indigenous people of my generation, the history of treaty-making on this land has been made almost completely invisible. I grew up in downtown Toronto in the 1980s, a child of Jewish intellectuals who emigrated from the United States; my parents saw the city as a sleepy Anglo bastion with a multicultural twist. Our family walks in the ravines and on Toronto Island left me with indelible memories of landscape, especially of the shoreline and the rivers flowing under and through the city toward the lake. But my movement through the city's landscapes never made any connection to the past and present of the land's original peoples. I never even questioned the name Toronto—from the Kanien'kehá:ka word *tkaronto*, "where there are trees in the water," a reference to the fishing weirs built by the ancestors of present-day Indigenous peoples in the rivers between Lake Ontario and Lake Simcoe (sometimes called "Lac Taronto" on settler maps; see Loft, "Remember"). My tenth-grade Canadian history teacher presented the stories of this land as a closed book from which we had to memorize dates of events with seemingly no relevance to our present lives. How could any understandings begin to seep into my body when the knowledge of what had taken place on this land was absent, inert, buried, and obscured?

Now, I still see how my students struggle to absorb this history in a meaningful way, even in the post–Truth and Reconciliation Commission of Canada (TRC) moment of ubiquitous land acknowledgements and state-sponsored gestures toward "reconciliation."[2] This was evident at the first workshop I

2 For a critique of liberal settler-colonial frameworks of recognition and reconciliation, see Coulthard.

invited Ange Loft to give at Glendon Campus of York University in 2017, in a fourth-year performance theory and practice class. Loft offered what she calls a Talking Treaties Quick Creation Workshop: three hours packed with history, testimony, images, drawing, and performance-making. For Loft the "quickness" of the quick creation process is a way to get participants moving without getting bogged down in endless reflections, "a trick to get you to say something before you think too much" (interview). Talking Treaties workshops offer participants more content than they can immediately absorb: images, symbols, words, and histories pour over us, intentionally without giving us time to explore each one in depth. These elements then become prompts for drawing, fragments of writing, and quickly sketched performances as a way of translating this material into embodied understandings. Loft might ask participants to write a phrase on a symbol-printed card in response to a prompt, then pass that card to someone else to read; or she might give pairs ten minutes to make a performance using craft materials and objects like stones, cloth, or paper. Some of the most generative prompts are visual symbols drawn from wampum belts, which (as I explore below) are key memory-keepers of treaty relationships. As Loft says, "These seemingly safe symbols are up to interpretation and they're up to your level of engagement and how deep you want to go. You could draw two lines, and I could tell you about the Two-Row Wampum, and we can go really deep into sovereignty and self-sustaining and agreements and keeping your promises and re-quickening. Or it's two sticks, or skinny legs" (interview). Generally, this openness leads to evocative artistic responses in the moment, and to later processes where images and ideas can translate into more elaborate performance work. But this time the rush of words and images allowed unaddressed conflicts and resentments to surface.

The fall 2017 Talking Treaties workshop began like other Talking Treaties workshops, with participants arranged around a long table topped by a long strip of brown kraft paper with a scattering of coloured pastels.[3] After

3 Loft adapted this tabletop drawing exercise from Jumblies founder Ruth Howard (Howard, personal correspondence).

a slide-show talk on treaty history, Loft played an audio collage of interviews from the project. These included conversations with members of the Mississaugas of the Credit First Nation, who spoke about advocating for a settlement in partial compensation of the loss of their land in the deceptive "Toronto Purchase" (Freeman; Sault). As we listened to the collage of voices, Loft encouraged the students to use white, blue, and black pastels to draw lakes and rivers, along with words and symbols inspired by the words they heard. The students moved in a ragged circle around the long table, sketching, scribing, and adding to each other's drawings. One student of Mexican origin, who at the time was wrestling with his own submerged Indigenous ancestry, began to draw black diagonal lines and scribbles, crossing out the images of other participants. For him, this was a representation of the colonial erasure of his past, the way that his home country's Indigenous origins and practices have become obscured by the nationalist formation of *mestizaje*. Some of the other students looked at him quizzically. A white male student began to get irritated and complained that the Mexican student was scribbling over his own drawings, erasing them. The Mexican student replied that his actions were nothing compared to the erasure in the form of genocide and land theft that his ancestors had experienced. Loft called a break, but the two students "took it outside," threatening each other verbally and then physically pushing and shoving in the hallway near the classroom. I called the program coordinator; we called in a mediator from Student Affairs. The three of us spent the next hour with the two students, trying to nudge the white student into understanding his actions and working toward some kind of détente between the two. Their bodies were enraged and blocked, their backs were up, and the best we could manage was a promise to give each other space and distance in the class going forward. At the end of the session, I snuck back into the workshop to watch the "quick creations" the other students had concocted using the simple materials that Loft had brought.

TREATY AS LIVING RELATIONSHIP

I shouldn't have been surprised at the eruption of verbal and physical violence in the classroom, which burst out of the unacknowledged grievances and unconscious settler privilege that the treaty histories and interviews had surfaced. Violence is a frequent outcome when irreconcilable understandings of history, territory, and identity rub up against each other. In the Indigenous practices that the Talking Treaties project extends, treaty mediates these conflicting understandings, containing violence and establishing a reciprocally recognized way of being based on shared needs and desires. In her workshops, Loft explains how the creators of Talking Treaties eventually came to understand treaty-making on three main levels. There is what she calls "original law," or establishing "right relations" between all living things. Then there are the more formal treaty agreements made to bring peace within and between Indigenous nations, such as the creation of the Haudenosaunee Confederacy and the Dish With One Spoon covenant between the Anishinaabe and Haudenosaunee. Finally, there are the agreements made between Indigenous nations and colonial authorities, whether broad or specific. As Loft recounts these different forms of treaty making, we are encouraged to fill a small paper card with drawings of symbols or icons inspired by wampum-belt iconography, rather than with detailed notes—and so my account here depends on pictorial memory, along with subsequent reading and conversations. Yet the gestural act of drawing, responding to spoken words with hand-sketched images or symbols, is an appropriate embodied response to the weave of relations that Loft describes.

The "original law" that Loft identifies as a form of treaty-making resonates with the work of many Indigenous theorists: from the "grounded normativity" that Leanne Betasamosake Simpson sees underlying diverse Indigenous practices, to John Borrows's rooted conception of Indigenous law and legal systems, to Heidi Kiiwetinepinesiik Stark's description of treaties as a "living relationship" based on the guiding principles of "respect, responsibility, and renewal" (Simpson, *As We Have Always Done*; Borrows, *Drawing Out Law*; Stark). My inherited European understandings of law and treaty are stretched by these expanded and rooted conceptions of law: what Simpson calls the "ethics, values and practices" that ensure that "human beings live in balance with the natural world, their family, their clan and their nation" (Simpson, "Looking After" 32). As Simpson writes, such ethics, values, and practices are embedded in Indigenous teachings and social-political structures, growing out of lived relations with the land and all its inhabitants. These practices and treaties guide embodied relations not only between human beings, but also between humans and non-human nations (in the sense of sovereign collectives): the fish nation, the deer nation, or the beaver nation. Stark retells the story of "the woman who married a beaver" to illustrate how Anishinaabe-beaver relations honour the treaty relationship between those nations, requiring the regular exchange of gifts and the renewal of reciprocity and respect. As Stark writes, "The exchange of gifts—the beaver's life in exchange for tobacco and housekeeping items—also maintains the pleasant and mutually beneficial relationship between the Anishinaabe and the beavers. The ongoing success of this relationship depends on the Anishinaabe's practice of returning the bones of the beaver to the water, as this allows the beavers to come back to life and return home" (146). For Stark, these "cooperative arrangements . . . between different kinds of beings in the world" contain "foundational principles" that guide Indigenous nations' approaches to treaty-making between humans (Bruce White, qtd. in Stark 146). Attending to the treaties between human and animal nations reveals that treaties are not a "one and done" type of agreement, as European law understands them, in which land is exchanged for money and goods. Rather, they are a mode of what might be called "making kin" (Borrows and Coyle; see also Haraway). As Simpson puts it: "The treaty outlines a relationship that when practiced continually and in perpetuity, maintains peaceful coexistence, respect, and mutual benefit" ("Looking After" 35). And as Stark's example shows, embodied and material practices—the exchange of gifts, the offering of tobacco, the return of the beaver's bones to the water—are a crucial part of those living relationships.

The Indigenous understanding of treaty as "living relationship" can be clearly seen in the treaties made between Indigenous nations prior to European colonization, and in the early treaties these nations made with colonial powers.

In workshops and presentations, Loft's examples of treaties between Indigenous nations include the agreement between the Haudenosaunee and Anishinaabe to desist from violence and care for the resources of the Great Lakes region—known as the Dish With One Spoon agreement to the Haudenosaunee and Our Dish to the Anishinaabe. The image of the Dish With One Spoon, depicted in a circle of purple-and-white cowrie shells on the treaty's wampum belts, suggests a common vessel that provides sustenance for all nations, and a single eating implement (with no knives) that must be shared. As Simpson writes, the Dish treaty set out principles for sharing territory that would act as a guide to future relations: "It was designed to promote peaceful coexistence and it required regular renewal of the relationship through meeting, ritual, and ceremony" ("Looking After" 37). This processual and relational understanding of treaty-making extended to the early treaties between Indigenous peoples and settler groups, including the Two-Row Wampum, originally made in 1613 between the Kanien'kehá:ka and the Dutch. This agreement's wampum belt shows the two nations as two purple bands on a field of white, representing two boats travelling separate paths, engaging in mutual exchange but respecting each other's customs and not interfering in each other's affairs. Again, the treaty offers a regulative framework for relational embodied practice, rather than a strict set of terms and conditions. Historians note that this Indigenous understanding of treaty-making as living relationship was to some degree adopted by European powers, who were eager to gain Indigenous people's trust and military support (Rath). This changed, however, in the nineteenth century, when a shift in the balance of power meant that European legal frameworks could be used more directly as a tool of dispossession. Treaties became increasingly a matter of legally depriving Indigenous nations of land title—as in the so-called Toronto Purchase of 1787, which offered the Mississaugas of the Credit a batch of trade goods in exchange for the surrender of their traditional territory on the shores of Lake Ontario.[4]

---

4 See Sault for a short history of the colonial deceptions of this treaty, which was rewritten in 1805 to cover a much larger territory, and of the land-claims settlement finally accepted by the Mississaugas of the Credit in 2014.

GATHERING GESTURES AND MATERIALS

In Loft's view, a more generous model of Indigenous-settler treaty-making was the Treaty of Niagara, a sweeping affirmation of Indigenous and British respectful relations held in 1764. Following the defeat of New France in the Seven Years' War, more than two thousand Indigenous leaders representing over twenty-four nations congregated at Fort Niagara, along with British representatives, to ratify the Royal Proclamation of 1763 and extend the Covenant Chain of Haudenosaunee-British alliance to many other nations. Anishinaabe legal scholar John Borrows describes how the 1763 Royal Proclamation, which simultaneously recognizes Indigenous rights and provides a legal framework for extinguishing land title, must be understood through its performative ratification at Niagara the following year ("Wampum"). Borrows shows how during the Niagara treaty council, prior treaties such as the Two-Row Wampum and the Covenant Chain were held up on both sides as a model for Indigenous-British respectful coexistence. The documentary record shows that these wampum belts were literally *held up*—raised and brandished to provide a mnemonic of past agreements that would guide future "living relationships." As in other instances of Indigenous treaty-making, the treaty council extended over several days and involved the exchange of countless presents, including animal pelts and trade goods, along with tobacco ceremonies, speeches, and other acts. These embodied/material performances, such as the tobacco ceremony, were not additions to or adornments of the legal treaty. Rather, for its Indigenous participants, the entire council—its spoken words, gestures, movements, materials, sounds, and collective acts—*was* the treaty (Raymond DeMallie, qtd. in Stark). For Borrows, this understanding of *council as treaty* means that documents such as the Royal Proclamation cannot be interpreted simply through their written words. Embodied acts of treaty ratification are a crucial part of treaty-making. And these acts were recorded—in the written descriptions of treaty participants, but also in oral memory (which Indigenous knowledge keepers passed down scrupulously and accurately, until the disruptions of oral memory caused by colonization) and in the creation of wampum belts.

The use of wampum belts in treaty-making was widespread among the nations of the Eastern Woodlands and Great Lakes long before European colonization. Strung with purple-and-white cowrie, they offer strong visual symbols of the central image of a treaty—as in the Dish With One Spoon or the Two Row Wampum. Radiating power and importance, wampum is a visual-material-symbolic memory-keeper of living relationships. The presenting of a wampum belt "impressed a whole scene and set of relations," including words, actions, power relations, gestures, ceremonies, songs, and non-linguistic sounds (Rath 315). In the words of Kanien'kehá:ka orator Odianne, at an Iroquois-British treaty council in 1684, a belt of wampum is a "Remembrancer" intended to "Stamp Understanding" into its recipients (qtd. in Rath 308). Wampum gives form to a new reality—a changed set of living relationships—and memorializes that change. Indigenous leaders would lift the wampum of Niagara at subsequent treaty councils to remind the British of their relational obligations. Again, as Borrows describes, these wampum belts were physically held up, raised in the hands, so that their power could be felt in the body and shared. This power then rubbed off on the treaty documents as well. First Nations frequently requested durable parchment copies of the written treaties, which were also often presented and lifted up at subsequent treaty councils (Borrows, "Wampum"). Wampum and treaty documents, in different ways, became "remembrancers" of living relationships that settlers all too often ignored and betrayed.

The image of a row of human figures linking arms, depicted on the Covenant Chain and Niagara belts, offers a gestural mnemonic of treaty as an embodied, living relationship. "To the Haudenosaunee," Loft writes, "the term used for the Covenant Chain had a meaning associated with clasped arms. There is an arm gesture, which involved grasping the forearms, which was commonly used to mean binding friendship. To show this union at an early pact for peace on the St. Lawrence, a French priest described a Haudenosaunee diplomat who: *Took hold of the Frenchman, placed his arms within his, and with his other arm, clasped that of the Algonquin, calling it the knot that binds us*" ("Remember" 19). How to allow this physical gesture of binding friendship to be felt in the bodies of people today? In October 2021, as part of an online workshop about visual symbols of treaty-making, Loft asked participants to clasp our own arms and to move gently "from that centre space between your wrists" (Polishing the Chain). Even isolated on Zoom, the clasping of our own arms was a gesture of care, perhaps of dancing while cradling a baby. It opened up a connected way of moving through an embodied gesture rooted in history.

This image of connection and friendship has special meaning for Loft, a Kanien'kehá:ka artist from Kahnawake territory exploring treaty relationships on the land of the Mississaugas of the Credit. Bringing together Indigenous artists across different territories can invoke difficult and conflicted histories, including those between Indigenous nations. As Loft writes, a reading of the Yellowhead Belt mentions that her community of origin is described as having already emptied the Dish, of not caring for the land and sharing with others ("Remember" 26). She wonders: Did they take more than they needed?

> Probably. I'll need to do more research about my community's relationship to the Dish. What old grudges are affecting how we talk about this place? How do we keep learning from each other, layering new findings, knowing they don't negate old knowledges? I imagine us locked together, hand to forearm, propping each other up, strong enough to keep the bowl from being emptied again. ("Remember" 26)

The Talking Treaties work brings this imagining into action, extending treaty relationships and translating them into visual, material, and embodied languages—including the language of large-scale participatory spectacle performance.

LANDSCAPE CHOREOGRAPHIES

In Loft and her collaborators' work with the Talking Treaties project, powerful mnemonic images from wampum belts and other sources are translated into movements and materials. Sometimes the images "stamped" into our understanding involve actual stamping, as in the block-printed tags and little books that audiences and workshop participants take away with them as reminders of their experience. The wampum symbols also become prompts for "choreographic explorations," including "landscape choreography," the "big giant outdoor images . . . made out of whatever's at hand" that Loft creates in charged historical spaces (Loft, interview). As part of these giant images, performers and audience members are physically put into motion, encouraging them to absorb histories and symbols into their bodies. As Loft says, "You've got to literally pull the images out and then get them to think about what they mean, while moving around" (Polishing the Chain).

In the *Talking Treaties Spectacle*, these images include the circular movement of performers and audiences promenading around the grounds of historic Fort York, echoing the circular Dish With One Spoon. The shared Dish, Loft recounts, was originally a beaver tail, a delicacy among the Great Lakes nations (Polishing the Chain). During the *Spectacle*, a mascot-sized dancing Beaver loses their tail, which is then carried by a group of performers who move along the stone walls of the old fort. The performers deliver rhythmic, chanted text pulled from interviews and historical documents, leading the audience in a circle around the fort's grounds. As audience members, we are pulled into that circle, following the performers, moving from place to place—an embodied mnemonic of the Dish that we must relearn how to share. Below the fort's walls, at the level of the audience, Loft pulls a cart with a sound system from which the words of interviewees echo; musicians and mascot-sized puppet performers lead to the next performance location, and community performers and audience members follow in a ramshackle parade. The movement of several performers using mobility devices underscores the need for equitable access to the land. Later in the show, as the performance engages the successive dispossessions of the Toronto Purchase, the circular movement by which the performers lead the audience becomes frantic and sudden: not the measured curving of the Dish, but a jagged flight as the Mississaugas are pushed farther and farther from their home.

The *Talking Treaties Spectacle*'s visual and performance language is both historically grounded and playful, an epic pageantry that Loft calls "large-scale with scraps" (interview). Legible images are created from group movement, choral music, multiples of flags and banners, giant quilts, quasi-historical

Fig. 1. Community performance troupe in the *Talking Treaties Spectacle*, 2018. Photo © Mark Fawcett, Jumblies Theatre + Arts.

costumes, and performing objects crafted in drop-in community workshops. Both iterations of the project—the first as part of the Indigenous Arts Festival in the counter-Confederation anniversary year of 2017, the second as an independent project in 2018—took place at Fort York, a historic site of low colonial military buildings, stone walls, and grassy lawns. As a British military garrison, it hosted treaty meetings between Indigenous nations and colonial authorities. Now the fort sits atop the buried Garrison Creek, surrounded by Toronto's downtown expressways and proliferating condo towers. It is one of the few downtown spots where you can see a wide-open sky.

Fort York currently doesn't host "living history"-style performances, where employees wear outmoded garb and act out "life as it was" displays, but this is the kind of performance audiences might expect in this colonial space (see Magelssen). Loft and her collaborators, including historian and writer Victoria Freeman, subvert these expectations with their playful approach. The moment in the *Spectacle* closest to historical re-enactment comes in "Symbolically United," a scene written by Freeman and performed in the fort's blockhouse. Staged on and around a giant four-poster bed, the scene is a lovers' duet featuring Mohawk leader Molly Brant (played by Anishinaabe/Ashkenazi performer/scholar Jill Carter) and wealthy merchant and colonial superintendent Sir William Johnson (played by Anishinaabe actor/puppeteer Jesse Wabegijig). The couple tumbles on the bed, bickers, and makes up, as Molly helps William prepare for the extension of the Covenant Chain at the gathering of Nations at Niagara. Their comic flirtations and exaggerated historical drag—William's powdered wig, Molly's tumble of curls and bustle dress—are counterposed to the betrayal of the treaty that the audience knows will come. This betrayal is underscored by four servants who recite statements of warning from the Indigenous Nations who refused to attend the gathering at Niagara, along with letters between colonial authorities who describe how to foment jealousy and conflict between Nations. Yet the scene mostly revels in the erotic and political spark between these two powerful historical figures. As Molly says to William, "We have an ongoing relationship, some might say, a Marriage. While all the world insists our peoples cannot live together, we prove the lie" (Loft and Freeman). We don't quite believe Molly, who seems more interested in the luxuries that William provides her than the well-being of her people. But it opens a sense of possibility to see Indigenous performers stage this marriage as historical burlesque, even if in real life it has thoroughly broken down.

As a self-contained theatrical scene, "Symbolically United" is an exception to the performance style of the *Spectacle*, which collages verbatim text, group movement, and material performance into a fast-paced promenade-style pageant. Both text and movement are delivered rhythmically, often in choral style. Poems contributed by volunteers are transformed into fragments of text set to a beat or pulse, as in the repeated "Field of Voices" poems that punctuate the performance. The first of these poems offers audiences a generous allowance of confusion when dealing with the overload of historical content in the *Spectacle*:

> I have a lot of questions
> What, who, why
> But I'm afraid
> Get over it!
> Memory, learn it all
> Misunderstood, memory
> It might come out a little incoherent or rambley . . .
> (*Field of Voices Poems*)

Recited by groups and accompanied by the performers' rhythmic gestures—arms raised and lowered, heads bobbing up and down—the text becomes a mnemonic of how to approach the treaty relationship, and a way of understanding that relationship in an embodied way. Loft tells me, "As a performer, when I memorized texts, I liked to see it in my body. Like, be able to feel through it and know where I'm playing off people rhythmically . . . If somebody went to the show a couple of times in a row, they would be able to memorize those things" (interview). I find myself chanting these little phrases to myself in the weeks after the performance: "I have a lot of questions / what, who, why . . . " I'm afraid, too: of getting it wrong, of asking the wrong questions. But really, "get over it!" Memory is always misunderstood, and a little incoherence is just how we get started. The rhythm helps stamp this generous invitation into my bodily understanding.

DANCES OF ASSEMBLY

The rhythm of the group text and movement carries over into the physical rhythms of solo performers. The two figures guiding the audience in the *Spectacle* are the Beaver and Britannia, mascot-like dancers in oversized, big-headed puppet costumes.[5] Cartoon-like icons pulled from Toronto's historical crest, they are animated by gifted and energetic dancers. The big-headed Beaver, especially, boogies as we move from place to place, delighting the kids in attendance. Loft recalls: "The actors we put in there are hilariously good movers, just funny movers. [Performer] Candy [Blair] can powwow dance wearing a beaver, apparently. I didn't even ask them to do that. They just whipped it out" (interview). Much of their movement is generated by prompts connected to wampum symbols, Indigenous practices, or historical iconography. Loft describes this process: "Even those movers in Britannia and the Beaver, their movement sequences were a personal

---

5 In the first version of the *Spectacle* in 2017, Britannia was a regal and tall backpack puppet, but this led to audience confusion, and in 2018 she was replaced by a more comic and anime-like mascot character (Loft, interview).

Fig. 2. Community performance troupe in the *Talking Treaties Spectacle*, 2018. Photo © Liam Coo, Jumblies Theatre + Arts.

exploration of ground, centre and sky. Or directionality, and how do you move to a place far away? Even Britannia had these beautiful 'the ground is mine' moves" (interview). As they guide us around the site, their movement is both elegant and goofy, fast footsteps alternating with graceful sweeping arms. Again, movement becomes a way of assimilating an often "rugged" history into the body in a playful way (interview). When the big-headed Beaver and Britannia beckon us to join in their fancy footwork, it's hard not to find yourself dancing along.

Another embodied way of reckoning with this history comes at a slower time scale, in the successive drop-in community workshops where participants create the material elements that will be used in the performance. These elements include a giant quilt of braided rivers flowing between and under the streets of Toronto to the lake; animal-printed pennants; ship sails mounted on bamboo sticks; scores of fabric beaver pelts that get tossed across the lawn; and a large pile of trade goods given to the Mississaugas as part of the Toronto "Purchase"—including 120 mirrors, ninety-six jugs of rum, twenty-four kettles, and twenty-four laced hats, each object wrapped in calico-printed fabric.[6] In performance, these objects are piled around fabric-wrapped miniature apartment buildings and set against the actual Toronto skyline in a wind-up-toy dance of assembly. The piling of trade goods materializes the deceptive exchange between colonial authorities, who saw these items as payment for land, and the Mississaugas of the Credit, who understood them in the treaty-making tradition as proof of good intention and ongoing relationship.

Fig. 3. Community performance troupe in the *Talking Treaties Spectacle*, 2017. Photo © Liam Coo, Jumblies Theatre + Arts.

As with many community-based projects, the collective production of these materials is a crucial part of the creation process. Over many months, different participants—neighbourhood residents of mixed abilities in Jumblies's studios, drop-ins at Native Child and Family Services of Toronto on Dundas Street, workshop participants from multiple sites—work slowly on assigned tasks: braiding fabric rivers or wrapping trade goods in calico-printed cloth. Throughout the process, numerous facilitating artists (including designers, makers, composers, and choreographers) lead hundreds of diverse community members in the collective work of creation and fabrication. Loft describes how this "hand stuff"—the slow act of making things together—offers another way to absorb a difficult and complex history

6 The "flowered" calico pattern, a product of British colonialism in India, was wildly fashionable among both settler and Indigenous women; Loft describes how wrapping these colonial objects in calico works to "soften" them in performance (interview).

Fig. 4. Community performance troupe in the *Talking Treaties Spectacle*, 2017. Photo © Liam Coo, Jumblies Theatre + Arts.

"in a chill way" (interview). "Why are we braiding all this fabric?" she asks. "Because we're re-braiding all of the rivers onto this giant map of Toronto. Clearly it starts a conversation" (interview). The understanding that historical knowledge can be absorbed into the body through acts of physical making runs through the Talking Treaties project, which encourages participants and audience members to embroider, draw, and print "as a way to process what you're taking in" (Loft, interview).

In performance, the materials in the *Spectacle* also work to take us out of the strictly human realm. They remind audiences that treaty is not only a matter between humans but encompasses other beings and the land. During the show, a definition is quoted rhythmically by the whole group several times: "Treaty: A long-term relationship to take care of the land and the relationships between humans and non-human peoples on that land" (Loft and Freeman). Watching a giant beaver shimmy around the old colonial fort, or maybe even joining in that joyful dance when the beaver beckons, is a way to remember these relationships. Another way is to take up Loft's invitation, as part of a performance lecture held midway through the show, to consider ourselves as embedded in a wide weave of relations. After a lecture/slide show on treaty history, we are led by Loft through a series of prompts inspired by the Haudenosaunee Thanksgiving Prayer on the things to consider "before all else." Our attention is guided from low to high, starting from the roots, rocks, and critters below the surface of the earth to the ground and its waters and plants to those creatures moving below us and at our height to the tall trees, air, birds, sun, and sky. Each of us has been given a little ribboned tag block-printed with a symbol drawn from wampum or other sources—a bowl and spoon, waving rows of rivers, and dozens of other icons. On the other side, we're invited to write words that complete the following phrase: "Before all else . . . we will consider . . . when we . . . " After writing our responses, we pass the tags between us, so that later in the *Spectacle* we read out each other's words. At the end of the show, we leave with someone else's tag, a reminder of those fundamental relationships we should consider "before all else." For weeks, I move around the city with that little ribboned tag sticking out of my jacket pocket, a remembrancer of the relationships that should guide my steps, words, and actions on this land.

POLISHING THE CHAIN

In the months after Ange Loft's workshop and the *Talking Treaties Spectacle*, I try to allow these embodied experiences and teachings to flow through my practice and to find new forms. In fall 2019, Loft generously agrees to return to Glendon for another "quick creation" workshop, this time as part of a devising process for a production course. Picking up on themes and techniques from the Talking Treaties project, a group of students works with me to create a verbatim/multimedia/immersive/puppetry/movement piece called *The Housing Show*, which we present in early March 2020 (Levine and Shapiro). The performance is about housing precarity and inequality in Toronto, but also about what it means to call for more equitable housing on Indigenous land, inspired by the understandings of treaty learned from Loft's workshop. *The Housing Show*'s final section, "Land and Water," takes place around a structure of illuminated kraft-paper buildings, with the audience moving about promenade-style across paper pathways. Shifting images are projected on the rear wall and on the floor—treaty documents, colonial maps, a lapping shoreline, and student drawings from the Talking Treaties workshop. Four lines of performers move river-like through the audience toward the centre of the space, repeating a string of gestures in a water-inspired choreography.[7] There they speak text drawn from interviews about the meaning of home, followed by a "land back" acknowledgement written by one of the students. The show's final cue is to light the trees outside the theatre, which become visible through the tall windows in the wall behind the projection scrim. The wintry branches call us back to the actual land that we need to take care of and share in a more just and equitable way. It's a quiet gesture, inspired by the history in our bodies learned from our engagement with the Talking Treaties project.

I continue to attend workshops, talks, and presentations by Loft and her collaborators, including a too-short afternoon spent at the Small Arms Inspection Building in Mississauga where a Talking Treaties installation is set up as part of the first Toronto Biennial of Art (2019). The installation features videos of costumed performers adapting moments from the *Talking Treaties Spectacle*, performed along the banks of the Etobicoke Creek and other historically significant sites across Toronto. As part of the installation, we are invited to make little embroidered patches in response to histories of treaty-making and treaty-breaking. Loft will later use these embroidered patches as prompts for "choreographic explorations" as part of another manifestation of the Talking Treaties project, *Dish Dances*, at the 2022 Biennial (Polishing the Chain). At an online workshop on "The Visual Language of Wampum Diplomacy," Loft shows a photograph of a line of Indigenous dancers moving through the woods holding beaver pelts above their heads—the same fabric beaver pelts tossed across the lawn in the *Talking Treaties Spectacle*. The embroidered patches, the dancers carrying beaver pelts, these are part of the relay of movements and materials in the Talking Treaties project. Over

7 *The Housing* Show featured projections and design by Duncan Appleton and choreography by Meredith Thompson.

succeeding years, a residue of a performance becomes a "remembrancer" of relationships that can then find new embodied expression. In this approach to movement and materials, Loft and her collaborators continue to enact treaty, carrying relationships of reciprocity and respect across time with the help of powerful mnemonic supports.

In a time of near-constant public discussion of "reconciliation" and treaty history, where panels and talks proliferate without necessarily altering relationships in the world, the Talking Treaties project offers an embodied and material path of engagement. Loft tells me how "sneaking" the first *Talking Treaties Spectacle* into the 2017 Indigenous Arts Festival at Fort York "after a day of powwow" showed "the benefit of having all Native people in a space already." She remembers: "I got some good feedback that first run. There was one guy who I'd seen around at rallies and these kind of things. And he was like, 'I thought this was just going to be a discussion panel or a talk. And this was so much better'" (interview). Moving with performers and audiences through these historically charged spaces opens up the possibility not only of teaching about treaty relationships, but of continuing to practise them in a real, embodied way. In her chapter published in the recent *Indigenous Toronto* collection, Loft alludes to this playfully. She writes, "I do a lot of the Talking Treaties performance work at Fort York, and I like to imagine its role as a place to keep the talk going, with dance, big puppets, and lots of people. If the federal government would like to host an annual 'Polishing the Chain' event there, I'm sure it could be arranged. I'll bring the giant beaver costume" ("Remember" 27).

Working with real histories in real spaces can also bring up more difficult feelings in the body. As Loft often says, the history that the project deals with is "rugged"—especially the history of the last two centuries, during which the Crown's promises at Niagara have shifted into settler-colonial dispossession, genocide, and cultural assault. Reckoning with this history in an embodied way can be painful. For *Dish Dances*, Loft is working with students from the Centre for Indigenous Theatre who come from diverse nations, often far from the territory of the Mississaugas (as she does herself). As she says at the online workshop on the visual language of treaty, this work on someone else's territory requires "acknowledging all the grief and the trauma and problems that happened before, knowing that people when they come into a new territory are carrying a lot of baggage. They're carrying a lot of grief, they have a lot to clear out. They have a lot to move through before they can make good choices and good communications in a place" (Polishing the Chain). To allow this movement to happen, Loft and her collaborators are finding sites near water, "places where we can go and sit together and have council, and just discuss and dance and be weird and talk about things that we can do in private, just between ourselves" (Polishing the Chain). These gatherings of Indigenous artists and performers have become central to the Talking Treaties project. And yet those of us who are non-Indigenous are not excluded from what comes out of these meetings. The Covenant Chain is about as rusty as you could imagine, but it can still be polished. Taking these histories into our bodies and working through them collectively in shared moments of performance can return us to the roots of treaty as ongoing relationship. Loft and her collaborators are inviting us in to polish the chain, to continue the conversation, and to renew the treaty relationship in an embodied way. It's up to us to take up the invitation.

WORKS CITED

"About Jumblies." *Jumblies Theatre*, jumbliestheatre.org/jumblies/about.

Borrows, John. *Drawing Out Law: A Spirit's Guide.* U of Toronto P, 2010.

———. "Wampum at Niagara: The Royal Proclamation, Canadian Legal History and Self-Government." *Aboriginal and Treaty Rights in Canada: Essays on Law, Equity, and Respect for Difference*, edited by Michael Asch, UBC P, 1997, pp. 155–72.

Borrows, John, and Michael Coyle. *The Right Relationship: Reimagining the Implementation of Historical Treaties.* U of Toronto P, 2017.

Coulthard, Glen Sean. *Red Skin, White Masks: Rejecting the Colonial Politics of Recognition.* U of Minnesota P, 2014.

Field of Voices Poems. Word document.

Freeman, Victoria. "'Toronto Has No History!' Indigeneity, Settler Colonialism, and Historical Memory in Canada's Largest City." *Urban History Review*, vol. 38, no. 2, 2010, pp. 21–35. 10.7202/039672ar.

Haraway, Donna. *Staying with the Trouble: Making Kin in the Chthulucene.* Duke UP, 2016.

Howard, Ruth. Personal correspondence with Gabriel Levine. 29 Jan. 2022.

Levine, Gabriel. *Art and Tradition in a Time of Uprisings.* MIT P, 2020.

Levine, Gabriel, and Shelby Shapiro. "Condo Towers and Buried Streams: Stories from *The Housing Show.*" *Liminalities: A Journal of Performance Studies*, vol. 17, no. 1–2, 2021. liminalities.net/17-1/housingshow.html.

Loft, Ange. Interview with Gabriel Levine. 21 May 2019.

———. "Remember Like We Do." *Indigenous Toronto: Stories that Carry This Place*, edited by Denise Bolduc, Mnawaate Gordon-Corbiere, Rebeka Tabobondung, and Brian Wright-McLeod, Coach House, 2021, pp. 17–28.

Loft, Ange, and Victoria Freeman. *Talking Treaties Spectacle.* Victoria's edits, 20 Sep. 2017. Word document.

Magelssen, Scott. *Living History Museums: Undoing History through Performance.* Scarecrow, 2007.

Polishing the Chain: Treaty Relations in Toronto. "The Symbolic Language of Wampum Diplomacy." *YouTube*, presentations by Alan Corbiere, Rick Hill, and Ange Loft, 29 Sep. 2021, youtube.com/watch?v=HFdxbqLiAAk.

Rath, Richard Cullen. "Hearing Wampum: The Senses, Mediation, and the Limits of Analogy." *Colonial Mediascapes: Sensory Worlds of the Early Americas*, edited by Matt Cohen and Jeffrey Glover, U of Nebraska P, 2014, pp. 290–322.

Sault, Margaret. "A Story About the Toronto Purchase." *Indigenous Toronto: Stories that Carry This Place*, edited by Denise Bolduc, Mnawaate Gordon-Corbiere, Rebeka Tabobondung, and Brian Wright-McLeod, Coach House, 2021, pp. 37–44.

Simpson, Leanne Betasamosake. *As We Have Always Done: Indigenous Freedom through Radical Resistance.* U of Minnesota P, 2017.

———. "Looking After Gdoo-Naaganinaa: Precolonial Nishnaabeg Diplomatic and Treaty Relationships." *Wicazo Sa Review*, vol. 23, no. 2, 2008, pp. 29–42. 10.1353/wic.0.0001.

Spatz, Ben. *Blue Sky Body: Thresholds for Embodied Research.* Routledge, 2019.

Stark, Heidi Kiiwetinepinesiik. "Respect, Responsibility, and Renewal: The Foundations of Anishinaabe Treaty Making with the United States and Canada." *American Indian Culture and Research Journal*, vol. 34, no. 2, 2010, pp. 145–64. 10.17953/aicr.34.2.j0414503108L8771.

"Treaties." *Government of Ontario*, 2021, ontario.ca/page/treaties.

TRANSNATIONAL FEMINIST INQUIRY IN PLACE-BASED LEARNING

AHALYA SATKUNARATNAM[1]

I. MEMORY

It was the last day of my campus interview at Quest University Canada on 4 March 2014. A faculty member on the search committee kindly offered me a ride to the Squamish Adventure Centre, where I would take a shuttle to the Vancouver International Airport for my flight back to Chicago. In the last minutes of the car ride, he asked, "Isn't ethnography the same as memoir?" He proceeded to suggest that ethnography and opinion were solely individual perspectives and, as such, potentially untrue and definitely insignificant in their singularity.

I tried in the last minutes of the car ride to share what I knew of feminist ethnography: that it requires deep research, extended commitment, and unwavering responsibility to acknowledge power among people in cultural practices, including the practice of research and publication. I tried my best to formulate that feminist ethnography is different from opinion.

Relieved to say goodbye as I closed the door of the car, the subtly charged conversation left me nervous. Still, it wasn't the first time (nor would it be the last) when a search-committee member would confront my work and the disciplines in which I situate myself: cultural studies, women's and gender studies, and dance studies. It was one of many challenges I faced at Quest University Canada, where I taught for seven years.

1 Dedicated to :gyauustees.

II. MIGRATION

This reflection shares parts of my journey in transnational feminist inquiry as I migrated from one world, the unceded lands of the Council of Three Fires—the Ojibwe, Odawa, and Potawatomi Nations—and many other Indigenous people, including the Miami, Ho-Chunk, Menominee, Sac and Fox, Kickapoo, and Illinois Nations (commonly referred to as Chicago), to teach at Quest University Canada, located on the ancestral, traditional, and unceded territories of the Sḵwx̱wú7mesh peoples (the municipality of Squamish), and to live on the unceded territories of the xʷməθkʷəy̓əm (Musqueam), Sḵwx̱wú7mesh (Squamish), and səlilwətaɬ (Tsleil-Waututh) peoples (also known as the city of Vancouver). Migrating for the opportunity to continue to teach cultural studies and feminist and dance ethnography, I employed the methods of these fields to grapple with my own existence as a recent settler and as an educator teaching in this specific place for the first time.

Until I taught at Quest University, most of my teaching career and life had been rooted in Chicago. There, I was able to share histories and idiosyncrasies of specific places and neighbourhoods, of local electoral politics and policy. I could turn to familiar aspects of the city in order to develop connections between practice and theory—a foundational exercise in my classroom. Moving to the west coast of Canada destabilized my knowing. I was not familiar with Stanley, Vancouver, or Fraser—names that circulated in the Lower Mainland of BC. I did not know details about the histories and contemporary lives of Indigenous people in this region. I had not been informed about the waves of settlement in the area.

In this reflection, I share how migration moulded my teaching through two courses, "Ethnography of Squamish" and "Violence, Trauma, & Representation." The courses I share were very much part of my syllabus creation for Quest and were created alongside my experiences with the university. They were created as part of my migration journey and my own learning to prepare myself to teach in this new place, and to also shape Quest University, as I and many others would work to shape it.

This reflection is about teaching to students and an institution. As I tried to allude to in the opening memory from my job interview at Quest, I would have to continue to navigate assumptions about the fields in which my research and teaching is situated—cultural studies, women's and gender studies, and dance studies. Feminist and dance ethnography considers the basis of individual experiences alongside examinations of the larger culture. That practice itself, like several disciplines, is forged through continuous investigations and (self-)critique. Along with similarly minded colleagues who shared disciplinary approaches and social visions, we investigated the culture of the university and charged the institution to move beyond misappropriations of concepts and practices and cursory conceptions of our fields.

In constructing these memories for *Power Moves*, I am reminded of Michael Lambek's work, which I assigned in the course "Violence, Trauma, & Representation": "To remember is to articulate one's relationship to it—never morally or pragmatically neutral" (240). This reflection is not an ethnography. Compiling this reflection on my teaching at Quest, I have been making sense of syllabi, rereading the texts that I assigned, and looking over any notes saved on my computer and in physical folders that I kept since leaving Quest in 2021. I cannot find course plans. The personal journals that I maintained years ago were disposed of when I left the institution and Vancouver (to start a new position in Chicago). I am writing about something that I didn't intend to write about. I let go of records to intentionally let go of place and experience as I migrated again.

III. THE UNIVERSITY

Quest University Canada was located in the Garibaldi Highlands of the town of Squamish, where views of the Rockies and glacial rivers surround the campus. The university was founded in 2007 by former president of the University of British Columbia, David Strangway. It was the first private, not-for profit, liberal arts and sciences university in Canada. Quest prided itself on not having departments, majors, or tenure (faculty were on continuing contracts that increased in length over the duration of our employment).

Also unlike most universities, Quest was small, with a maximum capacity of seven hundred students. Classes were capped at twenty students. The university was structured on the block plan, where students enrol in one course at a time and faculty teach one course at a time. Courses ran three and a half weeks with three-hour classes daily Monday through Friday. Over its short, sixteen-year existence, Quest encountered many legal and financial disputes that stemmed from its founding as a private institution through the Sea to Sky University Act passed by the Legislative Assembly of British Columbia. Board members and land developers utilized the not–for-profit status of the university to evade taxes through "philanthropy" (Thibault). In 2020, Quest filed for protection under the Companies' Creditors Arrangement Act (CCAA), a tool employed by financially troubled corporations to avoid bankruptcy and allow creditors to receive payments for amounts owed. With its first class graduating in 2012, the university graduated its last class in April 2023 and has since suspended academic programming indefinitely (Mackin).

On the Sea-to-Sky Highway from Vancouver to Squamish, a sign marks the town of Squamish as the "Outdoor Adventure Capital of Canada." Quest students, many from the west coast of Canada and the US, from independent and home-schools, seemed well-versed in the outdoor-adventure practices. Several students were elite athletes specializing in outdoor sports. There was also a number of international students, some of whom attended elite and international schools globally. For many years, Quest's freshman experience course, Cornerstone, demanded students be in the outdoors for two full days of hiking and outdoor activities (including swimming across a glacial river with a matchstick in order to start a fire on the other side). Until a larger discussion about accessibility and student and teacher safety changed these activities, they were celebrated as unique and drawing from a particular community, as shared in the 2012 article published in *The Globe and Mail* by Erin Millar:

> I'm blindfolded and barefoot, standing on a cool mossy patch with one arm grasping the trunk of a hemlock tree in a futile attempt to feel somewhat secure. The forest is quiet except for a river flowing

> nearby. Suddenly the oppressive silence (I'm a dedicated urbanite) is broken by the sound of a slow drum beat seemingly hundreds of metres away. I reluctantly let go of my hemlock and take an uneasy step toward the sound.
>
> Toran Savjord, vice-president of operations and development of Quest University and leader of this exercise, has assured me and my 13 classmates that making our way through the forest in this manner will be worthwhile. We're meant to reflect on how it feels to push ourselves out of our comfort zone and how we can tackle any challenge no matter how uncomfortable or unfamiliar. The students later describe the experience as meditative, enjoyable, even revelatory. All I can think of as I paw my way over logs and roots is how gross it would be to have a slug squished between my toes.
>
> For the past 10 days I've joined a class of first-year students at Quest University to get a firsthand taste of the unique education offered at this unusual school. Little did I know when I began this assignment that, in addition to reading Rousseau and relearning how to calculate square roots, I would gather firewood and jump in a glacier-fed lake. It has not been a week of armchair journalism.

The experience of the outdoors and place seemed part of Quest's identity. Before its shutdown, if you were to go to the Quest University website, under "Student Life" you would come across a banner with a GIF of a student lying on a nylon hammock tied between two trees. Somewhat perfectly, behind them is a view of the sharp edges of snow-topped mountain ranges of the town of Squamish. The quote in white text across the moving image states, "Quest has allowed me to develop a sense of home here and feel continuously inspired" ("Student Life"). In my first year living in the town, I tried to ski, cross-country ski, mountain bike, kayak, hike (the steepest of hikes), and sail. I would laugh at myself, conscious of my active effort to try to belong through these very difficult sports. At Quest, many of my colleagues were regulars in participating in these outdoor activities. I failed at these activities, physically and socially. But I wanted to examine this self-appointed capital of outdoor

Fig. 1. A screenshot from the now-defunct Quest University website. The image appeared as a banner above the "Student Life" section of the website.

sports. I wanted to know about this land and this culture. What was visible and what less so? And although, as that moving image from the Quest University website shares, Squamish and Quest were so easily called "home" for the four years of students' lives as they pursued their undergraduate degrees, perhaps we could question what that practice of assuming a home means.

IV. ETHNOGRAPHY OF SQUAMISH

Ethnography of Squamish was a course that aimed to introduce students to feminist ethnography through a study of our own location—Quest University and the town of Squamish. The course was a window into feminist embodied-qualitative research of place and practice, taking into consideration the position of "outsider." The course considered dilemmas, practices, and implications of research and asked students to think about place critically. We read and discussed human-subject research and dance ethnographic practices in the unceded territories that are occupied by British Columbia and across borders and in different contexts. Ethnography of Squamish considered colonial inheritances that shape research and colonization and the significance of the Northwest Coast. We delved into practices of colonization, the notion of economy and ownership of land, and the politics of outdoor sports.

The central questions that centred the course were: What is the town of Squamish? What is Quest University? What is home? *Feminist Ethnography* by Dána-Ain Davis and Christa Craven was the core text and offered methodologies for the class. Davis and Craven provide a helpful start to the practice of feminist ethnography:

> 1. Feminist ethnography attends to the dynamics of power in social interaction that starts from a gender analysis. By gender analysis we mean that a feminist ethnographic project takes into account all people in a field site/community/organization, and pays particular attention to gender by honing in on people's statuses, the different ways in which (multiple) forms of privilege allow them to wield power or benefit from it, and the forces and processes that emerge from all of the above. (9–10)
>
> 2. It is our job as feminist ethnographers to be attentive to positionality as we embark on our research and discuss the inevitable (and sometimes multiple) impacts of our identity. (81)

Many students had favourable ideas of interviews, personal correspondence and connections, and surveys as "authentic" and "untainted" and "honest" representations. I wanted them to consider the "impacts of identity" by considering the navigations of social relationships in terms of power and positionality as emphasized in the works of feminist ethnography and to reflect on the meaning of settling in Squamish in the contemporary moment. Over the duration of the course we kept a record of the questions we might want to pursue in researching within the community and amongst ourselves. I approached several residents of Squamish through various contacts and websites. All agreed to being approached and interviewed by Quest students for the purpose of this course. For that, I obtained Quest University's Research Ethics Board approval. The two questions that guided these interviews were:

> 1. Could you share your thoughts on this place called Squamish and what you know of its history?
>
> 2. How long have you lived here in Squamish and do you consider this place home? Why or why not? What makes a "home" for you?

I wanted students to have the experiences of conducting interviews and observations and with being observed. I divided the class into groups of four students. Two students would conduct the interview with a resident of Squamish; the other two observed the interviews and the conduct of their peers. The interviewers would transcribe their interview. Those that observed the interview would also provide a transcription and observation notes of the interview. The group activity asked them to reflect on their different perceptions and observations in order to critically think about their descriptions and assessments of culture—perhaps there were unanswered questions, perhaps they didn't know much about the subject and couldn't follow up with a question during the interview—these were the moments that were produced through critical analysis and group engagement with ethnography.

We did read Indigenous and non-Indigenous histories and scholarship on the area, but as ethnographic practices shared with us, textual knowledge wasn't the only form of knowledge students should pay attention to in considering place. Quest didn't have any protocol agreement with the Squamish Nation at the time.[2] Although I was part of the First Nations Initiative that was to develop a formal protocol agreement between the Squamish Nation and the university, the program was at a standstill after the University's board of directors removed the university president, who had started the initiative.

A formal protocol lays out several agreements and practices between the university and the Nation including services, payments, and commitments for the future. It also determines a line of communication so that the Nation is not overburdened by "asks" from the university, staff, and students. A lack of protocol agreement made me unwilling to simply approach the Squamish Nation or acquaintance for any services for the university. Adequate process from the university (including payment) and adequate treatment in terms of demands and record keeping of demands could not be guaranteed without

2 I discuss more about the failures of the initiative in a chapter in *Rethinking Women's and Gender Studies Vol. 2* (see Satkunaratnam).

a formal protocol agreement. As such, the best options for the class were to book tours with established organizations/businesses within the Squamish community. We attended two field trips, one to the Squamish-Lil'wat Cultural Centre in Whistler and one with Talaysay Tours and Deanna Lewis of the Squamish Nation.

For the final project, in small groups, students had to design a way of sharing their interview materials through an installation that reflected on the theories and methodologies of research from the assigned readings. Sometimes students didn't agree on how to present their research and refused to work with each other. These moments demonstrated the difficulties and responsibilities of presenting and sharing someone's life and one's own "impact of identity."

I taught Ethnography of Squamish one more time, two years later. There was still no protocol agreement and the university was still reeling from the firing of the president by the university board of directors. The troubles on the board seemed to be financial. But the faculty were divided—many supported the removal of the president. They were suspicious of his investment in the First Nations Initiative and other initiatives focused on equity and labour and felt these initiatives replicated the norms (and difficulties) of the universities Quest wanted to distinguish itself from. These initiatives, they felt, were financially demanding and irresponsible.

Alongside the dismissal of the former president, the work of the First Nations Initiative was disbanded. The contracts of the consultants who worked with us were not continued. :gyauustees, a Squamish and Nuuchahnulth teacher was invited by the new president to keep an office at Quest while he worked on independent initiatives—it was not a formal position and there was no protocol agreement. :gyauustees and I would meet often over refilling coffee at the faculty lounge and while walking in the hallways. I had mentioned my courses and he would drop by my classes on occasion to listen and share his perspectives and knowledge. He invited the Ethnography of Squamish class to his home on reserve lands.

V. MEMORY

> Last night I dreamt that a student's room was flooded due to my oversight. All their belongings were soaked. As I tried to save their things, I was trying to save myself from being fired. (Satkunaratnam, personal journal)

To drive the university van for the field trip to :gyauustees's house, I hired a student driver who was enrolled in the course and approved to drive university vehicles. The van would hold the majority of the students in the class, while my small car would hold two students, :gyauustees, and myself. After checking in with the student driver and making sure all the students were situated, I walked to my car with :gyauustees and the two students travelling with me. Before we could even sit down in my car, the student driver drove off, taking the majority of the class with him. The driver didn't wait for the guide and homeowner, or the professor. My vehicle made it to :gyauustees's home—about a twenty-minute drive from campus—but the university van had yet to arrive.

We received a phone call and were informed the van was in another area, trespassing on another part of the reserve land. It was stuck in a huge ditch on an unpaved dirt road in the forest with tires submerged in a water-filled, muddy hole. By the time we reached the van we learned that the students who were in the van had already called *more* Quest students to arrive at the scene. They hoped the other students could tow the van out with a personal truck and tow straps. No one waited for :gyauustees or me to consider what to do before inviting more people to the scene on these lands.

A van this stuck in mud was not going to be pulled out by a passenger vehicle and tow straps. It was raining in the rainforest and the ground was softening. The vehicle was sinking lower and lower into the mud. As hours passed, it continued raining moderately and it was getting cold. I imagined this Quest van sitting stuck in the mud through the winter until spring, the land hardening and softening and firming up finally to release the van. I imagined this van with the large letters “Quest University Canada” sitting through the seasons. I was horrified and disgusted. Students kept telling me that I just looked so sad. I was very sad. I asked all the students (aside from the student driver of the van) to leave with the students who had come hoping to assist.

I then called a tow company. A flatbed truck arrived but couldn’t go farther down the trail road. A tow truck arrived about five hours after the start of what was to be a three-hour field trip. As the rain continued, the tow truck sunk deeper in the softening land. It was stuck. I couldn’t look at the scene anymore and said to :gyauustees, “I just need to pray.” We sat in the car, holding hands, and prayed and talked as the tow truck driver attended to the scene.

After winching their truck to a tree, the tow truck driver was able to pull their own vehicle out of the mud. The tow truck stayed winched to the tree and eventually pulled the van out. The land literally got us out. That tree in that earth helped our vehicles get out. It was 6 p.m. in the late fall, and night had arrived.

Because this was reserve land, private land, my roadside-assistance membership was invalid and there was an additional fee. I paid with my credit card to get the university van towed. I drafted an incident report and sent it off to the dean. As an outcome, students would no longer be allowed to drive vans for the university.

For the next class, :gyauustees suggested we hold a circle to discuss what was in our hearts from this harrowing experience. Many addressed that they tried to stop the vehicle from leaving but were told by the driver that he knew what he was doing. Everyone wanted the outcome to be different. Students also spoke to the dynamics of silencing and power in those moments—among themselves. Who was listening to whom. Trust was broken on many different sides. I wondered what I could have done to have avoided this. I thought about my own decisions and actions as an educator and settler. I thought about the lack of protocol agreement. I would not teach the course again.

VI. VIOLENCE, TRAUMA, AND REPRESENTATION

I built my course Violence, Trauma, & Representation to focus on visual culture and collective forms and practices of representation. Students were to be introduced to theories and cultural/artistic practices that connect self/collective with location/place. Understanding vision and memory as mediated forms was foundational to thinking about how we engage with and create collective representations. As I continued to consider my own learning in place, the course culminated with a field trip to Vancouver where groups of students designed teach-ins about local monuments of their choosing.

We started with W.J.T. Mitchell's, "What is an Image?":

> Images are not just a particular kind of sign, but something like an actor on the historical stage, a presence or character endowed with legendary status, a history that parallels and participates in the stories we tell ourselves about our own evolution from creatures "made in the image" of a creator to creatures who make themselves and their world in their own image. (504)

Over the three and half weeks of the course, we considered images/representations and their connections to memories and understandings about place and people. I remember some themes that were particularly strong for me in offering the foundations of thinking critically about representations of collective place, identity, or experience:

1. Collective remembering via the work of Maurice Halbwachs's *On Collective Memory* and Paul Antze and Michael Lambek's *Tense Past.*

2. Economies of the visual via Susan Sontag's *Regarding the Pain of Others.*

3. Indigenous experiences and resistance via the National Centre for Truth and Reconciliation's exhibition and *The Survivors' Flag,* Jean

Barman's *Stanley Park's Secrets*, and Alanis Obomsawin's *Kanehsatake: 270 Years of Resistance*.

4. War and state practices of remembering that have taken place across the world via examples of Hiroshima, the Vietnam War, September 11, and the Global War on Terror.

The final project asked students to consider these practices to analyze a monument in Vancouver. Small groups of four to five students designed and conducted a thirty-minute teach-in for a monument of their choice. They were to help us understand the monument through outside research while considering the content from the course. The teach-ins discussed the images that emerge, circulate, and are "understood" through the monument, both preceding and following its creation: How is this monument "an actor on the historical stage" and what images, narratives, and collective memories are created and shaped via this still object?

As we discussed and learned from analyses on visual culture, inquiries of self and collective, and historical examinations of place and practices of place-making, I engaged with learning about myself in place while forming a collective—particularly with my students and interested colleagues (and as timed passed with friends and acquaintances outside of the university). We built a culture of questioning assumptions of home and envisioning, critically, what home could mean and should mean more ethically for ourselves and our relationships with whom we were connected in place and time.

VII. MEMORY

Our day of teach-ins began at this monument. Although very close to my apartment, I never stopped at the base to look at it. I passed it by bus or on foot often. Upon seeing it, there was a clear difference in form from the commonly seen Olympics-associated logo. This structure was much larger than those that mark the ski hills of Whistler Blackcomb or Cypress. Its proportions were different. The points where the rocks came together were filled differently from the smaller versions that marked the sites for the 2010 Winter Olympics

Fig. 2. *Inukshuk* by Alvin Kanak, located in English Bay, Vancouver. This monumental sculpture was created for Expo 86, but has since been appropriated for the 2010 Olympics and by Tim Hortons. Photo © Ahalya Satkunaratnam.

I had encountered the structure and image before—widely spoken of as an "inukshuk," it is stamped across Tim Hortons Canada 150 Timbit boxes. I knew of its appropriation as a logo for the 2010 Winter Olympics, which were held across Coast Salish territory. The association with the Olympics prevented me from taking too much notice of the structure, but participating in the teach-in with my students, I learned of a particular monument's crucial connection to the Olympics. The creation of this work by the late Alvin Kanak of Rankin Inlet, Nunavut, was for Expo 86—twenty-four years prior to its inspiration for the 2010 Olympics logo. What does it mean to associate this marker from 1986 with the 2010 Olympics, and to have learned to disregard the other stories?

Inukshuk, the title of the monument, is a mispronunciation of the Inuktitut "Inuksuk." In their teach-in, the students referred to Nadine Fabbi's essay, "The Inuit Inukshuk and the 2010 Olympic Logo," pointing out that the monument was chosen by the Olympic committee judges "because it is simple, happy, welcoming, has a sense of energy and, while universal, speaks to the particular location of Vancouver."

How does a marker of Nunavut speak to the particular location of Vancouver? How is it universal? My students led the class to read the plaque at the bottom of the structure:

Fig. 3. The plaque that accompanies *Inukshuk* by Alvin Kanak.
Photo © Ahalya Satkunaratnam.

The plaque states so little of the Inuit, First Nations, or Indigenous history. Kanak is minimally attributed. Only his name and place are noted. There is nothing else of his work or life; beyond its name, no details of place are given. The students shared some significant findings by Fabbi in her essay, which I would return home to read in its entirety, inspired by their research and attention to the monument.

Fabbi noted that Kanak was not invited to the unveiling ceremony in 2005 of the 2010 Olympic logo and did not receive recognition for his work. Fabbi's piece also discussed the resistance to the usage of this image for the Olympics, as it ignored work by local Coast Salish/First Nation artists of the Northwest Coast, but also because, as Legislative Assembly of Nunavut minister Joe Allen Evyagotailak stated,

> I find it very sad that the 2010 Olympic logo will be an inuksuk when hamlets in Nunavut are struggling to keep recreation facilities open. (qtd. in Fabbi).

But the continuous gifting that is shared on the plaque paints a different type of relationship—it highlights a different practice. Its interest is in the transactions of sponsors and government bodies—those relationships—and their gifts. It also covers over the practice of taking—of the inspiration, the art practice, the structure, the land. Those relationships are not highlighted. The plaque embodies contradiction. My conception of the image as a tool of the Olympics stopped me from considering a much longer and difficult history around this monument so close to where I was living. That longer and much-needed complicated story, one where an artist made a work and shared it on an international stage in 1986, and the numerous transactions of representation, land, and bodies prior to, between then, and now were exactly what I needed to consider.

VIII. REFLECTION

> No one goes anywhere alone, least of all into exile—not even those who arrive physically alone, unaccompanied by family, spouse, children, parents, or siblings. No one leaves his or her world without having been transfixed by its roots, or with a vacuum for a soul. We carry with us the memory of many fabrics, a self soaked in our history, our culture; a memory, sometimes scattered, sometimes sharp and clear, of the streets of our childhood, of our adolescence; the

> reminiscence of something distant that suddenly stands out before us, in us, a shy gesture, an open hand, a smile lost in a time of misunderstanding, a sentence, a simple sentence possibly now forgotten by the one who said it. (Freire 23)

Paulo Freire's works transformed me when I first read his influential *Pedagogy of the Oppressed* as an undergraduate student in Chicago. Like for many globally, the value he placed on the recognition of world views and distinct histories of people and places drastically empowered me as a student and as an educator. It made me think critically about how we all are moved and influenced by our distinct and connected worlds. Freire's work moved me toward the teaching practices I hold today and share here in this reflection.

The methodologies of cultural studies via feminist and dance ethnography, and along with them investigations into the transnational, offered me a tremendous journey of learning and doing in my classroom and in my former workplace. The commitments to being place-based in our learning are wrought with the politics of our arrival (for me, as a settler, several times over) and the institutions, including the classroom, that brought us there. I was forced to encounter that history of arrival in an institution that was proudly new, and, as such, a newcomer and outsider. It didn't give me the feeling of stability and (perhaps) approval that comes with older institutions and their long-standing, marketed, and accepted sense of worth and history (even if constructed). I am grateful to feminist inquiry and its many inheritances that pushed me to ensure my courses weren't just sharing a discipline and knowledge, but a practice that was ultimately resonating with the class in place, on those unceded territories, and through the acknowledgement of the construction and making of the university itself.

Writing these memories has been sweet, allowing me to consider the type of collaborative learning that took place through these courses. Students would invite authors of the texts we read to campus to be part of the Power, Race, and Privilege student-organized symposium. Research projects developed out of these courses examined culture in place and the power dynamics within that practice, including that of research: the usage of the word "Squampton" in Squamish to refer to the town ("Squampton: An Appropriation Or The (re) Making of Empire"), Confederate Army inspiration in Vermont public high school mascots ("Once a Rebel, Always a Rebel: Mascots, Memory and the Confederate Legacy"), the power dynamics of land development/continuous colonization ("(Re)Colonization Through Tourism: A Study on the Potential Impact of PGA Golf and Beach Resort in South Cat Island Communities"), and settler culture ("The Presence of Wonder: An Examination of White Settler Communities in Toronto").

Writing these memories has been difficult while considering what was taking place institutionally at the same time I was teaching these courses. Finance was a major issue for the university, tied up with a philanthropic scheme around the land development of the school. With the closing of Quest in April 2023, it would be revealed more widely that the university was a tax-shelter scheme for philanthropists and the land (and its development) was at the centre of it (Chua). There were politicians and elected officials, land developers, lawyers, "philanthropists," and educators that profited immensely from the financial and development scheme that was Quest. Many students who took my classes (alongside other faculty who focused on power and positionality) would call out the board, lenders, and land developers who benefited from contracts with Quest and knowingly pushed the university toward insolvency.

Alongside the financial issues, at a faculty and student level, any discussion of power—whether that be equity, Indigeneity, race, or gender—in institutional practice was considered costly and discriminatory and a matter of personal opinion. The First Nations Initiative was considered the president's cash cow—and after the president's firing in 2017, faculty who were involved were pulled into endless meetings and communications demanding the records of expenditures. But the initiative was successful in pushing Quest to create its first position in Indigenous Studies. The short list was comprised mainly of settler candidates. Many students who had taken courses in critical race studies, gender and women's studies, and Indigenous Studies had organized to ask questions at the candidates' job talks. At each talk, the students posed a question to the potential candidate: "Do you believe an Indigenous scholar should fill the first Indigenous Studies position at this university?" Students found power to ask questions that the search committee were unable and unwilling to pose. They shared their grievances with the local newspaper. The university responded by calling the candidates unqualified and justifying their position through a Squamish advisor who sat on the search committee. We sought payment for this advisor and for them to have a vote on the committee, but the university denied both requests. As one of the few faculty of colour at Quest, teaching these courses were forms of building knowledge about issues of justice and a way to create in the institution a needed community committed to mobilizing.

My reflection is about what it meant for me to be given the time to learn, live, and teach on the unceded territories of Sḵwx̱wú7mesh peoples. It is also about teaching a university a discipline of examining culture through a transnational feminist and dance ethnographic lens. Writing this reflection from my apartment in Chicago reminds me of the work I must do as I live here. Seven years have passed since I first left this place and a new group of students is in front of me experiencing the pressures of life in 2023. Paraphrasing Freire, I carry the memories of many fabrics woven in my work and life on Sḵwx̱wú7mesh territory, moving me to continue transforming my teaching practice.

WORKS CITED

Antze, Paul, and Michael Lambek, editors. *Tense Past: Cultural Essays in Trauma and Memory*. Routledge, 1996.

Barman, Jean. *Stanley Park's Secret: The Forgotten Families of Whoi Whoi, Kanaka Ranch, and Brockton Point*. Harbour, 2006.

Chua, Steven. "A Timeline of Quest University's Financial Troubles." *Prince George Citizen*, 8 Mar. 2023, princegeorgecitizen.com/human-resources-education/a-timeline-of-quest-universitys-financial-troubles-6666992.

Davis, Dána-Ain, and Christa Craven. *Feminist Ethnography: Thinking through Methodologies, Challenges, and Possibilities*. Rowman & Littlefield, 2016.

Fabbi, Nadine. "The Inuit Inukshuk and the 2010 Olympic Logo." *K–12 Study Canada*, Spring 2006. *Henry M. Jackson School for International Studies*, jsis.washington.edu/canada/wp-content/uploads/sites/20/2019/07/Inukshuk-2006.pdf.

Freire, Paulo. *Pedagogy of Hope: Reliving Pedagogy of the Oppressed*. Translated by Robert R Barr, Continuum, 2004.

Halbwachs, Maurice. *On Collective Memory*. Edited and translated by Lewis A. Coser, U of Chicago Press, 1992.

Kanak, Alvin. *Inukshuk (Kanak)*. English Bay, Vancouver, 1986. Monumental sculpture.

Lambek, Michael. "The Past Imperfect: Remembering As Moral Practice." *Tense Past: Cultural Essays in Trauma and Memory*, edited by Paul Antze and Lambek, Routledge, 1996, pp. 235–54.

Mackin, Bob. "Quest University Says It Was Caught Off-Guard When Landlord Put Campus for Sale." *BIV*, 27 Feb. 2023. biv.com/article/2023/02/quest-university-says-it-was-caught-guard-when-landlord-put-campus-sale.

Millar, Erin. "The Great Experiment: Quest University's Radical Step in Higher Education." *The Globe and Mail*, 22 Oct. 2012, theglobeandmail.com/news/national/education/canadian-university-report/the-great-experiment-quest-universitys-radical-step-in-higher-education/article4620451/.

Mitchell, W.J.T. "What Is an Image?" *New Literary History*, vol. 15, no. 3, spring 1984, pp. 503–37.

Obomsawin, Alanis, director. *Kanehsatake: 270 Years of Resistance*. National Film Board of Canada, 1993.

Satkunaratnam, Ahalya. "Inclusion." *Rethinking Women's and Gender Studies*, edited by Catherine M. Orr and Ann Braithwaite, vol. 2, Routledge, 2023.

———. Personal journal. 2019.

Sontag, Susan. *Regarding the Pain of Others*. Farrar, Straus and Giroux, 2003.

"Student Life." *Quest University*, 2022, web.archive.org/web/20230308034800/https://questu.ca/student-life/.

"The Survivors' Flag." *National Centre for Truth and Reconciliation*, nctr.ca/exhibits/survivors-flag/.

Thibault, Alissa. "What Went Wrong with Quest? BC Politicians Raise Concerns About University's Financial History." *CTV News*,16 March 2023, bc.ctvnews.ca/what-went-wrong-with-quest-b-c-politicians-raise-concerns-about-university-s-financial-history-1.6316267.

FURTIVE MOVEMENTS: FRAGMENTS AGAINST SURVEILLANCE, AS TOLD WITH DANCE AND OTHER DISCIPLINES

MJ THOMPSON

When the New York City Police Department's Stop-and-Frisk program was ruled unconstitutional in 2013, the racist bias at its core was affirmed to all. At the same time, another significant detail came to light. Among the most cited reasons given by police for conducting stops was "furtive movements": an ambiguous phrase, a qualitative assessment, and the kind of language that, once uttered, has the effect of promising easy codification and legibility. Yet such an understanding would belie much of the work of movement research and scholarship since the 1970s, which attests to the fluidity of meanings for gesture, dance, and ordinary forms of human movement. What follows is an attempt to reckon with the category of furtive movements through the movement lens, and via an incomplete set of fragments written to undermine the solidity of the phrase itself. In the following short passages, I aim to think with and through dance performance to see how movement knowledge might help to destabilize a discourse that has largely been made through the disciplines of law, policing, philosophy, and, more recently, geography.

Black Studies scholar Christina Sharpe has challenged the notion of "furtive movements" as they are configured through Stop-and-Frisk, linking them to fugitivity and the trauma of the escaped slave. Sharpe points to the contextual logic of furtivity, as forced and enforced corporeality, the body targeted, reified, and nonetheless in motion in spite of criminal discourse and the state. She writes, "Whatever furtive movements are or are not, any movements while black may be interpreted as furtive" (830). Her 2012 reading both anticipates the available scholarship, its attendant practices, and the legal ruling of 2013 and invites further work in reading what is meant by the phrase "furtive movements" to begin with.

Moving between disciplines and building on this work primarily from a dance perspective, I write about a (false) category of movement, on the one hand made and compelled by a disciplining white gaze and codified through policing and legal discourse with so much ambiguity as to become a container for any racist impulse, and on the other hand a really (real) category, experienced and lived directly by Black and Brown bodies in the ordinary comings and goings of daily life. Whereas "furtive movements" point to a history of surveillance bound to the fallacies of racist ideology, a second fallacy lies in a bogus faith in the ability to read and predict movement as a singular meaning and unified pattern. My aim is to work against further codification, the binaries of language that function as its core tool, and the limits and enclosures that such writing and thinking tend to make real.[1] Movement knows better.

I. FURTIVE MOVES AS (FALSE) CATEGORY[2]

In 2013, in the United States District Court class action case Floyd v. City of New York, Judge Shira A. Scheindlin ruled that Stop-and-Frisk—the police program of stopping and searching pedestrians based on visual appearance and the grounds of "reasonable suspicion"—was unconstitutional. Over 198 pages, including testimony from fifteen plaintiffs, some of whom had been stopped more than once, Scheindlin's ruling found the practice violated the constitution in two important ways: it stopped individuals without legal basis

1 Please note that I write as a non-Black scholar; my lived experience is as an Irish Italian descendent, formerly Roman Catholic, Anglo currently living in Tiohtiá:ke/Montreal. My pronouns are she/her.

2 My thanks to Anne Flynn, who urged me to write about this subject after we saw a piece on Stop-and-Frisk by Trevor Noah on *The Daily Show*, 30 September 2016; to the artists Ellen Furey and Malik Nashad Sharpe for their creative work and performances; to my research assistant Tristan Clairoux for bibliographic support and conversation; and to the multiple readers who offered comments on versions of this draft.

in violation of the Fourth Amendment, and it targeted individuals based on their race in violation of the Fourteenth Amendment. In what is a stunning portrait in numbers of the delimiting of pedestrian freedoms, Scheindlin notes that of 4.4 million stops conducted between January 2004 and June 2012, over 80 per cent of those were Black or Hispanic citizens. This data plays out across different periods and modes of surveillance in American history, as discussed in Simone Browne's writing about the long history of the racialized disciplinary society. Browne notes, "Surveillance isn't new to black folks. It is the fact of anti-blackness" (11). Yet power exerts its pressures slowly, in dispersed and cruddy ways, as evidenced in the court case;[3] the most frequently cited "reason" offered by police officers for conducting a stop was "furtive movements" ("Document 373" 11), I wondered, "How did movement function here as cover for and an instrument through which to enact systemic oppression?"

The NYPD required officers making a stop to fill out a report worksheet, a UF-250 (Fig. 1). The first part of the form dealt with the question of reasonable suspicion; officers are required to tick one or more answers to the question, "What were the circumstances which led to stop?" Options here included: "carrying objects in plain view used in commission of crime; fits description; actions indicative of 'casing' victim or location; suspicious bulge; actions indicative of acting as a lookout; actions indicative of engaging in drug transaction; furtive movements; actions indicative of engaging in violent crimes; and wearing clothes/disguises commonly used in commission of crime" ("Document 339-3" 34). The language here suggests furtivity as a kind of catch-all term, subject to wide interpretation and bias.

A second part of the worksheet focused on reasons for preceding to frisk, including "inappropriate attire—possibly concealing weapon; verbal threats of violence by suspect; knowledge of suspects prior criminal violent

3 Sally Marston points to power's dissemination in and through the terrain of everyday, and thus elusive, acts. Elizabeth Povinelli describes the "cruddy" nature of power—that is, its decentralized, banal dispersal through small, quotidian acts. See, especially, Mat Coleman's reading of their work in light of police power.

APPENDIX B
Blank UF-250 Form

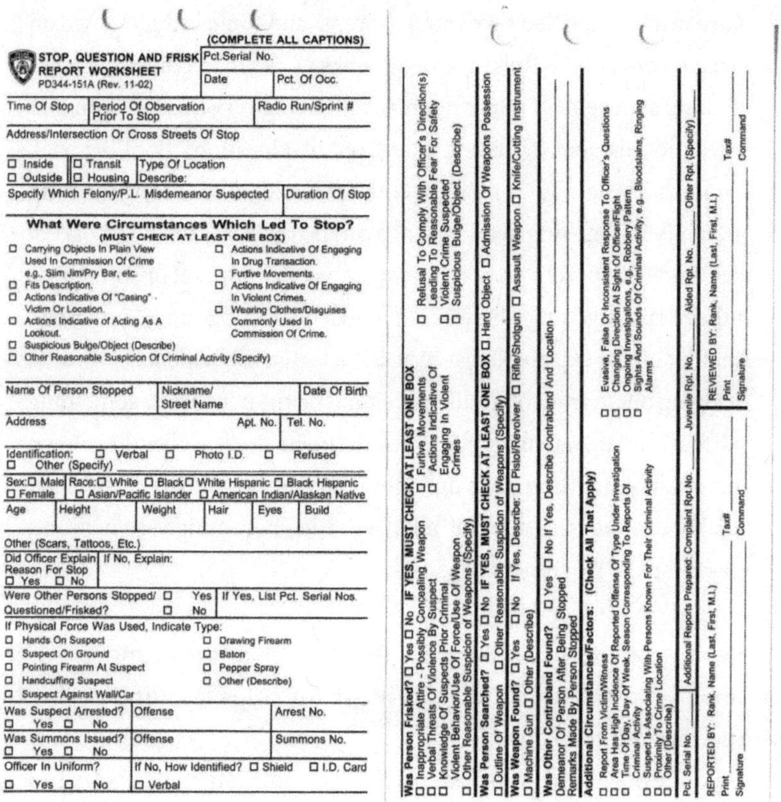
(COMPLETE ALL CAPTIONS)
STOP, QUESTION AND FRISK REPORT WORKSHEET
PD344-151A (Rev. 11-02)
Pct.Serial No.
Date | Pct. Of Occ.
Time Of Stop | Period Of Observation Prior To Stop | Radio Run/Sprint #
Address/Intersection Or Cross Streets Of Stop
☐ Inside ☐ Outside | ☐ Transit ☐ Housing | Type Of Location Describe:
Specify Which Felony/P.L. Misdemeanor Suspected | Duration Of Stop

What Were Circumstances Which Led To Stop?
(MUST CHECK AT LEAST ONE BOX)
☐ Carrying Objects In Plain View Used In Commission Of Crime e.g., Slim Jim/Pry Bar, etc.
☐ Fits Description.
☐ Actions Indicative Of "Casing" Victim Or Location.
☐ Actions Indicative of Acting As A Lookout.
☐ Suspicious Bulge/Object (Describe)
☐ Other Reasonable Suspicion Of Criminal Activity (Specify)
☐ Actions Indicative Of Engaging In Drug Transaction.
☐ Furtive Movements.
☐ Actions Indicative Of Engaging In Violent Crimes.
☐ Wearing Clothes/Disguises Commonly Used In Commission Of Crime.

Name Of Person Stopped | Nickname/Street Name | Date Of Birth
Address | Apt. No. | Tel. No.
Identification: ☐ Verbal ☐ Photo I.D. ☐ Refused ☐ Other (Specify)
Sex: ☐ Male ☐ Female | Race: ☐ White ☐ Black ☐ White Hispanic ☐ Black Hispanic ☐ Asian/Pacific Islander ☐ American Indian/Alaskan Native
Age | Height | Weight | Hair | Eyes | Build
Other (Scars, Tattoos, Etc.)
Did Officer Explain Reason For Stop ☐ Yes ☐ No | If No, Explain:
Were Other Persons Stopped/Questioned/Frisked? ☐ Yes ☐ No | If Yes, List Pct. Serial Nos.
If Physical Force Was Used, Indicate Type:
☐ Hands On Suspect
☐ Suspect On Ground
☐ Pointing Firearm At Suspect
☐ Handcuffing Suspect
☐ Suspect Against Wall/Car
☐ Drawing Firearm
☐ Baton
☐ Pepper Spray
☐ Other (Describe)
Was Suspect Arrested? ☐ Yes ☐ No | Offense | Arrest No.
Was Summons Issued? ☐ Yes ☐ No | Offense | Summons No.
Officer In Uniform? ☐ Yes ☐ No | If No, How Identified? ☐ Shield ☐ I.D. Card ☐ Verbal

Was Person Frisked? ☐ Yes ☐ No IF YES, MUST CHECK AT LEAST ONE BOX
☐ Inappropriate Attire - Possibly Concealing Weapon
☐ Verbal Threats Of Violence By Suspect
☐ Knowledge Of Suspects Prior Criminal Violent Behavior/Use Of Force/Use Of Weapon
☐ Other Reasonable Suspicion of Weapons (Specify)
☐ Furtive Movements
☐ Actions Indicative Of Engaging In Violent Crimes
☐ Refusal To Comply With Officer's Direction(s) Leading To Reasonable Fear For Safety
☐ Violent Crime Suspected
☐ Suspicious Bulge/Object (Describe)
Was Person Searched? ☐ Yes ☐ No IF YES, MUST CHECK AT LEAST ONE BOX ☐ Hard Object ☐ Admission Of Weapons Possession ☐ Outline Of Weapon ☐ Other Reasonable Suspicion of Weapons (Specify)
Was Weapon Found? ☐ Yes ☐ No If Yes, Describe: ☐ Pistol/Revolver ☐ Rifle/Shotgun ☐ Assault Weapon ☐ Knife/Cutting Instrument ☐ Machine Gun ☐ Other (Describe)
Was Other Contraband Found? ☐ Yes ☐ No If Yes, Describe Contraband And Location
Demeanor Of Person After Being Stopped
Remarks Made By Person Stopped
Additional Circumstances/Factors: (Check All That Apply)
☐ Report From Victim/Witness
☐ Area Has High Incidence Of Reported Offense Of Type Under Investigation
☐ Time Of Day, Day Of Week, Season Corresponding To Reports Of Criminal Activity
☐ Suspect Is Associating With Persons Known For Their Criminal Activity
☐ Proximity To Crime Location
☐ Other (Describe)
☐ Evasive, False Or Inconsistent Response To Officer's Questions
☐ Changing Direction At Sight Of Officer/Flight
☐ Ongoing Investigations, e.g., Robbery Pattern
☐ Sights And Sounds Of Criminal Activity, e.g., Bloodstains, Ringing Alarms
Pct. Serial No. | Additional Reports Prepared: Complaint Rpt. No. Juvenile Rpt. No. Aided Rpt. No. Other Rpt. (Specify)
REPORTED BY: Rank, Name (Last, First, M.I.) Print Tax# Signature Command
REVIEWED BY: Rank, Name (Last, First, M.I.) Print Tax# Signature Command

Fig. 1. The UF-250 report worksheet filled out by New York Police Department officers after a Stop-and-Frisk.

behavior/use of force/use of weapon; other reasonable suspicion of weapons; furtive movements; actions indicative of engaging in violent crimes" (35). Written up from the aggregate experiences of officers conducting stops over many years and "cabined by both federal and New York State case law," the UF-250 concretizes furtive movement as a category of suspicion, possible arrest and legal action through ambiguous language, and the practices of visual assessment.

What are furtive movements? *Floyd et al. v. City of New York* offers considerable vocabulary here, based on the testimony of two officers:

> "Furtive movement is a very broad concept," and could include "a person changing direction," "walking in a certain way," "acting a little suspicious," "making a movement that is not regular," "being very fidgety," "going in and out of his pocket," "going in and out of a location," "looking back and forth constantly," "looking over their shoulder," "adjusting their hip or their belt," "moving in and out of a car too quickly," "turning a part of their body away from you," "grabbing at a certain pocket or something at their waist," "getting a little nervous, maybe shaking," and "stuttering." Another officer explained that "usually" a furtive movement is someone "hanging out in front of a building, sitting on the benches or something like that" and then making a "quick movement," such as "bending down and quickly standing back up," "going inside the lobby . . . and then quickly coming back out," or "all of a sudden becoming very nervous, very aware." ("Document 373" 14–15)

I quote at length to mark the ways that so-called furtive movements as described within criminal discourse are, of course, multiple, shifting, non-specific, and subjective.

Legal discourse affirms this, as per Sharpe's understanding above. In *Floyd et al. v. City of New York*, Judge Sheindlin stated that an officer's impression of whether a movement was furtive or not "may be affected by unconscious racial biases" (44); and more, that "furtive movements, standing alone, are a vague and unreliable indicator of criminality" (47). In his preparatory report for the case, the sociologist Jeffrey Fagan found that the category "lacks precise definitions or standards, and [is] vulnerable to selective and highly contextualized interpretations" (*Second Supplemental Report* 32).[4] More, these categories tended to be formulated on group-based identifiers rather than individuals, since they rely on accrued experiential knowledge of police officers and trials.

4 See also, Fagan, *First Supplemental Report* 52–55.

Fagan notes, "These are not individual markers of suspicion but in fact are constructed categories" (*Second Supplemental Report* 49). Balancing quantitative research with qualitative, he cites retired NYPD officer Peter Mancuso who said, "Furtive movements . . . tells me that the cops are out there winging it a bit . . . they're really not looking for individuals" (*First Supplemental Report* 53). Testimony of this order, along with Fagan's research and mundane evidence such as the UF-250 form itself, affirm the problem on a structural level. Through the magic (that is, the veiling of cause from effect) of bureaucratic processes and daily habit, the racist impulse at the heart of the designation "furtive movements" takes on categoric, and criminal, form.

Yet while *Floyd et al. v. City of New York* determines the category of "furtive movements" to be biased and rules that Stop-and-Frisk is unconstitutional, there nonetheless remains a kind of belief running through the transcript—belief in surveillance as a necessary part of policing; belief in gesture as being legible; and belief in a solidifying effect that comes with any sustained engagement with a given terminology—something I risk repeating here. At the trial the argument was against the subjectivity of interpreting the category rather than the act of categorization itself as problematic. The considerable language thrown at unpacking the category of "furtive movements" suggests there is something there to be isolated and identified, even if ruled unconstitutional. At the same time, little attention is paid to the phenomenology and sociocultural aspects of gesture and human comportment as a complex set of relays between cultural pattern and individual interpretation. Returning to the frame of dance, nothing is said of movement's ontology: its gestural detail and coding, its rhythms and ephemerality, and its charged embodied status that tend to challenge the felt truth of perception and sight. Movement holds complex patterns and stylizations that mark cultural and individual histories not readily available at first glance. More, movement carries everyday contingencies, subject to and stylized by shifts in consciousness, energy, and context.[5] Such aspects of ordinary human movement offered a

5 On dance and ontology, see Maxine Sheets-Johnstone and Sondra Fraleigh. On dance as culture—that is, enduring, shaped by history, experience, and tradition—see Cynthia

covert strategy, seemingly bound to visible "evidence," through which to enact a brutal regime of surveillance on Black and Brown citizens in New York. The ontologies of movement, however, are what dancing bodies have much to say about—and this critical element seems absent from the discourse thus far.

II. FURTIVITY AS EFFECT OF STATE VIOLENCE

An initial glimpse of how dance asks us to consider furtivity might lie in the short film *Ditch Plains* (Fahrenholz), a tense carousel of scenes depicting post-apocalypse New York.[6] Driven primarily by danced action and developed in tandem with its stars, the Brooklyn-based hip-hop dancers Ringmasters Crew, director Loretta Fahrenholz describes the film as a "performative documentary" (Bell) a phrase that starts to get at the seamless melding of dance and street scenes—real and imagined—that make the work so unnerving. Shot at night in the aftermath of Hurricane Sandy, the thirty-minute film is a loosely plotted, porous narrative of the city at night: there are long shots of empty streets, damaged homes, dead bodies. On the documentary side, we see post-storm housing detritus in Far Rockaway; lines of people queuing up for gas; and neighbourhoods dark with power outages, as first-responder vehicle lights flash in passing. In tension with these quiet scenes of a city in recovery, there is performance. Bodies lie still in crumpled postures, splayed out on the ground. Or else bodies come alive to walk the streets, moving in distorted, staccato ways, as per the zombie gestural vocabulary popularized by the horror genre. Ringmaster Corey, Jay Donn, and an extraordinary company perform a range of street techniques—flexin, pauzin, tuttin, jookin, and more—in linked, episodic depictions of rage and grief, loss and resilience. It is

---

Jean Cohen Bull (Cynthia Novack); Katrina Hazzard-Gordon; Deidre Sklar; Brenda Dixon Gottschild; Sally Ann Ness; and Carrie Noland and Sally Ann Ness. On dance as ephemeral—that is, in motion and thus resistant to commodification and challenging to the visual grasp—see Peggy Phelan; and as cultural relay, see Thomas F. DeFrantz and Philipa Rothfield.

6 My thanks to dance studies scholar VK Preston, who introduced me to this film while presenting in my class Performance and Pedagogy at Concordia University, fall 2016.

a vision of the particular catastrophe of Sandy—with its inequities of devastation across different neighbourhoods—and a more general sign of catastrophe writ large across the United States via racial capitalism and climate change.[7]

One scene draws our attention specifically to the experience of furtivity as an effect of state violence. Midway through the thirty-minute film, Ringmaster Corey (Gutta Love) and Spyda da Hat Man enact an encounter between police and a pedestrian in a scene that pits inner monologue against public speech, dance against posture, gesture and comportment as choreography. Spyda/the cop appears first wearing jeans, jean jacket, and cap, his clothing outlined in neon. He begins to dance with liquid movement, popping and locking with silky-smooth footwork that demonstrates maximal control and access to the space of the sidewalk. Then he stands waiting on a corner. Corey/the pedestrian approaches him, moving slowly. A piano tinkles, at once casual, banal, and ominous.

A dialogue unfolds, excerpted below only in part so as not to rehearse the brutality of white policing:

> **COREY:** *(inner voice)* Stop following me, Officer, get outta my head.
>
> SPYDA'S COP *harasses.*
>
> *(inner voice, as hat is taken)* Don't do that, don't do that, Officer . . .
>
> SPYDA'S COP *moves* COREY *into the shadows, takes his hat, gives verbal abuse.*
>
> *(inner voice)* If he search me right, he may find a little smoke smoke. And he may take me down for that.
>
> *Instead,* SPYDA'S COP *doesn't really search, just torments:*

7 On Sandy's inequities, see Erin Bergren, Jessica Coffey, Daniel Aldana Cohen, et al. On racial capitalism, see Robinson; and Gilmore.

Cop: Say "sir!" . . .

Corey: *(inner voice)* No one escapes, not even me. This is not *The Matrix.*

The scene performs a double vision, at least showing profiling as a violation of the physical and psychic space of the Black pedestrian, and as an enforcement of racial hierarchies rather than any legitimate search for illegal items. The movement is especially revealing. For Spyda/the cop as a character, mobility seems to come easily, both in terms of his body's own global movements as well as in the manner by which he directs Corey/the pedestrian's movements: alternately smooth, or punctuated, he is virtuosic, in control, expansive in space and expressivity. He directs this power at Corey/the pedestrian, slowing him down, backing him up, making him stop. Then stealing his cap, bullying and tormenting, before turning from him and slipping into pure dance. Corey, by contrast, moves with great restraint, demonstrating what might be called a careful "tactics of withholding," to borrow Saidiya Hartman's phrasing (12). Here, Corey works the ordinary and the unmarked in everyday movement: walking, standing, slouching, containing. He compresses his body, dropping the shoulders, hands in pockets, slowing down, folding his arms across his chest. Here, the "ordinary" movements associated with the pedestrian contrast the tense fluidity of the cop's dance; more, they are isolated by the performer and camera, as if to underscore that he cannot afford to move differently.

Returning to Christina Sharpe's thinking, she describes furtive movements as "stuttered movements" (829), marking the compelled and conscious nature of this mode of comportment. The word suggests a flickering, stop-start rhythm: a kinesthetics that resonates with the materiality of film itself as the rhythmic projection of light in space. Equally, the term resonates with a history of writing about everyday movement that notes the role of consciousness and attention in distorting "natural" modes of ordinary movement (see Thompson). And yet, perhaps mimicking the ricochet, viral effect of terror that poisons its perpetrators too, if "stuttered" describes Corey/the pedestrian's movement, it nevertheless equally describes the rhythmic qualities of Spyda/

the cop. Spyda/the cop begins from a stationary position, on the sidewalk, standing in a strong, adversarial pose that situates his body perpendicular to the object of his surveillance. His head is cocked and turned to face the pedestrian, elbow bent and pointing at a right angle, hand on his belt. I read this as a wind-up pose, the kind we see when someone is focusing on a target and about to swing or shoot. He then begins turning in circles, traversing the sidewalk with gliding footwork and upper torso isolations that allow him to face all directions in sequence and carry him away off screen. Here, the elegant fluidity of movement conjoins with a rhythmic punctuation of popping and locking that suggests the highly technical as well as the pixellated and the glitch, invoking modes of digital capture.[8]

If the performance of furtive movements remains ambiguously in the scene, the effects of the "furtive" as a construct are exact. Between his bounded movement and inner dialogue, exterior cool and inner critique and fear, Corey/the pedestrian marks the impact of such stops. Whereas the threat is real—the cop "may find a little smoke smoke" and arrest might be imminent—the intent of the cop exists on the level of harassment. For Corey, gesture as truth is not a given, and the "accuracy" of reading gesture is beside the point. Together, the dancers show Stop-and-Frisk as failed in terms of law enforcement, yet highly functioning in terms of how it promulgates terror: addressing itself not to any real present (the weed in the pocket) but to white fantasies of future movements, where whiteness may be understood in part as the drive to fixicity, immobility, and control.[9]

Dance, however, works differently in terms of how it understands and presents movement, and its ways are rendered all the more fraught on film. The performers of *Ditch Plains* expansively bring together dance, speech, gesture, and choreography for the camera, overlaying multiple expressive codes. Here, I turn to dance scholar André Lepecki's essay on choreography as an apparatus of capture, which describes choreography, as distinct

8 Boško Blagojević notes the pixelated effect in his short review of *Ditch Plains.*

9 My understanding of whiteness as a discourse of power is indebted to scholarship by David R. Roediger, Maurice Berger, Richard Dyer, Toni Morrison, and Cheryl Harris.

from dance, as "a mechanism that simultaneously distributes and organizes dance's relationship to perception and signification" ("Choreography" 120). As an Enlightenment form, he writes, choreography figures as authority: paternal, state, judicial, and "a project that, moreover, removed dance from its social terrain (the communal yard) and placed it in a private courtly chamber, thus subordinating dance to signification, to full presence and to archiving" ("Choreography" 120). In *Ditch Plains*, the authority of camera and signification remains incomplete. With minimal context and dialogue, with fragmentary narrative and potent dance and gestural performances, knowledge is never entirely given to viewers. Even as the choreographic plan of the dancers and camera brings contemporary African American street dance and experience into sharp focus, the film leans heavily into the horror genre, collapsing the real and the fantastic, the everyday context of the street and the extreme effects/affects of life under racial capitalism. In doing so, the dancers of *Ditch Plains* at once show and resist, exceeding the choreographic drive to inscription.

What do I mean by exceed? One way to think about this is how the film's sense of grief and loss is countered by Jay Donn's joyful performances of affect, motion, and resistance. He shrieks and grimaces at the camera; he threatens and torments Corey in multiple scenes, part inner demon, part anger-management translator. In the film's closing moments, he performs a stylized march—slowed, chopped movements—through the middle of an empty car-lined street into the early morning, owning it. Another exemplar of what I take to be a portrait of dance's capacity to exceed capture[10] involves a solo street dance, wherein the performer's body, illuminated and marked in neon light detailing, exceeds the schematic and explodes and decomposes into space. In one of the only special effects of the film, a trick of animation begins to scatter the neon outline, breaking apart the dancer's form and obliterating the body into an excess of light, illegible pixels on a screen. If the dancers of

10 See Rizvana Bradley's essay "Black Cinematic Gesture and the Aesthetics of Contagion," which argues for a distinction between choreography and gesture as a core aspect of dance materials.

Ditch Plains point to the inequities of access to movement and the surveillance of Black life as fact, failure, and psychic trauma, the film equally seems to refute associations between movement patterns, forms of movement capture, and any settled meaning.

Dance scholars and dance anthropologists have long noted the limits of reading dance and gesture across disciplines, mediums, and cultures.[11] Hip-hop scholar and performing artist d. Sabela Grimes, for instance, has argued for greater appreciation of community-bound understandings of knowledge: that is, the particularity of gestural meaning in context. Dance scholar Thomas DeFrantz has admonished white dancers and scholars for claims to "understand" Black work, marking how the complexities of contemporary Black performance are made in and through the histories, socialities, and modes of collectivity bound to Black life. These defy quick translations, thoughtless citations. More, he has written of the imperative not to reduce work to the shameful category of "race." Instead, and citing DeFrantz at length,

> Blackness has to do with an approach, like this one, to discourse to gesture to art to family to expression. To life, *l'chaim*. Blackness is indeed incomprehensible, and it is entirely real and everyday. It has to do with outsiderness in white contexts and nothingness in black spaces; yes, because in black spaces no one is black because we stop being black except in relation to you. Of course. But in black spaces we don't "just exist" without race, because that is not a possibility in the context of this planet or in the context of contemporary performance. There is no outside of race, as there is no outside of history. But race is not blackness. Blackness does; blackness inspires; blackness confirms and consecrates. Race inhibits; it constrains. It shuts down. Blackness allows for. For love. ("I Am Black" 11)

With these lessons in mind, born out in the gift of Jay Donn's and the Ringmasters Crew's extraordinary performances, I see *Ditch Plains* as a

---

11 See Desmond; Foster; and Sklar.

performative text, with one scene in particular gathering the powers of choreography, dance, and gesture to critique the aims and effects of Stop-and-Frisk. Whereas furtive movements have been read as secretive or threatening, the dance film shows us furtivity as contextual and compelled through state violence—a condition of Black life under a white surveillant gaze.[12] More, the work foregrounds Black bodies in motion, resistant to arrest, categorization, and facile interpretation. "Furtivity," then, may appear—fleetingly!—as the creative, strategic, and logical response to white repertoires of surveillance.[13]

III. SURVEILLANCE AND THE MOBILITY REGIME

If *Ditch Plains* as a performance lens offers a critical affective portrait of surveillance, the story it tells neatly follows social sciences scholarship, particularly in the areas of geography and sociology, which has documented the experience of surveillance for pedestrians who are forever adjusting routes to and from work, managing mundane movements over sidewalks and streets to avoid harassment. This research offers another take on the furtive, constructed through policing and surveillance techniques, bound to the codification and control of everyday movement. Writing in 2002, sociologist Zygmunt Bauman identifies control of movement as a core strategy of state control: "Differentiation of mobility chances is one of the few strategies avidly

---

12 This understanding resonates deeply with Fred Moten's work on fugitivity; he writes, "Fugitivity, then, is a desire for and a spirit of escape and transgression of the proper and the proposed. It's a desire for the outside, for a playing or being outside, an outlaw edge proper to the now always already improper voice or instrument" (131).

13 I say fleetingly to resist underestimating the power of dominant forces to surveil and impose conditions on the surveilled. Furtivity, of course, depends on where you stand; seen through the practices of NYPD law enforcement, which build on histories of surveilling Black bodies in the United States, the term is used as a category of criminality, mobilized to control and delimit the movement of Black citizens. Yet, from the perspective of the surveilled, the term and its practices may point to something else notable amid the oppression—that is, as imaginative strategies for responding to state aggression and propelling resistance.

and consistently pursued by the governments of more affluent areas in their dealings with the population of less affluent ones" (83).

His words underwrite work by geographer Ronen Shamir, who notes that while globalism has argued for the easy flow of goods and people across borders, the result has been heightened mobility for some, with highly restricted mobility for most. Shamir includes the phenomenon of Stop-and-Frisk as part of a mobility regime, whose "point of departure is that the differential ability to move in space—and even more so to have access to opportunities for movement—has become a major stratifying force in the global social hierarchy" (200). The mobility regime, he writes, "is predicated, first, on the classification of individuals and groups according to principles of perceived threats and risks; and, second, on an emergent technology of intervention that provides the technical/statistical means for creating elaborate forms of such social distinctions" (200).

Whereas the early euphoria associated with globalism appeared tied to ideals of universal human rights and access, Shamir argues that the mobility regime exploits a tension between globalism's sense of proximity and technology's sense of social distance to create widespread suspicion and legitimize the use of multiple and widespread screening mechanisms, including massive data archives and mining programs like CompStat[14] or Real Time Crime Center[15]

---

14 CompStat is short for "computer comparison statistics," a program designed in 1994 for the NYPD in response to out-of-date crime data. "Compstat uses timely crime statistics to push precinct commanders to greater awareness and command of the immediate on-the-ground crime situation . . . Within each of the City's 76 precincts, Compstat is used to compile information on crimes, victims, times of day crimes took place, and other details that enable precinct officials to spot emerging crime patterns. The result is a computer-generated map illustrating where and when crime is occurring. With this high-tech 'pin-mapping' approach, the police can quickly identify trouble spots as well as causal relationships and then target resources to fight crime strategically. Precinct commanders now work closely with precinct detective squad commanders on countering the developing crime patterns within their precincts." See "Compstat: A Crime Reduction Management Tool."

15 A data warehouse that provides instant record access and geographic imaging for police officers in the field.

that allow instantaneous and unprecedented access to individual biometrics and histories (Kaufman).

Scholarship of the mobility regime marks the rise of pre-emptive policing across major urban centres around the globe and points to the escalating scale of programs like the NYPD's Stop-and-Frisk. But a second shift in scale lies in the expanding technologies of surveillance, starting with manual forms like Stop-and-Frisk, which privilege individually performed acts of observation and movement, compliant with a notion of body presentation as recognizable and legible; and moving to biometrics, such as iris, retina, and face scans, reliant on digital replication as truth and fact; and biospatial modes, such as gait analysis and pattern-of-life analysis, which foreground pattern and habit of movement over space and time. Such modes of surveillance, whether manual, camera-based, or algorithmic, rely on codification of furtive movements *and* the structures of vision and visual imagery to analyze and "recognize" individuals and/or movement deemed questionable.

Geographer Emily Kaufman describes the dangers of overlapping technologies in her essay about two Brooklyn neighbourhoods during the height of New York's Stop-and-Frisk program, coining the term "biospatial profiling" as the mechanism through which "police practices racialize crime and criminalize everyday life in demarcated zones" (74). She describes tactics that include the targeting of particular areas; the conducting of manual forms of control, such as Stop-and-Frisk; and the gathering and accumulation of data in systems that record all encounters with police, however nominal. Rather than representing any hierarchy, she notes, these are deeply entwined strategies of control. In New York, for example, though very few legitimate arrests were made, those stopped nevertheless had their names entered into the massive criminal database that served to create and entrench a history of criminal suspicion on an otherwise innocent individual.

Distinctive modes of technology come fully loaded with distinctive threats. A technology such as gait analysis, for instance, is exemplary in its use as a "passive" biometric that does "not require a subject's knowledge or consent" (Kaufman 77). Whereas with face scans, an individual often knows they are being scanned and may—at least in theory—"agree" to comply, and gait is far more readily assessed at a distance and without consent. Again, researchers believe gait to be a highly accurate marker of individual identity: "cameras know you by your walk" (Giles). In many cases, these forms suggest that aspects of criminality may be read on the body, recalling dubious nineteenth-century ideas linking physiognomy to character.[16] At the same time, these technologies privilege movement's predictability and habitualized pattern generally as repeatable, meaningful, and determinant.

Beyond the hideous impulse to manage movement at scale, what irks me further is the unspoken and naive positivism of the logic. All these techniques and technologies of surveillance rely on a misconception of vision as truth and movement as legible, even as the positionality of the observer is increasingly obscured. Jonathan Crary, in his key 1992 work on the performativity of sight, describes the observer "as an effect of an irreducibly heterogeneous system of discursive, social, technological, and institutional relations" (6). Crary shuts down any imagined neutrality for the observer and reminds us that, in the gap between perceiver/perceived, there is much room for error.

IV. ANOMALY AS CRIME

In what remains of this essay, I aim to take on this positivism as it relates to human movement, first by challenging what I see as flawed logic in early theorizations of surveillance—built on abstractions of the body, conceived as lines, patterns, and pixels, and written from within a tradition of European philosophy that has tended toward universality—and then by thinking with a particular dance piece in order to understand the body as anomaly. In his expansive account of attempts to schematize the moving body across the twentieth century, French theorist Gregoire Chamayou follows how different actors within the arts, science, and industry developed parallel and evolving methodologies to track human movement. From experiments in the

---

16 Formative texts include Johann Kaspar Lavater's *Essays on Physiognomy for the Promotion of Knowledge and the Love of Man*; and Ludwig Klages's *The Science of Character*. For recent work focused on algorithms and surveillance, see Chinoy.

avant-garde, such as Picasso's light drawings to early forms of dance notation, the arts appear as early innovators in imagining the possibilities of how this might be done using a wide array of tools—the pen, the camera, and light itself. Chamayou situates dance notation and choreography as no more than one pivot point in the complex history of chronogeography—the tracking of individual movement activity through time and space.

Discussing the increasing interest in such tracking, Chamayou maps the tension between perceptions of *individuals* as unique and *dividuals* as pattern, between Michel Foucault's model of the disciplinary society and Gilles Deleuze's society of control. He writes, "The technologies in question certainly focus on the search for 'signatures' . . . but they also spread out today in open milieus like the apparatuses of control. They focus on individualities conceived as indivisible chronospatial units, but, to constitute them, they also mobilize dividual material, aggregated in databases and treated in an algorithmic fashion." He points out a basic tension at the core of how these technologies work, and his interest lies in the escalation and broad distribution of data collection that moves the practice beyond Deleuze's society of control, with its emphasis on dividuals, into what he calls, "targeted societies."

Chamayou grounds his thinking in several drawings from the Paul Klee notebooks, drawings that influenced Deleuze in his framing of the control society, that delineate distinction between the individual as the line from which nothing can be taken or added without changing the integrity of the figure and the dividual, which is pattern-bound by repetition and divisibility. He links the individual to Foucault's disciplinary society, with its emphasis on state power, and the dividual to Deleuze's society of control, with its emphasis on networks, big data, and forms of access. Chamayou finds a third way here:

> The corresponding object of power here is neither the individual taken as an element in a mass, nor the dividual appearing with a code in a databank, but something else: a patterned individuality that is woven out of statistical dividualities and cut out onto a thread of reticular activities, against which it progressively silhouettes in time as a distinctive perceptible unit in the eyes of the machine.

Chronogeographical individualities, he writes, belong "neither to discipline nor to control, but to something else: to *targeting* in its most contemporary procedures, whose formal features are shared today among fields as diverse as policing, military reconnaissance and marketing." According to Chamayou,

> These are, in a sense, *normativities without norm*. Their notion of the normal is, in fact, strictly empirical: it is *learned* by the machine on the basis of an analysis of frequencies and repetitions in given sets of activities. It is then a discrepancy within such patterns of regularities—an *anomaly*, rather than an *abnormality*—that will trigger the red-orange alert on the analyst's screen.

Under pattern-of-life computation, the anomaly becomes the target, the unexpected enemy. And all who slip under the technological gaze are subjected to a kind of standardization, wherein variation, difference is marked, again, as trouble.[17]

Before I return to dance, I want to underscore that both Chamayou and Deleuze use the knowledge of the artist to build their theorizations. Each refers to Klee's painting *Gitter tanz* (185, fig. 2) and I wondered, what practice-based understandings might have slipped away in their usage? In mapping out his general idea of pictorial means, Klee privileges relations between fixed points in space—rhythm—as a way to convey movement and produce energy in a drawing. Klee writes, "Figuration must be connected with the concept of movement. In the general case mobility ends in rigid rest . . . The manner of mobility in a composite principle is completely balanced in itself. It achieves this through the regular spacing of the firm points and by the equivalence of the to and fro of movement among the firm points" (26).

Among other things, *Gitter tanz* shows this production of rhythm, generated by the overlay of representational strategies—the patterned line, the

17 These technologies equally raise the issue of algorithmic bias, an important point of critique of surveillance practices, and a reminder that there is no "neutral" gaze. For recent work in this area, see Safiya Umoja Noble, *Algorithms of Oppression: How Search Engines Reinforce Racism*, or Megan Garcia, "Racist in the Machine."

Fig. 2. Paul Klee (1879–1940), *Gitter tanz* [*Lattice Dance*] (1934), watercolour and pencil on paper on cardboard, 48.3 x 30.5 cm. Privatbesitz, New York.

structure, the dividual—and the free-formed line, the individual, carefully in dialogue to create the image. Yet Klee is careful to note that such representations move in two directions: toward the microscopic, where "elements hitherto perceived as structures would gain a thoroughly individual aspect" and the macroscopic, whose effects include "localized temporal structure, structural degradation, but also the creation of new individuals" (96–97). Another way to put this is that structures form and break down; points in space are relative. Klee notes, "Creation is thus in both directions an infinite, complex, intricate construction" (99).

Chamayou distinguishes between bodies and their trajectories of movement yet lands on the idea that these patterns take all unknowns as anomaly, rather than targeting specific pathways. Whereas Klee reminds us that he is explicitly working with effect and illusion in line rather than in life, theorization—including Chamayou's—has tended to elide the specificity of real bodies and the ability of "targeting societies" to identify and mark deliberate targets. In similar fashion, biometrics and pattern-of-life technologies tend to equate the schematic—the edge, the line, the fragment (Simon)—with a generalized body. Reconstituted parts assembled through mediated representations come to stand in for all live bodies.

But mediated representations of bodies cannot be equated with live bodies. Allen Feldman, for example, has described the rise of widespread surveillance practices as a "structural mutation" of the public sphere. For Feldman, writing in the wake of the American "war on terror," digital surveillance extracts important gestural and behavioural details, turning "the citizen into a digital silhouette" (340). Here, the surveilled body is "fragmented," "intentionality is digitally deleted," "acts and gestures are temporarily elongated," resulting in a "holographic composite" (340). Feldman's work is important for how it foregrounds the body, the perils of decontextualization, and the limits of mediatized sight.

To summarize: digital capture of movement at once dismembers and distorts bodies in motion, making its search for anomaly a self-fulfilling prophecy. For Chamayou, this means we are all potential anomalies under the camera's eye, in what could perhaps urge us toward a solidarity of resistance.

And yet. Returning to Simone Browne's research, she notes that the discourse of surveillance has tended toward the universal, a fact that has contributed to the masking of its disproportionate application to Brown and Black bodies. The challenge is to name and dismantle the racist impulse in finding specific bodies while simultaneously disallowing the solidity of perception that places moving bodies into binary projections (legal/illegal, white/Black) and stable categories. Here, I turn once more to performance and dance for a counter view. Rather than serving as direct account or illustration of furtive movements, *SOFTLAMP.autonomies* (2018) offers a critical tool for thinking about moving bodies generally and furtivity specifically. What more can dance teach about phenomena like the body as line, movement as habit and pattern, and the limits of predictive and pre-emptive surveillance?

V. BETWEEN PATTERN AND BREACH

To dig deeper into what dance offers, I want to describe an astonishingly beautiful and powerful work that reveals, to my mind, so much about why attempts to rationalize and codify human movement in the interest of control or production must inevitably fail. Where the mediated performance of *Ditch Plains* allowed for a depiction and critique of the effects of surveillance, live performance tends to offer what mediation and the digital frame cannot. *SOFTLAMP.autonomies*[18] by Montreal and London–based performer/choreographers Ellen Furey and Malik Nashad Sharpe (a.k.a. marikiscrycrycry) is a rigorous sixty-minute duet bound by vigour and stillness, repetition and simultaneity; highly challenging in its durational aspect for both performers and viewers. With its low-fi aesthetic—low affect, low drama, low differentiation—and tight unison performance of repeat choreography, the work drives hard at notions of pattern but in the end refuses to give any comfort in predictability of form. Program notes describe the work as a kind of meditation

18 I attended the premiere on 23 April 2018 at Théâtre La Chapelle, Montreal, as well as performances on 29 April 2018 at Studio 303, Montreal, and 9 January 2019 at American Realness, New York.

on power, "suggesting possibilities beyond authoritarian and coercive visions" ("SOFTLAMP.autonomies") and if it can be said to be "about" anything, it might function as a study in collaborative effort, authorship, and solidarity.

Before describing the work, a note about the performers. Ellen Furey took classes at the Grotowski Institute in Poland and studied dance, voice, and theatre in Toronto before moving to Montreal in 2010; she is interested in "discursive and collaborative processes emphasizing the messiness and power of subjectivities" ("Bio"). Malik Nashad Sharpe earned a B.A. in Experimental Dance from Williams College and a certificate in Contemporary Dance from Trinity Laban Conservatoire of Music and Dance in London; his work addresses "themes of violence, alienation, horror, melancholia and the horizon" ("Malik Nashad Sharpe"). They asked that I not assign identity categories in the writing of this work, and whereas viewers may perceive variation, here I follow their lead in resisting the violence of the named category.

The dance begins on the floor, with Furey down on her side and Sharpe reclining on one elbow, torso upright, with burning incense sticks in one of each performer's hands. Wearing white track pants, sneakers, and hoodies, their face makeup is bold: red circles, red/blue lips. In the darkened space, their white-costumed bodies appear as striking contrasts: they are sculpture-like, nearly still, imperceptibly shifting position in silence while smoke coils upward. For roughly the first twenty minutes, they appear in this way, occasionally shifting location, slipping into a hip-hop-like freeze, for example, as if falling backward, arms and legs reaching up. The ultra slowness builds tension: What did you see? What did you expect to see?

The music starts with a fizzy drop as a low-affect, under-produced rap song titled "Pillen," an ode to pharmaceutical pleasure sung in German by the Austrian rapper Yung Hurn, begins looping for roughly twenty minutes. The dancers move to centre stage and begin performing a seamless phrase in tight unison. Furey described the creative process as "long form improvising with objects and costumes and wigs and singing songs and thinking about nationalism and authoritarianism." A key source lay in what she described as "commercial dance": many of the moves stitched together for this phrase look slightly familiar, as in a hip-hop crotch grab, a jazzy extension and drop,

Fig. 3. Ellen Furey and Malik Nashad Sharpe in *SOFTLAMP.autonomies.* Photo © Ian Douglas, provided courtesy of American Realness.

a lyrical pirouette, the arms of a Scottish dance, the bent knees and elbows of a Wing dance, and so forth. The work feels deeply citational, quoting multiple social-dance techniques, only to move swiftly on—no context, no plot, and with enough speed to trouble the viewer's sense of sight.

What emerges is an extremely energetic movement phrase that repeats, then repeats again and again, with the dancers facing different aspects of the performance space. The audience gets to see the phrase, then see it again. And again. Repetition, performed in unison, underscores the rule of choreography and the interpretation of the individual. The dancers claim a huge amount of space, working the entire floor of the stage, pushing against walls that appear as obstacles and supports. For over twenty minutes they give us intense synchronized physicality and, yes, a demonstration of both hard work and teamwork. Then the unison begins to unravel slowly: there are ruptures and accommodations, the technique shifts and breaks down, distorts, fails, becomes something other. And then full stop. For an extended period, there is near stillness, in which we hear only the ragged breathing of the performers, their action paused, in poses on the floor. When the dance phrase and

Fig. 4. Ellen Furey and Malik Nashad Sharpe in *SOFTLAMP.autonomies*. Photo © Ian Douglas, provided courtesy of American Realness.

song begin again, they come this time with human sounds: Furey and Sharpe begin uttering a single note, at first just an utterance, as if reaching for some proper note or meaning. Then louder, escalating to slow cries of anguish or exhaustion: "Awwww . . . !" They cry out, repeatedly, and we sit in darkness, shifting in our seats, complicit as watchers, reflecting on what we've seen and what it means to work this hard. The piece ends with the pair still moving, feet pulsing, running in place, as the music plays on and the theatre darkens, save for a thin white horizon line appearing behind them.

An early impetus for the work lay in the phenomenon of YouTube dance videos; Sharpe and Furey were "intrigued by these very short catchy phrases" and thinking: "What if it lasts?" (Furey and Sharpe, post-show chat). Not just a minute-long bit on YouTube. Not just gesture beamed through networks and written in light. In its citational aspect, the dance appears to show us bytes of movement that in some way recall the digital: excised, decontextualized, objectified, and on replay. But here liveness performs the difference. Within the extreme conditions of their performance—the sustained duration of intense effort—the dancers mark a slippage at the sharp edge of technique, choreography, and ensemble unity. This is future movement: individual acts and economies of stylization, agency, accommodation, and resistance performed in relation to the other dancer and the audience's gaze. Under the intensity and duress of sustained performance, bodily movement—understood phenomenologically as "form in the making" (Sheets-Johnstone 28)[19]—confounds pattern and predictability.

Let's go back to Klee's dividual/individual tension, which appears in sharp relief in *SOFTLAMP.autonomies* thanks to its duet structure. As interpreters with distinctive training and bodily archives, both in terms of their academic formation and their cultural histories, we notice the minutiae of difference in performing bodies and performance style and get a sense of the habitus as that particular constellation of cultural pattern and individual agency, dividual and individual. What remains shared and on view is form itself: the looped phrase that repeats, the bodies carving space as line, shape, and force. Here, the work teases at form's potential as common vision across bodily positions and collective memories. Form serves as shared anchor point of perception. Yet form is never simply that. Furey and Sharpe remind us that live bodies as generators of movement work differently than their digital avatars.

Here lies dance's critical counter-vision to movement as rationalized by the surveillance discourse. In *SOFTLAMP.autonomies* the global movement arcs widen or shrink; gestural details are blurred or simplified; precision unravels, yet other values step in: strategies of reduction? virtuosity? adaptability? what else? The dancers appear to my eyes to shift between seeming to "mark"[20] the movement, and leaning harder into effort as fatigue—or anger?—takes hold. Bodies loosen, tire, change shape through time and effort, slip in and out of precise line, fall and fail: technique and habitus, as repositories of cultural

19 See the longer passage, which offers the following description: "Since movement is never complete at any one instant or point, never fully there, consciousness exists its body in movement as form continuously projecting itself toward a spatial-temporal future; hence, as form-in-the-making" (28).

20 To mark movement is to manage effort differently; dancers mark movement when they are learning a choreography or move, focusing on the acquisition and memory of the technique or step rather than the performance of the move.

pattern, become strange. Finally, predictability of line—whether seen to reside in the choreography, technique, or habitus—falls apart, shifts, reorients under the labour, duress, and continued effort of extended durational performance.

In his essay theorizing dance as freedom, André Lepecki invokes exhaustion as devotional, internally driven, and thus a model of resistance ("Choreopolice").[21] He offers the term "choreopolicing" for the set of tactical strategies of movement control—say, the kettling of protesters, for example—at the heart of contemporary policing. "Choreopolitics," on the other hand, suggests the possibility of movement toward freedom (as in, say, a public protest). For Lepecki, who like Chamayou evokes Deleuze's control society and grappling with a sense of conformity writ large at a mundane scale that prioritizes the functional activities of capital, the dancer offers a revolutionary vision: "It is the dancer who, in the most policed, controlled spaces (say even in the tightest of choreographic scores), has the potential to activate the appearing not necessarily of a subject, but of the highly mobile political thing" ("Choreopolice" 20).

His reading of work by Sara Michelson's *Devotion Study #1*, centred in the sustained spinning of dancer Nicole Mannarino, decomposes her exhilarating effort and repetition not as "martyrdom" but as self-driven agency. Yet this tends to obscure the complex material relations between choreographers and dancers, artists and audiences, producers and artists—inspired, compelled, or otherwise nuanced—all of which inform the theatrical space and shape notions of agency. Whereas Lepecki zeros in on dance's potential for modelling the appearance of a political subject, I want to think more closely about dance as specificity *and* slippage, wherein movement, and *embodied* movers, have the potential to at once invoke particular bodies, dance traditions, and cultural forms of expression *and* undermine any idealized or stabilized understandings.

Power, it's been said, circulates, yet part of the work of mobility regime scholars has been to identify the sticky, jammed nature of late twentieth-century mobility. Mat Coleman, working specifically on police

---

21 See also Lepecki's book *Exhausting Dance.*

power and borrowing from Sallie Marston and Elizabeth Povinelli,[22] reminds us of power's invisible nature: less the individual cop on the horse, more the policy, training, laws, and other systemic practices—the Stop-and-Frisk UF-250 form, with its tick-box labelled "furtive movements" and the ever-scanning eye-camera seeking out anomalous lines and edges, "capturing" visual images and sorting them into categories and problematics (Coleman). Such forms of power—banal, dispersed, and thus covert—resist our flow and tamp down on possibilities for change.

Instead, dance performance as I read it here suggests that the phenomenological and lived body in motion is a producer of anomaly generally and under extreme conditions specifically: for example, through the intense expenditures of energy, as per *SOFTLAMP.autonomies*, or when under scrutiny and surveillance, as per *Ditch Plains*. At minimum, dance as resistant to choreography and capture may direct our attention to the resistant malleability of the body as habitus,[23] at once patterned and in process via agency, intent, experience. At best it affirms the distinction between live and digital bodies, enactment versus representation. For the cop on the street or the camera in the sky, a moving body remains only ever schematic.

This essay is, I hope, a psalm to the energy, proliferation, and strangeness of bodies appearing in and through movement as phenomenon rather than a call for codification. In the dance offerings discussed in this essay, viewer gratification is not only not immediate, it is not the point. Knowledge is deferred in light of bodies doing what they do, radiating difference in multiples. Finally, the anomaly is the rule.

---

22 Marston points to power's dissemination in and through the terrain of the everyday, and thus elusive, acts. Povinelli describes the "cruddy" nature of power—that is, its decentralized, banal dispersal through small, quotidian acts. See Coleman.

23 Following Marcel Mauss's formation of the term as the total set of bodily comportments carried by an individual and shaped by psychology, sociology, and biology. See "Techniques of the Body."

VI. WE ARE ANOMALIES

There are easier ways, perhaps, to take down Stop-and-Frisk as exemplar and gateway to the scaled up, digital sweep of racialized surveillance. On moral grounds alone, with an eye to social justice and the terrible lessons of white capitalist colonial histories, one might simply say: full stop. And yet, in her pivotal work *Dark Matters*, Simone Browne observes that "race continues to structure surveillance practices" (12) and, citing John Fiske, she reminds us that the surveillance camera's eye continues to be white. Whereas part of her work identifies different practices such as lateness and loitering as forms of micro-resistance, it is equally true that these resistances—variations and interpretations on the capitalist drive to perform—will increasingly be labelled anomalous and targeted. As Lisa Nakamura has noted, "Surveillance does more than simply watch or observe bodies. It remakes the body as a social actor, classifying some as normative and legal, and some as illegal and out of bounds" (221).

Perhaps, then, dance offers another set of clues for pushback against the violence and perceived realness effect of sight—that is, vision as truth or evidence—as it operates through living bodies and in digital forms of observation and enforcement, with its aim to catch and interpret human movement through a set of electrical impulses rendered in light. Dance, and movement, complicates the fixed sense of knowing so often proposed by sight and surveillance. Thinking with dance means refusing simplified notions of the body as image, line, or symbol. To repeat, following Furey and Sharpe's strategies: bodies in motion function as machines of anomaly, generators of difference, and an excess of movement action, information, aesthetics, and imagery that belie codification and strict relations between sign and meaning. In doing so they remain critical sites of resistance, performativity—understood here as efficacy, or doing things in the world—and escape from restrictive codes of language and meaning. Dance eludes me, and it does you, too. That is, movement in its robust informational and expressive power always resists quick readings, easy binaries, and visual analyses taken out of context and out of culture. This fierce elasticity may be part of its key power to gather and bring together, rehearsing us toward multiple visions of the body and the social, toward the potential of solidarity, whatever that might mean going forward.

WORKS CITED

Bauman, Zygmunt. *Society Under Siege*. Polity, 2002.

Bell, Kirsty. "In Focus: Loretta Fahrenholz." Frieze, 23 Apr. 2014, frieze.com/article/focus-loretta-fahrenholz.

Berger, Maurice. *White Lies: Race and the Myths of Whiteness*. Farrar, Straus, Giroux, 1999.

Bergren, Erin, Jessica Coffey, Daniel Aldana Cohen, et al. *A Tale of Two Sandys. Superstorm Research Lab*, 2013, superstormresearchlab.org/wp-content/uploads/2013/10/srl-a-tale-of-two-sandys.pdf. White paper.

"Bio." *Ellen Furey*, ellenfurey.ca/bio.

Blagojević, Boško. "Loretta Fahrenholz." *Artforum*, 15 Jan. 2014, artforum.com/picks/loretta-fahrenholz-43043.

Bradley, Rizvana. "Black Cinematic Gesture and the Aesthetics of Contagion." *The Drama Review*, vol. 62, no. 1, 2018, pp. 14–30.

Browne, Simone. *Dark Matters: On the Surveillance of Blackness*. Duke UP, 2015.

Chamayou, Grégoire. "Patterns of Life: A Very Short History of Schematic Bodies." *The Funambulist Papers*, no. 57, 4 Dec. 2014, thefunambulist.net/history/the-funambulist-papers-57-schematic-bodies-notes-on-a-patterns-genealogy-by-gregoire-chamayou.

Chinoy, Sahil. "The Racist History Behind Facial Recognition." *New York Times*, 10 Jul. 2019, nytimes.com/2019/07/10/opinion/facial-recognition-race.html.

Coleman, Mat. "State Power in Blue." *Political Geography*, vol. 51, 2016, pp. 76–86. 10.1016/j.polgeo.2016.01.008.

"Compstat: A Crime Reduction Management Tool." *Government Innovators Network*. 2018, web.archive.org/web/20200817133638/https://www.innovations.harvard.edu/compstat-crime-reduction-management-tool.

Crary, Jonathan. *Techniques of the Observer: On Vision and Modernity in the Nineteenth Century*. MIT P, 1992.

DeFrantz, Thomas F. "I Am Black: (You Have to Be Willing to Not Know)." *Theater: Yale's Journal of Criticism, Plays, & Reportage*, vol. 47, no. 2, 2017, pp. 9–21. 10.1215/01610775-3785122.

DeFrantz, Thomas F., and Philipa Rothfield, editors. *Choreography and Corporeality: Relay in Motion*. Palgrave-MacMillan, 2016.

Desmond, Jane. *Meaning in Motion: New Cultural Studies of Dance*. Duke UP, 1997.

"Document 339-3." *Floyd et al. v. City of New York*. ccrjustice.org/sites/default/files/attach/2015/02/Charney%20Ex%20A-K%2011-25-13.pdf.

"Document 373." *Floyd et al. v. City of New York*. wsj.com/public/resources/documents/nystop0812.pdf.

Dyer, Richard. *White: Essays on Race and Culture*. Routledge, 1997.

Fagan, Jeffrey. *First Supplemental Report, 08 Civ. 01034 (SAS) Floyd et al. v. City of New York et al.*, United States District Court, Southern District of New York, 2010.

———. *Second Supplemental Report, 08 Civ. 01034 Floyd et al. v. City of New York et al.*, United States District Court, Southern District of New York, 2012.

Fahrenholz, Loretta, director. *Ditch Plains*. 2013. Short film.

Feldman, Allen. "Securocratic Wars of Public Safety: Global Policing as Scopic Regime." *International Journal of Postcolonial Studies*, vol. 6, no. 3, 2004, pp. 330–50. 10.1080/1369801042000280005.

Floyd et al. v. City of New York. 959 F. Supp. 2d 540. Judge Shira A. Scheindlin, 2013.

Foster, Susan Leigh, editor. *Choreographing History*. Indiana UP, 1995.

Fraleigh, Sondra. *Dance and the Lived Body: A Descriptive Aesthetics*. U of Pittsburgh P, 1987.

Furey, Ellen. Email to MJ Thompson. 26 Jul. 2019.

Furey, Ellen, and Malik Nashad Sharpe. Post-show chat. 29 Apr. 2018, Studio 303, Montreal.

———. *SOFTLAMP.autonomies*. Daniel Léveillé Danse, Théâtre La Chapelle, Montreal, 23 Apr. 2018. Dance performance.

Garcia, Megan. "Racist in the Machine: The Disturbing Implications of Algorithmic Bias." World Policy Journal, vol. 33, no. 4, winter 2016/2017, pp. 111–17.

Giles, Jim. "Cameras Know You By Your Walk." *New Scientist*, 19 Sept. 2012, newscientist.com/article/mg21528835-600-cameras-know-you-by-your-walk/.

Gilmore, Ruth Wilson. *Change Everything: Racial Capitalism and the Case for Abolition*. Haymarket, 2021.

Gottschild, Brenda Dixon. *Digging the Africanist Presence in American Performance: Dance and Other Contexts*. Bloomsbury, 1998.

Grimes, d. Sabela. Public talk. Concordia U, Jan. 2018.

Harris, Cheryl I. "Whiteness as Property." *Harvard Law Review*, vol. 106, no. 8, 1993, pp. 1707–91. 10.2307/1341787.

Hartman, Saidiya. *Scenes of Subjection: Terror, Slavery, and Self-Making in Nineteenth-Century America*. New York UP, 1997.

Hazzard-Gordon, Katrina. *Jookin': The Rise of Social Dance Formations in African-American Culture*. Temple UP, 1990.

Kaufman, Emily. "Policing Mobilities Through Bio-spatial Profiling in New York City." *Political Geography*, vol. 55, 2016, pp. 72–81. 10.1016/j.polgeo.2016.07.006.

Klages, Ludwig. *The Science of Character*. Translated by Walter Henry Johnston, G. Allen & Unwin, 1929.

Klee, Paul. *Notebooks: Volume 2, The Nature of Nature*. Edited by Jürg Spiller, translated by Heinz Norden, Lund Humphries, 1973.

Lavater, Johann Kaspar. *Essays on Physiognomy for the Promotion of Knowledge and the Love of Man*. Translated by Thomas Holcroft, William Spotswood & David West, 1794.

Lepecki, André. "Choreography as an Apparatus of Capture." *The Drama Review*, vol. 51, no. 2, Summer 2007, pp. 119–23.

———. "Choreopolice and Choreopolitics: Or, the Task of the Dancer." *The Drama Review*, vol. 57, no. 4, 2013, pp. 13–27. 10.1162/DRAM_a_00300.

———. *Exhausting Dance: Performance and the Politics of Movement*. Routledge, 2006.

"Malik Nashad Sharpe." *Arts Admin*, artsadmin.co.uk/profiles/malik-nashad-sharpe/.

Mauss, Marcel. "Techniques of the Body." 1935. *Techniques, Technology and Civilisation*, edited by Nathan Schlanger, Berghahn Books, 2009, pp. 70–95.

Morrison, Toni. *Playing in the Dark: Whiteness and the Literary Imaginary*. Harvard UP, 1992.

Moten, Fred. *Stolen Life (Consent Not to Be a Single Being)*. Duke UP, 2018.

Nakamura, Lisa. "Afterword: Blaming, Shaming, and the Feminization of Social Media." *Feminist Surveillance Studies*, edited by Shoshana Magnet and Rachel Dubrofsky, Duke UP, 2015, pp. 221–28.

Ness, Sally Ann. *Body, Movement, and Culture: Kinesthetic and Visual Symbolism in a Philippine Community*. U of Pennsylvania P, 1992.

Noble, Safiya Umoja. *Algorithms of Oppression: How Search Engines Reinforce Racism*. New York UP, 2018.

Noland, Carrie, and Sally Ann Ness, editors. *Migrations of Gesture*. U of Minnesota P, 2008.

Novack, Cynthia J. [a.k.a. Cynthia Jean Cohen Bull]. *Sharing the Dance: Contact Improvisation and American Culture*. U of Wisconsin P, 1990.

Phelan, Peggy. *Unmarked: The Politics of Performance*. Routledge, 1996.

Rivera, Ray, Al Baker, and Janet Roberts. "A Few Blocks, 4 Years, 52,000 Police Stops." *New York Times*, 11 Jul. 2010, nytimes.com/2010/07/12/nyregion/12frisk.html.

Robinson, Cedric J. *Black Marxism: The Making of the Black Radical Tradition*. U of North Carolina P, 1983.

Roediger, David R. *The Wages of Whiteness: Race and the Making of the American Working Class*. Verso, 2007.

Simon, Nivin. "How Does AI Recognize Your Gesture and Movements?" *Mantra AI*, 2019, mantra.ai/blogs/ai-in-gesture-recognition/.

Shamir, Ronen. "Without Borders? Notes on Globalization as a Mobility Regime." *Sociological Theory*, vol. 23, no. 2, 2005, pp. 197–217. 10.1111/j.0735-2751.2005.00250.x.

Sharpe, Christina. "Blackness, Sexuality and Entertainment." *American Literary History*, vol. 24, no. 4, 2012, pp. 827–41.

Sheets-Johnstone, Maxine. *The Corporeal Turn: An Interdisciplinary Reader*. Imprint Academic, 2009.

———. *The Phenomenology of Dance*. 1966. Temple UP, 2015.

Sklar, Deidre. "On Dance Ethnography." *Dance Research Journal*, vol. 23, no. 1, spring 1991, pp. 6–10.

———. "Reprise: On Dance Ethnography." *Dance Research Journal*, vol. 32, no. 1, 2000, pp. 70–77. 10.2307/1478278.

"SOFTLAMP.autonomies." *Daniel Léveillé Danse*, 2018, web.archive.org/web/20230131003151/https://en.danielleveilledanse.org/en-softlamp-autonomies.

Thompson, MJ. *Impure Movement: Mundane Body Techniques in 20th Century American Choreography*. Ph.D. dissertation, New York U, 2008.

CORPOREAL TURF: NOTES ON BLACKNESS AND DRAMATURGY

ANGÉLIQUE WILLKIE

This essay is part of an ongoing reflection. It will have a beginning; it will have an end. But that is neither the beginning nor the end of the questioning or of the thought process. They will both continue to evolve. Like a performance.

In 2018, Miguel Gutierrez, New York-based multidisciplinary artist, choreographer, and performer of Colombian origin, wrote an article in *BOMB Magazine* that allowed me to put words to unformed thoughts that have haunted me throughout my career. In "Does Abstraction Belong to White People? Thinking the Politics of Race in Contemporary Dance," Gutierrez quotes Afro American choreographer Donald McKayle:

> I always begin a project with the knowledge that I am dealing with people, with individuals, with human beings. And my approach is always visceral. I give moments that are visceral. Everything must come from within and everything must have meaning. When I choreograph, I never use people merely to create a design. I mean, abstraction is always present in an art form. And I use it, but I have never used human beings simply as a design element. My work has always been concerned with humanity in one way or another. Basically, I feel the beauty in man is in his diversity and in his deep inner feelings.

That statement was made by McKayle in 1973 in an interview with the *New York Times*. Gutierrez describes this citation as a way of helping him understand the tension that exists between what he calls "white modern dance" and "black modern dance." McKayle's need (and, by proxy, Gutierrez's also) to work from "within" is both aesthetic and profoundly political; his comments resonate for me as a call to artistic arms that remains valid fifty years later—a realization that in itself speaks to the current interrogations of our craft, and to my own predilections.

The title of this essay (or, rather, ongoing thought process), contains meaning for me in each of its component parts. "Corporeal" for me refers to the relational body, by which I mean the physical body and all that accompanies it (morphology, ethnoracial origins, age, gender, physical (dis)abilities, among others), as well as the way that the body engages with and is seen by the world (sociocultural background, sexual identity, languages spoken, religious beliefs, political preoccupations, etc.). Most importantly, this relational body is a site of both meaning-making and social inscription and is in constant and fluid engagement with its surrounding context/s. I think of "turf" primarily in the context of territory, with the notions of contested space, boundaries (and their transgression), belonging and autonomy embedded in my thinking. But there are also other inspirations that emerge from the term. In the online Merriam-Webster dictionary, among the definitions that come up for "turf" is grass, with its surface layer of soil held together by its roots. I think of the anchoring provided by those roots that are below the surface (or "from within" in McKayle's words), while the grass and surface soil are external (the potential "abstraction"?). There is also the idea of turfing someone—informal British English for throwing them out—which evokes for me the transgression of some limit and the right one has to eject the transgressor. The idea of corporeal turf then encompasses the territory of the body, implying autonomy, boundaries, potential contestation, etc., as well as what lies beneath its "surface," which I interpret as what is known in/to that body that cannot be known from outside that particular corporeality's engagement with the world.

In my reference to Blackness, I am looking beyond a specific ontology and toward an experiential knowing that is its own practice—a praxis. It is *a* lens through which I situate my light-skinned Jamaican self and my experiences in a world and an art form that are dominated by white, Eurocentric values, methods, and aesthetics. My unquestioning adherence to these values, methods, and aesthetics over many years has become the basis for my current interrogations, which sit at the axis of the very undefinability of Blackness and its very real experience: how it has consciously or unconsciously informed my artistic contributions; how it has been read *into* my artistic contributions; how its presence has informed the agency I experienced in creation. In McKayle's words, what are the "deep inner feelings" of my Blackness—these are the questions that rise to the surface of my thinking as I contemplate my art. Dramaturgy, for me, manifests in the fundamental source material and emergent through line of a creation and is responsible for identifying and cultivating the meaning embedded in, or unfolding through, the work in process. It expresses the ethos of that process, both informing and informed by the ever-evolving relationships between the original material being explored, its creators and/or performers, and the outside world. Ultimately, in the context of this essay, it is as much the ways in which I connect the notions of corporeality, territory, and Blackness as it is my individual navigations and negotiations as a Black artist in a creative process. Together, these notions provide the overall context for my reflections and set the stage for the ways in which I invite the reader to engage with them.

CURIOSITIES

My interrogations emerge primarily from my lived experience as a Black Jamaican woman who has enjoyed a successful career as a performer and dramaturge in a dance form that is primarily European, or at least Western in its origins. My dance training in the Martha Graham technique took place in the mid-1980s in Toronto, while the bulk of my professional career as a contemporary dance performer, teacher, and dramaturge took place over the twenty-five years I lived in Europe, throughout the 1990s and well into the 2000s. Arriving in Brussels, Belgium, at the height of what was known as the "Flemish dance wave," which had begun in the 1980s, I had the privilege to work with groundbreaking art-makers, including choreographers Alain Platel and Sidi Larbi Cherkaoui, theatre director Jan Lauwers/Needcompany, and as a singer with the "world-music" group Zap Mama. Currently, I enjoy a full-time position as associate professor in a prominent academic institution and continue to perform and to mentor artists, both locally and internationally.

In all of those contexts—with the exception of Zap Mama (we were all African diasporic women)—I experienced what it was to be the only, or one of very few, Black artist/s. The Europe I lived in seemed to pride itself on a kind of postracial mode of being in which my Blackness posed no issue. However, I was aware in Belgium that my privilege came from the fact that I did not belong to that country's colonial diaspora (the Congo or Rwanda) nor to its more recent immigrant population from the Maghreb, which suffers deep marginalization and Islamophobia. This meant that my presence in the Belgian artistic community was not provocative; rather, it assuaged any perceived need for representational diversity, notwithstanding whatever talent I was able to bring to those contexts. If anything, my light skin, Jamaican origin, and being a native English speaker were assets. It was not until I moved back to Canada and to North American sensibilities some ten years ago that I realized I had not felt "seen" for the specificity of my Black experience during those years spent in continental Europe. And, in full recognition of the complexities of the Black experience, I am not always comfortable with the heightened visibility that accompanies my Blackness in the Canadian context either.

Yet I recognize my need to embrace that complexity—the continued navigation between hyper- and invisibility; the ambivalence of wanting my specificity recognized and yet not wanting to be obliged to explain it; the need somehow for the stories my dance tells to reflect these ambivalences or perhaps simply to openly be informed by them. I am interested in the ways in which my lived experience as a Black woman from Jamaica living in Canada and Europe feeds my artistic contributions and their dramaturgies and nurtures the creative power and agency that come from my personal relational well. This for me is corporeal turf and I consider it a decidedly decolonial[1]

---

1 A term coined by sociologist Aníbal Quijano, **decoloniality** "undoes, disobeys, and delinks from this matrix [of modernity/coloniality]; constructing paths and praxis toward an otherwise of thinking, sensing, believing, doing, and living." Decoloniality is understood as a process of undoing. It is concerned with "the habits that modernity/coloniality

positioning. Honing in consciously on my own sensibilities and on the questions and ambiguities that arise from my particular Black body navigating white dance allows me to undo the layers of (colonial/white) conditioning that have been so significant to my dramaturgy.

Over the past five to ten years, there have been increasing concerns expressed by dance communities in North America and in Europe regarding the need to decolonize the art of contemporary dance—its training, its aesthetics, its creative methods, its programming and funding, who is in dance studios, who are dance audiences, etc. What is implicitly being considered in the calls for decolonization are the structural racist biases that are the legacy of Western society's development. Admittedly with some discomfort, I have often found myself wondering in what way these calls are relevant to me if I have actually enjoyed a long and successful career performing, creating and teaching contemporary dance on the international stage. What is that nagging questioning that has been with me over so many years? Yet another publicly displayed murder of a Black man—George Floyd in the summer of 2020—and the subsequent global reckonings provoked by the Black Lives Matter movement have brought me to a place of personal stock-taking and the acknowledgement that in my specific experience, decolonizing my dance includes situating my own background, i.e., addressing my Blackness and the ways in which it has been present, or not, in my artistic practice, and then speaking clearly (i.e., creating, teaching, performing) from that position. Simply "being an artist" is a universality that I have believed and aspired toward, but it does not in fact fully reflect the realities I live nor the ways in which I am perceived in various contexts.

One of the most notable experiences of my time in Europe was as a performer in Belgian creator Alain Platel's *La Tristeza Complice.* Platel's approach to creation is anchored primarily in a profound curiosity about people and the conviction that art has a social responsibility; his work does not shy away

---

implanted in all of us; with how modernity/coloniality has worked and continues to work to negate, disavow, distort and deny knowledges, subjectivities, world senses, and life visions" (Mignolo and Walsh 4). By contrast, the term decolonization refers to a shift in the power relations imposed by and through the structures of colonization.

from complicated subjects or bodies on stage. I was transformed as an artist by my experience with him and I realize that the beginning of my latent queries perhaps began with *La Tristeza*, as we called the piece. The performers enjoyed tremendous freedom throughout Platel's creative process and his talent in assembling the poetic collage of bodies and expressions that emerged was gentle and uncanny. Nevertheless, I wonder to what extent how I was "seen" could have been brought more consciously to the surface during the creative process, allowing me to embrace or refuse any projections accordingly. For example, neither during the creation nor in performance had I considered the potential impact of my duet with fellow dancer Koen Augustijnen, in which I sang "If Love's a Sweet Passion" from Henry Purcell's *The Fairy Queen* while he used his teeth to pull at my clothing and undress me. I discovered only many years later that a photograph of that scene graced the front cover of American dance studies scholar Ann Cooper Albright's 1997 book, *Choreographing Difference: The Body and Identity in Contemporary Dance*. In it she writes,

> In one section, for instance, a drag queen (played by Koen Augustijnen) repeatedly grabs a woman's body (Angélique Willkie). Pulling and picking at her skin, her hair and her clothes, he seems at once abusive and yet also desirous of becoming her. Watching a white man touch a black woman in such an abusive manner emphasized her passivity and at first I felt very uncomfortable with the sexual and racial politics of this scene. Nonetheless, these politics were complicated by the fact that this man was wearing a bra and lipstick, as well as the fact that he had earlier been the object of sexual harassment. In addition, the woman endured the whole event while doggedly singing a slow ballad. While I found the work to be disturbingly ambiguous at times like this, I also found it powerful and compelling. (xx–xxi)

Koen and I did not intentionally explore the dynamics of race or gender or passivity. What our respective corporealities represented in that moment together transcended any initial objective on our parts—and perhaps also Platel's. It is clear from Albright's reflections (who read the situation and our bodies as a white American woman steeped in the historical race relations of that country) that the kind of ambiguity and complexity that I am ultimately interested in exploring *as Blackness* was present in this scene—in spite of my lack of awareness.

My perspective was that of a Jamaican Canadian Belgian dancer who grew up in a context where most people looked like me or, at least, were all considered Jamaicans alike. Self-identification according to race was not a way of positioning myself in the Jamaica of my youth; social class and poverty were more significant as ways of being situated in that society. Immigrating to Canada with my family at the age of fifteen was a first introduction to me being seen as Black; but even if I had to deal with the realities of becoming a minority, I fortunately did not experience much direct racism. Coming from a relatively comfortable upper-middle-class background, I grew up believing I could do and be whatever I committed to, no matter where or amongst whom that took place. Some fourteen years later, I arrived in Belgium where I seemed not to be considered the same kind of "Black" as I had been in North America. It was another phase in my migratory past that has forcibly been characterized by adaptation, (successful) attempts at assimilation, and a certain hybridity. This meant a kind of identitylessness and convenient anonymity in Belgium that no doubt contributed to the freedom I felt to explore and to own whatever emerged in the creative process of *La Tristeza*, regardless of any other potentially contextual factors. If anything, I identified with Platel's concern for marginalized populations through the lens of the so-called haves and have nots, but not through the arbitrary signification that is race.

As I think back to my contemporary dance experiences at that point, I realize that since I still did not think of myself as a *Black* dancer, neither did I imagine that Blackness would be the lens through which others would see me. I naively thought I would simply be seen as a dancer—hopefully a good one. So I played! I had a bald head, so I wore a wig. I liked to sing, so we explored ways of making that complicated. I thought of women I had seen in European train stations, and those hidden on sidewalks and street corners I knew as a child. I wore their clothes and tried to disappear as they did. Koen was a heterosexual man with long hair, so he played dress-up and his transvestite character emerged. We liked working together, so we did. There was no particular conversation between us nor with Platel regarding the meaning-making we were engaged in—no shared reflections on our differences in race, sexuality, or gender. He simply left us the space to explore. The magic of Platel's work for me is its complex and yet simple humanity, its love affair with the minutiae of people, something I believe, in part, emerges from his confidence in the strange and wordless intuitions that constitute a successful collective artistic encounter.

Nevertheless, there is something about the agency of deliberateness that now holds my interest. Addressing possible interpretations of my creative interventions—knowing of course that it is impossible to predict the reactions of an audience—might have allowed me to fully invest my place in the evolving dramaturgy of that creative process. This current path of questioning is as much about my desire to interrogate how we function in dance creation as it is an opportunity for me to fully embrace my own artistico-political *raisons d'être* and the reality that my Black performer body is a socially and politically charged site that cannot be separated from meaning, creative content, or dramaturgical contribution.

DRAMATURGY IN DANCE

The practice of dramaturgy in dance, or how we make what we make, in my opinion, is fundamentally linked to the question of why we make what we make. When dramaturgical practice engages critically, it questions the concept of choreography, the process of creation, what is dance, the relationship to the audience, the body, the agency of the performer versus that of the choreographer, etc. There is no one way to practise dramaturgy. There are as many dramaturgies as there are processes, and it is a fundamentally artisanal discipline. Its becoming happens only by its doing. There is no positivist theory of dramaturgy, there is no instruction booklet; already, defining it is a subjective exercise. It is as experiential as it is experimental. I adhere to Flemish dance dramaturge pioneer Marianne Van Kerkhoven's suggestion that dramaturgy is not a truth that is imposed on a creation, but rather a constantly evolving thought process that is specific to each context. She described her practice as follows:

> The kind of dramaturgy that I am familiar with has nothing to do with the "concept dramaturgy" that has been in vogue in German theater since Brecht. [. . .] The kind of dramaturgy that I feel connected with, and that I have tried to apply in both theater and dance, has a "process" character: one chooses to work with materials of various origins (texts, movements, film images, objects, ideas, etc.); the "human material" (the actors/dancers) is decidedly the most important; the personality of the performers is considered as the foundation of the creation rather than their technical abilities. The director or choreographer sets to work with these materials; during the rehearsal process he/she observes how these materials behave and develop; only at the end of this process does a concept, a structure, a more or less defined form slowly emerge; this final structure is not known from the beginning. (qtd. in Cools 90)

Van Kerkhoven's reference to working with "human material" does not specifically suggest the broader notion of corporeality as I have expressed it here, nor does it address the agency that I hold dear in the idea of corporeal turf. However, her emphasis on "process" and on "working with materials of various origins" certainly suggests that dramaturgical practice has the potential to engage with what I would describe as corporeally sourced creative content (versus simple movement or theatrical exploration). Dramaturgy, as I know it, is a practice of listening, observation, improvisation, and sometimes provocation. Its form is fluid, by nature constantly adapting to its context, and it includes all facets of the creation. The emergent character of dramaturgy is rooted in the fact that its process, its reflection, its articulation, are intimately linked to live artistic exploration and therefore, potentially, to the sensibilities, propensities, and capacities of all individuals involved in the creative process. There is little doubt that considering "all individuals involved" goes counter to the usual hierarchies embedded in the creative process, which give clear priority to the vision of the choreographer. However, the development of decolonial dramaturgies relies precisely on meeting the challenge to not only allow but to facilitate and encourage the agency and opacity[2] of the performers.

According to Cathy Turner and Synne Behrndt, dramaturgy is always in progress, open to the disruptions caused by both rehearsal and performance (5). The possibility for disruption in and of itself implies a dynamic, contextual, and even political dimension to dramaturgical practice. It is this political potential of dramaturgy—in my opinion, a necessary ethos—that is of particular significance with regard to the socio-political charge, content, context that I believe is borne by and within each performer's relational body. Beyond their creative skills, it is this wider context that influences how they resonate with ideas, themes, or propositions, and I suggest that dramaturgy should not abstract these resonances from that wider context. My interest lies in how relational dramaturgies can become, or perhaps need to become, an active point of departure for creation. By encouraging the contextual threads that weave around and through my Black-woman corporeality to actively inform the creative process and its content, the stories that my dance tells have a better chance of speaking through my own sensibilities and agency, even alongside or in service of the vision of the choreographer. This is the basis for what I consider the corporeal dramaturgy of the performer: at the micro level it is the body within the piece; at the macro level, it is the body in its larger socio-political context.

WHAT BODIES?

The body is central to my understanding of and relationship to artistic creation. The intrinsic logic of dance implies the specific contribution of the bodies of the performers. As a young dancer, the approaches to technical training that I was exposed to were essentially based on the movement vocabularies of particular choreographers (Graham, José Limón, Lester Horton,

2 According to Édouard Glissant, the notion of opacity is a conceptual justification for irreducibility, for inexplicability, for the right to non-transparent difference (see his *Poetics of Relation*). I will come back to this notion in more detail later in the essay.

Merce Cunningham, etc.) and the dancer's primary objective was to perfect these proposed forms to be reproduced in choreography. That capacity to reproduce movement in the spirit of the choreographer's authorial signature is what defined a "good" dancer. (I did not consider my formative training in Jamaican folk dance of any significance at all at this point!) Improvisation—understood as my own movement research and exploration—was a distinctly different skill that did not seem pertinent to me because I did not imagine myself needing to develop my own choreographic vocabulary. In contrast, most of today's creative processes are almost entirely dependent on the dancers' improvisations, either as the performance material or, at the very least, to generate it. Recent creations I have been involved in either as performer or dramaturge have worked with scores and/or the negotiation of tasks, actively avoiding any aesthetics of sameness or exactitude and relying on individual and unique responses from each performer to the choreographic propositions. Nevertheless, as has been the case throughout most of my dance adventure, there is a certain dismissal or invisibility of my socially inscribed, racialized body in the different creative discourses, as if it has been unimportant relative to my talents and contributions. My status as a woman has been more evidently manifest and discussed, but my body in the world as a Black woman disappears when, in fact, that intersectional reality is critical to my relational body, its very specific relationship to the world, and to the stories it tells.

In *J'ai pleuré avec les chiens*, Canadian choreographer Daina Ashbee's work for the 2020 edition of Montreal's Festival TransAmériques (cancelled due to the pandemic), the program notes speak to the fact that the piece assembles five women between the ages of twenty-four and fifty-eight (myself) ("J'ai pleuré avec les chiens"). There is no mention of our ethnic backgrounds, but the reality is that I was the only non-white performer in the work of an Indigenous choreographer renowned for powerfully intimate performances using nudity and a certain violence in the movement propositions—I wonder about history; I wonder about the presence of my older, naked Black body alongside four younger white women; I wonder about "invisibility."

In July 2018, Quebec theatre director Robert Lepage created the production *SLĀV* for the Montreal Jazz Festival and it had to be cancelled. The production featured a predominantly white cast dressed in slave costumes, singing traditional African American songs and picking cotton. Audiences and critics rallied behind the binary notions of colour-blindness and cultural appreciation on the one hand, versus cultural appropriation and racism on the other. Lepage claimed that *SLĀV* was based on the foundations of theatrical practice. For him, that meant "to slip into the skin of the other in order to try to understand it. And, by the same, perhaps also to understand oneself." He continues, "From the moment that we are no longer allowed to slip into the skin of the other, where we are forbidden to recognize ourselves in the other, theater is distorted, prevented from performing its primary function and loses its reason for being" ("Annulation de *SLĀV*").

In reaction to the controversy, sociologist Myrlande Pierre talked about the expression of a "social malaise" and the fact that, in the context of *SLĀV*, a social and political charge was totally obscured in the final result of that performance, notwithstanding the noble intentions of its creators. There was a notable deficit in representation of the persons historically concerned by the production's dramaturgy and content. By persons concerned, I underline bodies concerned—the history of slavery is not disembodied. In this situation the body of the performer could not be seen as either neutral or universal. "Slipping into the skin of the other" was not an arbitrary exercise. An in-depth exploration of colour-blindness and postracialism is beyond the scope of this essay; suffice to say that, in my opinion, this particular example of cultural appreciation falsely depoliticized the bodies of both Black and white performers in a way that dissociated them from their broader lived, socio-political contexts and the power dynamics that are embedded in those contexts. Ironically, the two Black singers in the cast of *SLĀV* had to "leave their Blackness at the door" so to speak in order to universalize the entirety of the cast and content into a purely musical experience. As it turned out, the objections to the production revealed that the dramaturgies of these relational bodies could not be subsumed by an "abstract" and unrooted dramaturgy, and that perhaps performance and its creative processes need to move toward greater accountability with regard to their political situatedness.

As much as I am advocating for a deeper engagement with Black corporeality in dramaturgical thinking, I must also admit to a certain ambivalence with regard to its concrete manifestations in the creative process and how that might affect my agency. Did the Black (or even the white!) singers in *SLĀV* feel the need (and, if so, have the space) to express any concerns they might have had? Perhaps engaging in the project without hesitation was in fact an expression of agency! The social inscriptions on bodies cannot be erased, so my queries relate to how we acknowledge them in our art of the body and to what extent I/we have the agency to resist or to play with those projections in/through creation. In the case of Platel's *La Tristeza Complice* and Ann Cooper Albright's reading of the scene described, it's hard to say that I would necessarily have made a different choice with regard to the proposition had I imagined the impact for an audience of a white transvestite picking away at my Black female body. However, I might have felt significantly empowered to have been able to engage in a conversation about possible interpretations and/or even intentions on my part or that of the choreographer, particularly in the context of collaborative creation.

ACTS OF AGENCY

The collaborative creative process is one of mutual and consenting appropriation. It is what Marcus Boon calls "acts of possession and dispossession," and these acts take place throughout any artistic collaboration—they revolve around ideas, movements, personal stories, language, and a multiplicity of individual intentions and histories. This creative appropriation—i.e., possession and dispossession of creative material—can be considered legitimate in a situation where all parties begin by contributing from their acknowledged and respective turf. Any other situation becomes one in which power relationships, however well-intentioned, however invisible, are skewed. What does this imply for a choreographic dramaturgy? What is the performer's particular turf? As a Black dance artist, what have I brought into creations that I "possess(ed)," that I knew, and how was that recognized? What agency did this give me in those creative processes?

Confession Publique, a solo co-created with choreographer Mélanie Demers in 2021, has come to exemplify for me a performance that not only emerges from my corporeal turf, but also enhances the depth and scope of that turf as a source of dramaturgy, in the true sense of meaning-making—for me as performer as well as for the coherence of the work. As mentioned earlier, I see the corporeal dramaturgy of the performer as operating at both micro and macro levels—i.e., my body in the piece as well as that body in its broader societal context. In the case of *Confession Publique*, the micro and macro are inextricably intertwined. As the source material for the performance content, my corporeality is both the storyteller and the stories told. There is no decontextualization of my relational body from its broader web of influences and projections. In fact, on the contrary, we play wittingly with that web for its dramaturgical content—for example, the impact of displaying my older, Black, naked woman body on a platform reminiscent of the display of slaves or of the Hottentot Venus; or not allowing my (Black woman) voice to be heard by the audience as it is drowned out at various points in the performance. During the process, I engaged in acts of creative possession and dispossession as described by Boon in constant negotiation with the choreographer—my body, my stories, my willingness, my limits, what I felt I was ready to "give" to the process, what I felt needed to remain my secret garden, but all with the clear recognition that the choreographic craft was Demers's to hone. The result is an ode to agency and to opacity and to the power of my Blackness to speak for itself as dramaturgy.

The particular mix of my morphology, age, racial and ethnocultural origins, gender, relationship to my artistic disciplines, physical abilities, injuries, and, equally, the historical, institutional, political, and sociocultural contexts that inform my sensibilities, my personal and artistic perceptions that influence the ways in which I am perceived by choreographers and audiences—all of this (and more) constitutes the material from which my creation emerges. It is also the reality to which my creation speaks. Creating with, or rather from, an individual dramaturgy implies, for me, creating from a place of territorial corporeality, of turf, of agency, of opacity—none of these is neutral; none is universal.

WHEN AGENCY IS ABSENT

What might be an aesthetics of neutrality? Of universality? Of agency or its lack? The classical ballet of the French court was perhaps the summum of colonial normativity, privileging (white) non-differentiated, idealized (presumably universal) forms and bodies, rather than any differentiated individual content. It relied on a visual aesthetic rather than the kind of visceral humanity that Donald McKayle referred to in his 1973 interview. Describing the modernist conception of the subject as predicated on vision, art historian and theorist Amelia Jones writes that the "I" of the subject was a disembodied eye that turned all bodies into objects (37). One consequence of the prevalence of the disembodied visual was the othering of those who were visibly different, with little or no recognition of their individual subjectivity.

Saartjie Baartman, infamously exhibited as the Hottentot Venus throughout nineteenth century Europe for her steatopygic buttocks and genitalia is perhaps the penultimate example of a dehumanized performing Black woman "other," reduced to objecthood and denied all agency (there is some polemic as to whether or not she had agreed to being exhibited but with or without her consent, the dehumanization and objectification remain).[3] This imposition of an abject lack of subjectivity, of inner self, of turf, was the territory of the "other." It was in no way similar to the glamorous lack of individuality of the classical ballet reserved for white, universally normalized bodies.

This odd contradiction between the glorified anonymity and (white) sameness of a French court *Swan Lake* corps de ballet versus the degrading anonymity and vilified (Black) difference of a Saartjie Baartman is one that continues to haunt my thinking. One is chosen, the other imposed; one is

3 The fascination with Baartman's buttocks was so far-reaching that it is credited for the origin of the Victorian bustle dress, popular among upper-class women in the nineteenth century: "The origins of this accessory have an arguably complex history that is rooted in the exploitation of Black women. Specifically, the bustle is arguably directly inspired by Black body types. Through the repulsion and desire of Black women in European society, the bustle quickly became a staple among the elite" (Jackson).

reminiscent of light, purity, and transparency, the other of strangeness, inferiority, and even non-humanness. What we recognize as dance aesthetics have their origins in the evolution of this perception of bodies and its influence on universalized (white) dance, from the colonial period and its modernity through to postmodern and ultimately contemporary times. Despite a greater diversity of bodies being increasingly present (and still not sufficiently!), the frames of reference, both aesthetic and dramaturgical, do not inherently reflect the historico-cultural imaginaries of these "other" corporealities. Rather, in order to correspond (read: fit in), there has been a tacit understanding that they/we will adopt the universalized values that invisibilize our difference (read: invalidate our lived experience). This is yet another kind of anonymity—not glorified, not degrading, but abstracted, decontextualized, dehistoricized, made transparent. My need for decolonial dramaturgies sits here—i.e., in my desire to revisit, unabstract, and recontextualize my own story in all of its relational rootedness.

With specific relevance for the myth of universality, Miguel Gutierrez, a successful dance artist, is still provoked to wonder:

> How did I come to be colonized? And how did I find out that I had been colonized? Have I found out? . . . How did whiteness become, I shudder even to write this, safety—a lack of feeling, a lack of allegiances. It made space, or at least I thought it did, for me. For a me that had no history . . . Who has the right not to explain themselves? The people who don't have to. The ones whose subjectivities have been naturalized.

Corporeal turf is, in a way, a response to the need to explain myself in order to fully exist, and yet, at the same time, to have agency over what is explained and how it is done—if at all. Édouard Glissant's notion of opacity is a preciously useful lens. The Martinican philosopher advocates for an openness to the unknown, an unpredictability, and, ultimately, a non-transparency that is neither anonymous nor decontextualized. Speaking to difference as it is habitually "measured" or categorized, Glissant writes, "If we examine the process of 'understanding' people and ideas from the perspective of Western thought, we discover that its basis is this requirement for transparency" (189). He explains transparency as the need to reduce according to a scale of one's own reference: "I relate it to my norm. I admit you to existence, within my system. I create you afresh." He continues: "But perhaps we need to bring an end to the very notion of a scale. Displace all reduction" (190). Opacity becomes what he considers a "rightful" escape from supposed legitimacy and, by extension, from the Eurocentric criteria that define that legitimacy.

CONSTRUCTIVE OPACITIES

Glissant makes a critical contribution to my reflections on Blackness in particular but, also, to how I consider the potential of and responsibilities embedded in dramaturgical practice. What has been considered legitimate for Black bodies in dance has to a large extent been either "reduced" to a place of invisibility and assimilation into the universalizing aesthetics of Western concert dance, or exoticized as hypervisible "other" kinds of dance (for example, so-called African, ethnic, urban, and street dance, etc.—often considered neither professional nor concert-worthy). As calls for decolonization, antiracism, and equity in dance continue to manifest, what is dramaturgy's responsibility? How can we see the creative process and its eventual outcomes differently? It seems to me that the first step requires that we see the performers differently—that we allow their relational bodies to be an integral part of the process rather than secondary to it; that we invite a lack of "transparency" into our aesthetics and our modes of operation; that we renounce the illusion of universality and sameness in favour of real encounters with other historico-cultural imaginaries and lived experiences.

In his volume *Embodied Avatars: Genealogies of Black Feminist Art and Performance*, Uri McMillan looks at strategies for agency among Black women performers from the nineteenth century through to the present. Through the creation of so-called avatars, these women use their status as "performing objects" to gain empowerment and/or communicate a message that would otherwise go unheard. One of those artists is Lorraine O'Grady, an upper-middle-class daughter of Jamaican immigrants, in her late eighties at the time of this publication. In her own writing, she describes her illusions of living in a postracial America being shattered in 1980 by an encounter with a white performance artist who wore blackface. O'Grady was, in her words, "transformed from post black to black." This shift in the way she situated her identity is compelling. What brings us into Blackness? For me, it was not only George Floyd's murder that brought me into my Blackness; it was watching my two Black teenagers recognize with confusion and horror that their Black bodies were less worthy in our society. That was my call to arms, manifesting in extensive antiracism work at my university and a deep dive into the place of my Blackness in my art form.

O'Grady's work focuses mainly on representations of Black female subjectivity and issues surrounding the erasure and invisibility of difference. She explores notions of territory and proprietorship of the Black body, particularly female, and its role in her exercise of subjective agency. She became concerned with what she considered postmodernism's oversimplifications of social reality, which she felt relocated subjectivity away from the body and in favour of history in a way that conveniently continued to serve those in power. She argues that the body undoubtedly received the effects of that history and was shaped by them and that it forcibly remains the location of resistance. In response to a comment by a "non-artist acquaintance" that "avant-garde art doesn't have anything to do with Black people," O'Grady took her camera to the "largest Black space she could think of"—the African American Day Parade in the streets of Harlem, New York—to document the crowds for her series *Art is . . .* Fifteen Black actors and dancers, all dressed in white and travelling through the streets on a gold-fabric-covered float, reached out to the excited onlookers and had them pose inside empty gold picture frames. The piece spoke for itself.

She described it to a journalist:

> It's funny. The organizers of the parade were totally mystified by me and by the performance. The announcer made fun of the float as it passed the reviewing stand: "They tell me this is art, but you know

> the Studio Museum? I don't understand that stuff." But the people on the parade route got it. Everywhere there were shouts of: "That's right. That's what art is. *We're* the art!" And, "Frame ME, make ME art!" It was amazing. (O'Grady and Roth)

O'Grady's motivation for her *Art is . . .* project was to counter the idea that avant-garde art was irrelevant to Black people—not unlike Gutierrez's query that appears as the title of his article: Does abstraction belong to white people? Both artists understood the message that to participate in abstract avant-garde art meant NOT being Black or a person of colour because those realities and sensibilities have no place in that world; to be present there can only mean invisibly or as someone fully assimilated. The territory of the Black body therefore—Black people's corporeal turf—cannot be seen outside of the context of some level of resistance. Whether it is in defiance of imposed conditions of exclusion or invisibilization, objectification, and hypervisibilization, or even if it is an expression of joy, Black people's art becomes an opportunity to manipulate their subjective identities—a gesture of both art and agency.

In her reflections on the Black gaze, Black studies scholar Tina Campt describes how contemporary Black artists are pushing the boundaries of the simple representation of Black presence in art in favour of Black "livingness" (a term I borrow from Canadian Black studies scholar Katherine McKittrick[4]): "Here the radical question they are posing is: rather than looking *at* Black people, rather than simply multiplying the representation of Black folks, what would it mean to *see oneself through* the complex positionality that is blackness—and work through its implications on and for oneself?" (Campt 7, emphasis in original).

4 McKittrick's own words are best suited to define "Black livingness": "Telling, sharing, listening to, and hearing stories are relational and interdisciplinary acts that are animated by all sorts of people, places, narrative devices, theoretical queries, plots. The process is sustained by invention and wonder. The story has no answers. The stories offer an aesthetic relationality that relies on the dynamics of creating-narrating-listening-hearing-reading-and-sometimes-unhearing. The stories do not offer lucid tales or answers; rather, they signal ways of living in a world that denies black humanity (or, more aptly, the stories signal ways of black livingness)" (6–7).

Corporeal turf is about me cultivating my Black gaze, one that "shifts the optics of 'looking at' to a politics of *looking with, through, and alongside*" (Campt 7, emphasis in original) according to criteria that I determine. This is the basis for the decolonial dramaturgies that I am interested in generating at the micro level and being able to facilitate at the macro level; dramaturgies that emerge from and speak to Black "livingness" and that allow me to explore aesthetics and imaginaries that do not reflect any supposed universality.

OPAQUE BODIES

How do we decolonize the gaze? How do we undo the complex signification of skin without undoing the value of each individual's lived experience or indulging in tokenism? In his 2018 article mentioned earlier, Gutierrez recalls a comment made to a friend about the dance scene in New York City:

> I say how my current frustration is the lack of people of color in downtown dance artists' work. "Well, that's just who's in the community," she answers, unquestioningly, as if the white choreographers' casting choices have nothing to do with subjectivity or representational politics. That somehow their bodies can be signifiers for a universal experience that doesn't need to look at whiteness as an act of choice or as the default mechanism of a lazy, non-existent critique.

In the same way that this whiteness is an act of choice that privileges universal signification and transparency, (my equivalent of "lazy, non-existent critique"), so is working from and through Blackness a choice to prioritize specificity, opacity, and agency. But this is a long and convoluted lesson for dance.

The presumed universality of white corporealities finds its logical extension in the idea of a "natural body," and this notion, in turn, has played a significant role in the development of contemporary dance aesthetics and training. Crucial to the field of somatics as well as to the pedestrian movement vocabulary that anchored postmodern dance (the precursor to contemporary dance), the notion of the natural body is ridden with the fundamental values and politics of very specific, essentially white, sociocultural contexts. "Theorizing movement as a cultural site of meaning making," Doran George recounts that the "natural body" and its desirability emerged out of a white post–Second World War America filled with liberal ideologies and the rejection of authoritarianism (5). In the context of dance, this manifested in a shift away from the more prescriptive regimes of classical ballet and modern techniques (Graham, Limón, Cunningham, Horton) in favour of the perceived freedom and authenticity of natural, apparently aesthetic-free movement, epitomized by the famous Judson Dance Theater of early 1960s New York. A founding member of the Judson collective, Yvonne Rainer's "No Manifesto" appeared in 1965 as a call to the non-spectacular, to ordinariness as a thing of value. But not all bodies lived the same "ordinary"; not all bodies enjoyed the same "natural."

Black corporealities experienced a distinctly different reality in this period: in the United States it was still the heights (or depths) of the civil rights movement, with bus segregation only made unconstitutional in 1956 and the voting-rights act guaranteeing unfettered voter registration for Black voters only being passed in 1965. Across the oceans, many former slave colonies (including Jamaica) were fighting for independence from their former colonial powers in the 1960s, and the last human zoo exhibiting Black African families was closed in Brussels, Belgium, in 1958 after the world expo. At the same time, on both sides of the Atlantic, a complex (colonial) fascination with "things black" had Black music, Black dances, Black athletes, and Black style become the objects of hypervisible commodification, while often invisibilizing the very bodies that generated them. From Josephine Baker's "banana dance" (admittedly she was idolized rather than invisibilized) to Elvis Presley's borrowed dance moves to the subsequent globalization of breakdance and hip hop, Black "natural" has been desired and appropriated, leaving so many Black bodies hyped and stereotyped or forgotten and unrecognized. At the dawn of the "natural body" that anchors somatics and postmodern dance, it seems unlikely that Black bodies would have been able to identify with, much less indulge in, the perceived freedom and authenticity of natural aesthetic-free movement, appreciating the ordinariness of the (white) natural body. Any expectation that they should have been able to ultimately denies the realities of their lived experience, invisibilizing them and ignoring the subject matter, methods of creation, and aesthetics that could actually honour a Black gaze in Tina Campt's terms.

ALTERNATIVE DRAMATURGIES

Harking back to Gutierrez's reflection on the "safety of whiteness" as a place where he "had no history," I am reminded that invisibility through assimilation does not mean I am/we are seen. Few people seek to make themselves invisible beyond the survival strategies made necessary by hypervisibility. Blending into whiteness, dehistoricizing oneself is about the need to survive. This erasure includes rejection of one's own spaces, places, and stories. Not appreciating my formative training in Jamaican folk dance and, instead, stretching my feet under Canadian radiators in order to improve my arch speaks to the inheritances of Western dance aesthetics and values that I integrated without question—as if they were universal markers for the body, for culture, for art. In the context of dance and dance-making, if differences are respected, heard, honoured, how can there be universality in bodies? How do we acknowledge the undeniable intersectional realities of subjectivity, race, gender, age, and sexuality among others that we contend with in our society and allow them to not only be present (i.e., represented) in our art, but to actually *inform* the art? Holding the realities of racialized invisibility in dance at the forefront, Gutierrez addresses this admirably: "Am I a subject or a vessel, an agent or a channel?" The disruptive political potential of dramaturgical practices is perhaps a disruptive political responsibility if we are to further develop decolonial approaches to dramaturgy.

Acknowledging my corporeal turf and creating from that place allows me to consider a dramaturgical praxis that uses my Blackness as its principal lens. By a lens of Blackness I mean a perspective that recognizes the nature of Black lived experience as specific, expressive of a different socio-political and cultural reality, of different imaginaries, and therefore deserving of closer attention in both the content and dynamics of the choreographic process.

My reflections on the performativity of Black corporeality come from my experience of the socio-political and cultural charge that is inherent to the dramaturgy of the Black performer in a white dance world.

Performer and scholar E. Patrick Johnson writes,

> The interanimation of blackness and performance necessitates the codification of this relationship through intellectual inquiry . . . Black performance has been a sustaining and galvanizing force of black culture and a contributor to world culture at large . . . Similarly marginalized as the black bodies with which it is associated, black performance, while always embedded within institutionally sanctioned and privileged forms of performance, has often been neglected as an intellectual site of inquiry. (447)

Thinking about Black performance in this broader sense suggested by Johnson, I see the potential for Blackness as a method or praxis to enter contemporary choreographic processes beyond simple representation and identity, and consider how it might further inform decolonial dramaturgies, i.e., dramaturgies that explore alternative ways of meaning-making and logics for creation. Choreographer Ligia Lewis, whose work is deeply influenced by Black feminist thinking, comments on her performance, *minor matter*, which began as a response to the Black Lives Matter movement in 2016:

> Can you abstract a black body, and should you? . . . Although I am entirely engaged with the materiality of the body, looking at it through the lens of just formal abstraction is difficult. I prefer layered activities that engage a process of thinking in real time and inviting that into the work—making work thick and messy, rather than clean and beautiful . . . This idea of creating something from nothing is the backbone . . . Making something from nothing, for me, is a very hopeful gesture, despite seeming otherwise—and when I look especially at dance history, from a Western perspective, we don't have anything to look back on, because we've been written

> out of history. How do I try to make something from nothing? . . . I often think how to alleviate bodies of color from having to represent more than they can. That's why the voice is so important inside of this work, and this interrogation of subjectivity is so important. I try to get away from any identitarian stance in relationship to this, and arrive at something that's more slippery, and that's potentially more nuanced. I want to work through this notion of difference, multiplicity . . . Especially when you deal with race, everyone wants you to have a stance. I think a position is important, but to have an answer? . . . We're in a place where all of us just need to be in the process of asking more and more questions, and inviting problems into the work. (qtd. in Gastineau)

Lewis's observations of mess and multiplicity are reminiscent of Donald McKayle's diversity and deep inner feelings—McKayle's viscerality is Lewis's thick swamp. Alluding to Glissant and his reflections on transparence and opacity, the visceral mess is not resolution-thick; it is quagmire-thick. It requires wading through process and product differently (and difficultly!), acknowledging, even welcoming to be lost, to disappear, to be irrelevant, to survive, to fantasize, to "future" (the verb!), to "diasporically spider."[5]

There is a necessity to continue interrogating our dance and its capacity to speak to, through, and alongside our collective imaginaries—past, present, and beyond. The founder of the field of cultural studies and fellow Jamaican, Stuart Hall, wrote that

> . . . identities are about questions of using the resources of history, language and culture in the process of becoming rather than

5 In her article, "Diasporic Spidering: Constructing Contemporary Black Identities," dance artist and scholar Nadine George-Graves uses the metaphor of the Anansi spider—originally from today's Ghana and present in various forms throughout the African diaspora—to explore contemporary Black identities: "The multidirectional process by which people of African descent define their lives. The lifelong ontological gathering of information by going out into the world and coming back to the self" (33).

> being. Not who we are or where we came from so much as what we might become, how we have been represented and how that bears on how we might represent ourselves. Identities are therefore constituted within, not outside representation. Above all, identities are constructed through, not outside difference. (4)

How I explore my Black corporeality and offer it in public performance informs what it can become, and that is its potential universality—the sharing of my intimate specificity in representational forms that speak to and from my turf. This is where the dramaturgy really happens—in the place of decoloniality; this is where dramaturgical practice is at its full disruptive potential. Contemporary dance has an obligation to consider all possible opportunities to reflect on its aesthetics, modes of operation, and value systems—most of which speak primarily to its social and ethnocultural origins rather than to the range of experiences of its current practitioners. Our art must dare to explore other conceptual imaginaries and, consequently, dramaturgies. I offer this essay as a humble contribution to this ongoing and necessary process.

WORKS CITED

Albright, Ann Cooper. *Choreographing Difference: The Body and Identity in Contemporary Dance*. Wesleyan UP, 1997.

"Annulation de SLĀV: Robert Lepage dénonce 'l'affligeant discours d'intolérance.'" *Radio-Canada*, 6 Jul. 2018, ici.radio-canada.ca/nouvelle/1111157/culture-slav-robert-lepage-reaction.

Boon, Marcus. "On Appropriation." Marcus Boon, 1 Sep. 2007, marcusboon.com/on-appropriation/.

Campt, Tina M. *A Black Gaze: Artists Changing How We See*. MIT, 2021.

Cools, Guy. "De la dramaturgie du corps en danse." *Jeu: Revue de Théâtre*, vol. 116, no. 3, 2005, pp. 89–95.

Gastineau, Emily. "Minor Matter: An Interview with Ligia Lewis." Temporary Art Review, 22 Jun. 2016, temporaryartreview.com /minor-matter-an-interview-with-ligia-lewis/.

George, Doran. *The Natural Body in Somatics Dance Training*. Edited by Susan Leigh Foster, Oxford UP, 2020.

George-Graves, Nadine. "Diasporic Spidering: Constructing Contemporary Black Identities." *Black Performance Theory*, edited by Thomas F. DeFrantz and Anita Gonzalez, Duke UP, 2014, pp. 33–44.

Glissant, Édouard. *Poetics of Relation*. Translated by Betsy Wing, U of Michigan P, 1997.

Gutierrez, Miguel. "Does Abstraction Belong to White People? Thinking the Politics of Race in Contemporary Dance." *BOMB Magazine*, 7 Nov. 2018, bombmagazine.org/articles/miguel-gutierrez-1/.

Hall, Stuart. "Introduction: Who Needs 'Identity'?" *Questions of Cultural Identity*, edited by Hall and Paul duGay, Sage, 1996, pp. 1–17.

Jackson, Effie. "Saartjie Baartman, Victorians, and Bustles: A Hidden History." *Art & Object*, 19 Jan. 2023, artandobject.com/news /saartjie-baartman-victorians-and-bustles-hidden-history.

"J'ai pleuré avec les chiens." *Festival TransAmériques*, 2020, fta.ca/archive /jai-pleuré-avec-les-chiens-annulé.

Johnson, E. Patrick. "Black Performance Studies: Genealogies, Politics, Futures." *The SAGE Handbook of Performance Studies*, edited by D. Soyini Madison and Judith Hamera, Sage, 2005, p. 446–63.

Jones, Amelia. *Body Art/Performing the Subject*. U of Minnesota P, 1998.

McKittrick, Katherine. *Dear Science and Other Stories*. Duke UP, 2021.

McMillan, Uri. *Embodied Avatars: Genealogies of Black Feminist Art and Performance*. NYU P, 2015.

Mignolo, Walter D., and Catherine E. Walsh. *On Decoloniality: Concepts, Analytics, and Praxis*. Duke UP, 2018.

O'Grady, Lorraine. "This Will Have Been: My 1980s." *Lorraine O'Grady*, 2012, lorraineogrady.com/wp-content/uploads/2015/11/Lorraine-OGrady_This-Will-Have-Been-My-1980s_Art-Journal.pdf.

O'Grady, Lorraine, and Moira Roth. "Statement for Moira Roth re *Art Is . . .* " *Lorraine O'Grady*, 2007, lorraineogrady.com/wp-content/uploads/2015/11/Lorraine-OGrady_Statement-for-Moira-Roth-re-Art-Is_Unpublished.pdf. Unpublished correspondence.

Pierre, Myrlande. "La résonance d'un profond malaise social." Le Devoir, 30 Jul. 2018, ledevoir.com/opinion/libre-opinion/533450/la-resonance-d-un-profond-malaise-social.

Rainer, Yvonne. "No Manifesto." 1965. *Kenmore-Town of Tonawanda UFSD*, ktufsd.org/cms/lib/NY19000262/Centricity/Domain/116/No%20Manifesto.pdf.

"Turf." *Merriam-Webster*, merriam-webster.com/dictionary/turf.

Turner, Cathy, and Synne Behrndt. *Dramaturgy and Performance*. Palgrave Macmillan, 2008.

ABOUT THE CONTRIBUTORS

Natalie Álvarez is Professor of Theatre and Performance Studies and Associate Dean of Scholarly, Research and Creative Activities in The Creative School at Toronto Metropolitan University. She is the author, editor, and co-editor of five books, most recently *Theatre & War* (Metheun/Bloomsbury, 2023), *Sustainable Tools for Precarious Times: Performance Actions in the Americas* (Palgrave, 2019; winner of ATHE's Excellence in Editing Award), and *Immersions in Cultural Difference: Tourism, War, Performance* (U of Michigan P, 2018; winner of the Ann Saddlemyer Award). She is also the incoming co-editor of the *Theatre &* book series with Metheun/Bloomsbury. Her research focuses on immersive simulations in the public sphere, Latina/o/x performance, and performance activism in the Americas. She is also Principal Investigator of the SSHRC Insight study "Scenario Training to Improve Police Response to Individuals in Mental Crisis: Impacts and Efficacy" and co-lead of the Ministry of the Solicitor General–commissioned Mental Health and Crisis Response Education and Applied Training Program (MHCR), developed into a virtual reality program, which is now mandatory training for all police officers in Ontario.

Serouj "Midus" Aprahamian is Assistant Professor of Dance at the University of Illinois, Urbana-Champaign. He has been active in breaking, popping, and underground hip-hop dance styles since the late 1990s and has travelled throughout the world teaching, performing, and judging community-based events. He is the author of *The Birth of Breaking: Hip-Hop History from the Floor Up* (Bloomsbury, 2023) and his scholarly writings have appeared in the *Journal of Black Studies*, *Dance Research Journal*, IASPM *Journal*, and *The Oxford Handbook of Hip Hop Dance Studies* (Oxford UP, 2022).

Seika Boye is a writer, scholar, educator, and artist whose practices revolve around dance, movement, Blackness, archives and museums, and embodied pedagogies. She is Assistant Professor and Founder/Director of the non-curricular Institute for Dance Studies, Centre for Drama, Theatre and Performance Studies at the University of Toronto. Seika has worked as a professional modern/postmodern dance artist, as an archives and publishing assistant at Dance Collection Danse, and as a dance writer and editor. Dedicated to public scholarship, Seika curated the award-winning archival exhibition *It's About Time: Dancing Black in Canada 1900–1970* (2018) and co-curated *Into the Light: Eugenics and Education in Southern Ontario* (2019), which was the recipient of the Lieutenant Governor's Ontario Heritage Award. She is the inaugural recipient of Dance Studies Association Dance in the Public Sphere Award (2021). Her publications include writing for *Canadian Journal of History*, TURBA, *Dance Chronicle*, *Canadian Theatre Review*, *alt.theatre*, *The Routledge Encyclopedia of Modernism*, *Performance Matters*, *Dance Collection Danse Magazine*, and *The Dance Current*. Seika is the co-editor/contributor with Thomas F. DeFrantz, of *Configurations in Motion: Performance Curation and Communities of Colour* (3rd ed., 2017). She is Co-Investigator on the SSHRC-funded project "Gatherings: Oral and Archival Histories of Performance."

Mique'l Dangeli was born and raised on the Annette Island Indian Reserve, and is of the Tsimshian Nation of Metlakatla, Alaska. She is an assistant professor in the School of Creative Arts at the University of the Fraser Valley in Abbotsford, British Columbia. Her work focuses on Indigenous language revitalization, visual and performing arts, resurgence, sovereignty, protocol, and decolonization. Dangeli is a dancer, choreographer, curator, and activist. As one of the youngest advanced speakers and teachers of her people's language, she is dedicated to teaching Sm'algya̱x in community-based and university-accredited classes as well as mentoring learners and educational staff in their process of language acquisition and the creation of pre-K to high school programs. For the past fifteen years, she and her husband, artist and carver Mike Dangeli (Nisga'a Nation), have led the Git Hayetsk Dancers, an internationally renowned Northwest Coast First Nations dance group specializing in ancient and newly created songs and mask dances.

Camille Georgeson-Usher is a Coast Salish/Sahtu Dene writer, administrator, and artist using running to feel kinship of spatialities.

Gregory Hodge is a Social Service Worker graduate and peer support specialist in the forensics program at Ontario Shores Centre for Mental Health Sciences. He is a subject-matter expert with lived experience who teaches others on mental health and mental illness signs and symptoms. He is a long-time collaborator with Natalie Álvarez and Jennifer Lavoie on the SSHRC-funded study, "Scenario Training to Improve Interactions Between Police and Individuals in Mental Crisis: Impacts and Efficacy," co-facilitating Forum Scenario sessions to enhance officers' competencies in de-escalation.

Emily Johnson is a Yup'ik choreographer and artistic director, finding futures with more-than-human kin.

Evadne Kelly is a dance artist, educator, and interdisciplinary scholar who recently led and co-created projects that expose and counter histories and legacies of oppression in education. The projects, including the award-winning museum exhibition *Into the Light: Eugenics and Education in Southern Ontario* (intothelight.ca), formed collaborations with activists, scholars, and artists across various disciplines and sectors. Dr. Kelly completed her SSHRC-funded Ph.D. in Dance Studies from York University, which culminated in her book *Dancing Spirit, Love, and War: Performing the Trans-Local Realities of Contemporary Fiji* (U of Wisconsin P). She was a postdoctoral visitor in the Faculty of Health at York University before receiving subsequent postdoctoral awards at Re•Vision: The Centre for Art and Social Justice, University of Guelph. Building on her twenty-five years of professional dance experience, Dr. Kelly focuses her arts-based research and creation work on community-engaged and devised methodologies for social-justice aims.

Dr. Jennifer Lavoie is Associate Professor in the departments of psychology and criminology at Wilfrid Laurier University. She is a lead investigator on Ontario's Ministry of the Solicitor General–commissioned Mental Health and Crisis Response Education and Applied Training Program (MHCR), now a provincially mandated de-escalation training program for Ontario police officers. In collaboration with people with lived experience of mental illness, as well as industry and community partners, Dr. Lavoie led the development and implementation of the VR-MHCR, a groundbreaking virtual-reality education program designed to immerse first responders into a series of lifelike crisis situations with interactive characters to learn and practice de-escalation strategies. She has been recognized through Laurier's Award for Research Excellence (2017, 2020, 2023) and won the Society for Police and Criminal Psychology's Wayman Mullins Award for Best Journal Article (2023). She has published extensively in peer-reviewed journals about the nexus between mental illness and community safety.

Gabriel Levine is Associate Dean of the School of Humanities and Creativity at Sheridan College. He is the author of *Art and Tradition in a Time of Uprisings* (MIT, 2020) and of co-editor *Practice* (MIT/Whitechapel, 2018), and his writing is published and forthcoming in *Critical Inquiry*, *Performance Research*, *Liminalities*, *Journal of Curatorial Studies*, and *Canadian Theatre Review*, among others. He has released numerous musical recordings on labels including Constellation Records, and his puppet-theatre projects have toured internationally. He is a founding member of the avant-Yiddish band Black Ox Orkestar, and co-curator of Concrete Cabaret and OBJECTO Festival, which present experimental puppetry and object-performance to audiences in Tkaronto/Toronto.

Joseph M. Pierce ᏀᏔᎩᏠ ᎠᏰᏢ Cherokee Nation citizen, writer, curator, lines on fingers, sun circles waiting, water slipping through.

Karyn Recollet is an urban Cree scholar of a pedagogy of care.

Ahalya Satkunaratnam is Associate Professor of Humanities at Oakton College. Her book, *Moving Bodies, Navigating Conflict: Practicing Bharata Natyam in Colombo, Sri Lanka* (Wesleyan UP, 2021), won the 2021 de la Torre

Bueno® First Book Award from the Dance Studies Association. You can find her essays in publications such as *Rethinking Women's and Gender Studies (Volume 2)*, *Dance Research Journal*, *Women's Studies Quarterly*, and *SAMAR: South Asian Magazine for Action and Reflection*. 2022 marked the release of her first dance film, *AGNI*, an exploration of fire and war. She lives on the traditional and unceded lands of many Indigenous peoples, including the Council of Three Fires: the Ojibwe, Odawa, and Potawatomi Nations (Chicago).

MJ Thompson is a writer and teacher working on dance, performance, and visual art. Committed to popular culture and everyday aesthetics, she has written for a wide variety of publications, including *Ballettanz*, *Border Crossings*, *The Brooklyn Rail*, *Canadian Art*, *Dance Current*, *Dance Ink*, *Dance Magazine*, *The Drama Review*, *The Globe and Mail*, *Women and Performance*, *Theatre Journal*, and more. Her academic work is funded by the Social Sciences and Humanities Research Council in Canada, and her essays have appeared in several anthologies, including *Performance Studies Canada* (McGill-Queen's, 2017). She received the National Park Service Arts and Sciences Residency, Cape Cod National Seashore, August 2019, where she worked on a long-form essay about the embodied view (*Departures*, 2020). Her most recent book is *Louise Lecavalier: Dance, Labour, Culture* (Bloomsbury, 2025).

Performer, singer, dramaturge, and pedagogue **Angélique Willkie** spent twenty-five years in Europe performing most notably with Alain Platel/Les Ballets C. de la B., Jan Lauwers/Needcompany, Sidi Larbi Cherkaoui, Helena Waldmann, and as a singer with the Belgian world-music group Zap Mama. She is the recipient of the 2022 Prix d'interprète of the Prix de la danse de Montréal for her solo performance of Mélanie Demers's *Confession Publique*. Her dramaturgical work includes projects in dance-, music-, and circus-theatre. Associate Professor in the Department of Contemporary Dance at Concordia University and holder of a research chair in Ecologies of B/black Performance, her current research interests are firmly anchored in interdisciplinary artistic creation with a specific focus on decolonial dramaturgical practices and the dramaturgy of the performer.

INDEX

P

R